# Herding Cats

# Herding Cats

## A Life in Politics

S E N A T O R

# TRENT LOTT

ReganBooks
*An Imprint of* HarperCollins*Publishers*

HERDING CATS. Copyright © 2005 by Trent Lott. All rights reserved. Printed in the United States of America. No part of this book may be used or reproduced in any manner whatsoever without written permission except in the case of brief quotations embodied in critical articles and reviews. For information address HarperCollins Publishers Inc., 10 East 53rd Street, New York, NY 10022.

HarperCollins books may be purchased for educational, business, or sales promotional use. For information please write: Special Markets Department, HarperCollins Publishers Inc., 10 East 53rd Street, New York, NY 10022.

FIRST EDITION

*Designer:* Publications Development Company of Texas

Printed on acid-free paper

Library of Congress Cataloging-in-Publication Data has been applied for.

ISBN 0-06-059931-6

05 06 07 08 09 PDC/RRD 10 9 8 7 6 5 4 3 2 1

*For Tricia*
My steady companion and inspiration.
The wind beneath my wings.

# CONTENTS

# 1

# A PAINFUL CHRISTMAS

Pascagoula, Mississippi, December 20, 2002. Dawn appeared quiet and clear on the Friday morning that would change my life irrevocably. The winter sun turned the ripples on the Gulf of Mexico into that state of mottled silver so distinctive to the Mississippi coast. Even the Gulf itself was flat and glassy, a beautiful setting as the city around me plunged into the Christmas season. My house looks out over an expanse of grass and trees to the breakwater, and beyond that to the windswept Gulf Islands barely visible through the marine haze. From the back windows you can see a graceful neighborhood of distinctive homes meandering through the remains of a centuries-old grove of live oak trees, including some used to shelter horses during the Civil War.

I'd been pacing my historic beach residence since early morning, stopping occasionally to watch the pelicans dive into the Gulf, then soar from the surface with their catch. But my real purpose was to keep a wary eye on the ragtag army of press representatives who had appropriated private land to stake out my home from every angle. They had been there ever since the remarks I'd made about Senator Strom Thurmond at an affair celebrating his one hundredth birthday.

The Internet bloggers, television talking heads, and newspaper pundits had transformed those forty words into a racial furor ten days earlier. My innocent and thoughtless remark was treated by most of the media as a hanging offense. They had created a deafening hell with their voices, their ubiquitous cell phones, and even their rehearsal microphones, as their voices echoed brashly through my calm and sedate neighborhood. Their vans and satellite trucks—a collective eyesore on wheels—kept the engines running, the easier to crush rose bushes and snap the branches off green and red holly bushes as the vehicles darted this way and that.

Not even the gathering holiday spirit diminished their desire to film and record my family every chance they got—even if it was only for a few seconds.

My wife, Patricia (Tricia for short), sat at the kitchen bar writing out the last of the Christmas cards, making her presence known but distancing herself from the personal and momentous decision that was mine alone to make. Heirloom tree ornaments, only partially unpacked, lay scattered about the house, filling chairs and sofas. The season of joy to the world had been dampened; decorating would have to wait.

Every so often I ambled into my office to work on the political statement I was preparing, crossing out sentences, adding others—still trying to improve the language even as I briefly wondered whether I should make this statement at all. The media had already darkened my character; a formal statement might just fire them up again.

I'd returned to Mississippi, my spiritual life source, a week earlier to deal with the Thurmond drama on my home turf. As my pen scrawled across paper, I could hear the cars and trucks of dozens of Mississippians as they drove by in silent support. Occasionally, a young voice rang out, "We're with you, Lott. You're the man!" And I gratefully smiled before being swept back into the emotional undertow generated by the media just yards from the front door.

The phones had rarely been still. During this morning alone, I'd taken calls of support from three key Republican senators: Rick Santorum of Pennsylvania, Jon Kyl of Arizona, and Mitch McConnell of Kentucky, all of them close friends. They all pledged to back whatever decision I made. But I knew the heavy flak they were getting from other members of Congress and, more important, from their own constituents.

There also were calls from other GOP senators, terrified that the spreading political brushfire might engulf the Senate as a whole. The reality was obvious: The political world, at that instant, was focused on my small and quiet office in Pascagoula.

I glanced at my watch. It was about eleven in the morning—a perfect time for the networks to break into their daytime broadcasts and suddenly switch to Pascagoula. It was my cue to hit the airwaves. With good connections and a lot of luck, my statement would lead the evening newscasts of the major networks and, I hoped, bring a prompt end to my immediate suffering. Then the highly rated news anchors would finish the job. It would be a pleasure to stab the ranking Republican with their barbed words.

Sometime earlier, after painful conferences with my son, Chet, my daughter, Tyler, and Tricia, I'd decided to give up the position of majority leader of the United States Senate.

The decision was far from unanimous. Chet was furious. He also was certain—from his own Washington contacts—that I could retain the votes I'd always had and remain majority leader. "Almost every Republican with any power knows that your toast to Thurmond at this birthday party contained not a drop of racism," he said. "Go out there and fight this." Chet, a businessman and entrepreneur, had inherited my addiction to action—my compulsion to take something on and win it. He'd seen me do it time and time again. And I understood his fury over my treatment, by the press and even by President George W. Bush.

"I hear you," I said.

Tyler, a mom who also worked at the Metro Jackson Chamber of Commerce, didn't burst into anger. "Just see this through," she said. "You're majority leader now, and you will be reaffirmed in January. You're Trent Lott. You'll be standing when this is over." A few days later, she made an impassioned public speech in defense of my actions, pointing out that she had never seen a single racist action on my part. "Nor have I heard him utter a racist word or slur. Everyone's getting this wrong."

Tricia, always a rock at my side, somberly promised to line up behind whatever decision I made. But later, after I quit, a close friend told me she had slipped off to another part of the house for a good cry.

"Mom was outraged," Chet later said. "She just didn't want to burden you down with her emotions and her ire that this was undeniably unfair to you. It should never, never have happened. But she understood and accepted your decision."

For my part, I could see that the furor showed no signs of winding down. In fact, the nasty fallout was beginning to affect the mood and stability of the Senate, and the reputations of those brave enough to support me were beginning to erode.

There was little choice for me. I refused to hurt the institution I loved and had served for so long. I finished writing out my retreat in longhand late that morning, telephoned my loyal staff in Washington to convey my decision, and handed the statement to Tricia, who took it outside to the hungry press corps. "Who's the senior member here?" she asked. Someone—she can't recall who—stepped forward and took the piece of paper and spread it out on the hood of a car for all to see and photograph. "Now, will y'all go home?" Tricia implored. She wheeled around and went back up the steps, opened the front door, and saw herself on television in the small drama she had just left—a shock that magnified the moment and underscored the immediacy of the modern news cycle.

After all my editing, the statement came down to one sentence: "In the interest of pursuing the best possible agenda for the future of our country, I will not seek to remain as majority leader of the United States Senate for the 108th Congress effective Jan. 6, 2003."

Before long, the bulletin was dominating the "crawl" that runs along the bottom of CNN and other cable news channels. Wolf Blitzer made a perfunctory comment, and the network moved on to more important news—a portrait of Vermont's largest Christmas tree. I settled onto the couch to watch the yuletide unfold across the world. It looked as if we'd have a nice Christmas after all.

The nightmare was over; the tree could go up; my grandchildren were free to arrive unmolested by the press gangs.

But the next day, as I stretched and began to read the morning paper, I noticed that the news media—noisy and arrogant as ever—were still lurking about with looks of anticipation on their faces. Designated hitters from the delegation knocked on the door and presented a series of demands. The press would only leave if I came out onto the lawn and read a statement on camera. "Then," said one of them, "we promise to leave."

Though it was a slick form of journalistic blackmail, if I did what they demanded, they would retreat from battle. That would leave the yard to my rapidly arriving grandchildren.

"Okay." I said. "Let's get this over with."

I stepped onto the porch, wearing the casual clothes of the Christmas season, and moved into their midst as assertively as I could to give them the sound bite they craved. It was basically a reiteration of the formal statement made the previous day. One young reporter from ABC attempted to sneak in a few more prickly questions, but I silenced him. I looked him in the eye, then turned my back to climb the front stairs and said over my shoulder: "It's over, guys. I'm gone."

They, at least, were as good as their word. They disassembled their light poles and camera stands, packed up their gear, and were gone almost as quickly as they had arrived. "We can go out the front door again, Tricia," I yelled as I entered the house. Little things such as buying groceries and picking up cleaning were no longer a matter of carefully planned subterfuge.

The next day I received a call from President Bush and began disconnecting from the job I had savored with such purpose and joy. I took much consolation that I delivered to the Senate a much stronger, more flexible majority leader's office.

After a peaceful lunch—my first in two weeks—I drifted back to the study for the rest of the afternoon, catching up on a lengthening paper trail of news coverage. Later, as dusk settled in, I looked out again over the live oaks—thankful that I'd been able to end an ugly chapter of my life with dignity, in my own way, and in my cherished Mississippi home. My roots and those of my family went back into the history of this state, and its emotional grip on me had helped to shape my identity.

Sometime during the roar of misinformation over my Strom Thurmond remarks, I overheard a young television reporter damn me with faint praise by saying, "Senator Lott is still remarkable for one reason; he reached the pinnacle of power *in spite of being from Mississippi*." I had to chuckle at that. Actually, I ascended to the leadership of the United States Senate precisely *because* I was from the Magnolia State. After all, modern Mississippi and I grew up together.

# 2

# A SON OF MISSISSIPPI

I was born to Chester and Iona Watson Lott on October 9, 1941, in Grenada Hospital, which is in rural north-central Mississippi about one hundred miles from Jackson, the state capital. The circumstances that attended my birth said much about my rock-solid family, our work ethic, and our financial condition. My dad remained at my mother's side in the hospital just long enough to be reassured about her health, then rushed out to the two jobs that barely supported us. Similarly, my mother allowed herself a single day in the hospital before she bundled me home, then hurried back to work teaching elementary students at Calvary School. She had a babysitter look after me when she was teaching—and the school was within hailing distance of our house, so she was able to look in on me regularly. My mother worked long before it was cool for moms to hold jobs outside the home, because, quite simply, we needed the money. She fought her way through Holmes Junior College and took correspondence courses from the University of Mississippi at a time few women were permitted or managed to do so.

Blue collar was the precise definition of our family. We skipped from hamlet to hamlet as my father moved from job to job during my infancy, clawing out a living in a world still scarred by the Great Depression. In a matter of months, Chester Lott toiled as a pipe fitter, a crane operator, and, in his free time, as a sharecropper on someone else's land—a fate he shared with thousands in Mississippi and elsewhere in the rural South.

It was a backbreaking, frustrating, and often demeaning way to make a living, particularly when the war began to force its way—and its cash—into the state's poor economy. But Dad put on a brave face and tracked out of our farm door every morning with a jaunty step. And he always remembered to hoist me up over his head and kiss me good-bye. When he came home from his "borrowed land" about twelve hours later, he set a huge tub in the middle of the kitchen floor and soaked away the grime. Every few minutes, mother poured in another kettle of hot water fresh from the stove. Then there were prayers, the lowering of the kerosene, and bed.

Every day seemed like the day before, in what to Dad, at least, threatened to be a self-perpetuating cycle. In 1940, only two hundred Carroll County sharecroppers out of a total of 12,016 upgraded to their own land. But Dad was not going to accept life as a farmer without land. With whatever energy he had left every day, he scoured the state for jobs—particularly a position that involved mechanics.

Meantime, he plugged away at the sharecropper's life. Using a mule furnished by the landowner for a price, Dad cultivated twenty acres of a farmer's land to feed his family and further cultivated one of the landlord's sizeable plots to pay the rent and to return the advance he'd taken at the beginning of the season— money needed at home and to buy seed and fertilizer for his own crops. Dad had to sacrifice at least a quarter of the cotton he'd produced. The rest went to outfitting next year's crops. That made it impossible for him to save the money that would have given him a small measure of independence and a big dose of pride.

Today they'd call such labor subsistence farming. But today there are agencies to cushion farmers against the blows. Back then, it was little more than an economic prison.

On holidays and weekends, Mother would take me out to the cotton fields to watch Dad and his sturdy mule cultivate the land. We joked and laughed while Dad drank his coffee. Occasionally, Mother would pitch in and help pick the cotton until back pain forced her to stop.

I can still recall the musky aroma of the freshly lit fireplace and the exhausted look on Dad's face at the end of the day. These were harsh circumstances, and they were shared by two-thirds of the state's population. I remember hearing someone describe me as living a "hard and poor life." That was news to me, but it started me thinking about how in many ways I'd actually been fortunate. For one thing, I never felt for an instant that we were poor. There were not a lot of rich people in Mississippi, and almost everybody's dad was a farmer or a fisherman, a crane operator, or a truck driver. My dad was a sharecropper; he raised cotton on somebody else's land. But I never felt deprived. We always had what we required.

When I look back and hear the words, "poor, terrible Mississippi," I always remind myself that I have been royally blessed all of my life. I had a mother—a strong-willed Scotswoman—who paid the bills and made sure I went to Sunday school. I also had a father who loved me dearly. Although we moved a fair amount, that eventually turned out to be a politician's blessing.

When I was about to start second grade, we moved further north in Montgomery County—to a farmhouse situated in a fabled place named Duck Hill. The lumpish earthen pile of packed dirt that gave the hamlet its name had been greatly enhanced and fitted with rudimentary steps sometime in America's early days. It was not only a haven for ghosts, or so the tales went, but also an enchanting sight under the full moon. I could glimpse its undistinguished summit from my bedroom window, and I was soon swapping stories with my school chums about the Hill's curious and mysterious past.

The hillock had been named not for its appearance, but because it had been the lair of a Choctaw medicine man called "Chief Duck," who supposedly dispensed medicines, herbs, and potions to whites and Indians alike. And some of us kids thought his ghost haunted the mound, making it the cherished and inevitable destination on Halloween. The hill and thousands of acres around it had been ceded to Mississippi by the Treaty of Dancing Rabbit Creek in 1830, causing many white settlers—including some of my ancestors—to become prosperous landowners. But that occurred only after the Choctaws reluctantly agreed to decamp to a reservation in the far west.

Some say Chief Duck froze to death. And he may well have. Even in my childhood, the winters were agony. The blue northers continually roared down from the Great Plains to dump their sleet and snow on the already-soggy Montgomery County soil—famous for its porosity. On cold mornings I'd stick my head out of my grandmother's homemade quilt, take a peek at the frozen farmland, jump into my clothes, and dash through the house gathering up the slop jars. We had no indoor plumbing—nor did anyone we knew—so the slops had to be filled with fresh well water each day, placed in the bedroom, and then emptied a good distance out in the fields.

But an even more daunting experience blighted my life every morning. The outhouse! Since it was a good two hundred yards from the back door, I had to brace myself, lean forward into the sleet, then tear like heck to the swinging doors. The boards were often so cold you felt as though the skin on your rear was freezing to the surface. In those days, two-thirds of the state's dwellings were without plumbing and running water. The family that installed indoor plumbing climbed a few rungs on the ladder of life—not rich, but comfortable.

I remember the day—I was in the fifth grade—when Dad came home one weekend and began to install the luxurious additions of a shower and a commode. What a joy for a young boy! I stepped into the warm jets of the shower that Sunday night and felt like the luckiest kid in the county. My mother made certain that I understood the source of such luxury—hard work—and her lessons have remained with me to this day. They would later help to shape my political empathy for dedicated endeavor.

I don't have much sympathy for people who don't work to help themselves; I don't think the government owes you a living. My parents didn't get any government help, and they never had fancy jobs. Even though there were times when they didn't have enough money, they never thought of running to the government the way everybody does now. I was shocked when I got to Washington and found out what people thought the government should do for them. I know I sound like a Southerner. Well, I am, and I'm proud of that, too.

My parents were exceptional people who almost always rose above their troubles. And partly because of our straitened finances, partly because of some special factors, my parents never treated me as a child. They accepted me as an equal and to some extent as a premature adult. Beginning in the fifth grade, I had a lot to say about what the family did and did not do. And my advice and decisions carried great weight. Like most American families in those days, we lingered at the dinner table and talked about all the things that were important to us—from the permanence of Dad's job to the lay of the land in local Mississippi politics. I found myself preparing for these dialogues—you had to work a little harder when you were a fifth grader—and I am convinced the process contributed to the development of my future leadership skills.

I was tested early. My dad had a drinking problem that had grown worse over the years, and before too long I was well aware of it. He also had dalliances with other women, a fact known by many people in our area. As a consequence, my parents began to talk about getting a divorce—a subject that came up at our dinner table. I was dead set against a divorce and used my evolving powers of argument to say so in our open debates. "No, I won't agree with that," I said, on my feet and with emphasis. "I forbid it." And they listened—which doomed them to years of chronic fussing and fighting. My mother lived with Dad's imperfections, I believe, largely because of my dinner-table diatribes. I've always had strong opinions—a fact that won me the role of Lott family peacemaker.

There was nothing more important in my young mind than Mom and Dad staying married. So I continued for years to try and work things out between them. First I tried to tackle Dad's drinking, which was certainly the most obvious source of heartache. I was just finishing the fifth grade, but soon I found myself standing shakily before him and reciting chapter and verse about temperance.

Shame overcame him. After our father-son talks began, Dad took some pains to hide his problem. Yet when he was away he seemed to indulge more than ever. His tactics for subterfuge were sometimes clever, sometimes foolish. He'd never bring his whiskey into the house; instead, he'd hide his pints and half-pints around the yard.

But he just couldn't summon the strength to stop. Sometimes the temptation would render him helpless. He wouldn't even bother to creep off to a hiding place. I remember seeing him turn a pint bottle of whiskey way up and take a big slug. He'd smack his lips as if it were maple syrup instead of undistinguished, everyday bourbon. Then he'd notice me watching and sadly turn his head away. As it got worse, he took to pawning things to pay for his addiction. Even my favorite .22 rifle mysteriously disappeared one day; I was sure it went to some pawn shop.

In the sixth grade, I made an unusual proposal to him—actually, a form of blackmail that involved my daredevil side. At the time we still lived in northern Mississippi, and Dad was commuting back and forth to Pascagoula, where he had temporary work in a shipyard. The roads were dangerous under any conditions. With him drinking for much of the trip, Mom and I were terrified that he'd end up in the morgue of some small country hospital.

I'd spent a month constructing a tree house in the backyard, using the lightest boards possible so I could inch my creation out to the very ends of the branches. I also situated it as high up as possible, making it a perfect foil for Mississippi winds that caused it to shake and creak. My parents, naturally, were worried sick that I'd tumble to the ground.

One Sunday afternoon, Dad pleaded with me to give up my latest landed property. "If you fall," he said, "you'll break a sizeable number of bones in your body."

I answered him in kind. "You know, if you drink while you're driving, you'll break more than just bones in your body."

"Okay, you got yourself a deal," he said. "I won't drink if you don't go up there again—not even once." I should have noticed the hollowness in his voice—but I wanted our deal to work.

Inevitably, I kept my part of the bargain and he didn't. He couldn't. The addiction was just too powerful. But I kept on trying and assumed an even more powerful leadership role in the family, which I believe helped me to become an innovative and individual thinker. Mother encouraged this, impressing upon me that I could do just about anything I set my mind to if I worked hard enough. I collected on those dividends for life.

*    *    *

Ialso was blessed to be from a fabled Mississippi family that was
well schooled in politics. The family's political roots stretched
back into the nineteenth century to 1889, when my great-great
uncle John Lott ran for Mississippi state treasurer. He fielded an
exhaustive rural campaign, based at least partly on his status as a
Civil War hero: He had lost a leg on the killing fields of Gettys-
burg. I still have a faded flyer that clearly illustrates his peg leg and
full beard draped down over his chest. The faded document is an
endorsement by the Carroll County Board of Supervisors, which
included Carroll County Sheriff John S. McCain—the great-great
uncle of the current senior senator of Arizona, John McCain.

Unfortunately, John Lott was rather soundly beaten.

More successful was my mother's dad, Ed Watson, another
tough and colorful character, who served as justice of the peace
for a large chunk of rural Mississippi. With a .38 caliber revolver
tucked into a holster behind his long coat, my grandfather rode
the circuit on horseback, carrying justice to backwater towns and
villages that were sometimes inaccessible by automobile in the
1920s, '30s, and '40s. He basically settled misdemeanors—effectively head of a one-man court practicing untraditional law.

Grandpa was an interesting man, with a handlebar mustache
and thick black hair that was a sign of his carefully hidden Indian
blood. He had been a member of either the Cherokee or Chickasaw
tribe, though the family was divided on which. His work as a lawman sustained him because, outside of growing a few crops such as
sugar cane, a bit of cotton, and peanuts, he never had another job,
at least so far as I knew. But he raised and provided for six children,
including my mother and his middle son, Arnie Watson, who became heavily involved in state politics during the 1950s and '60s.

Arnie served as Carroll County tax assessor for eight years before graduating to the Mississippi State Senate, where he served

for twelve years. He was a rough and enduring politician. Eventually, his office was threatened by redistricting: His new district included a larger county and a more powerful sitting senator. But Uncle Arnie was undaunted: He bore down on the newly drawn redistrict with a furious campaign and unseated his storied opponent—one with a political silver spoon in his mouth.

My father's dad, Grandpa Aaron Lott, was a supervisor in Carroll County for twelve years—a charismatic man who stood six foot five, who filled every room he entered, and who eventually was elected president of the Mississippi State Supervisor's Association. He was defeated in his attempt at a fourth term by another Carroll County Lott. Carroll was a small county, and there were plenty of Lotts around—all of them descendents of my great-great-great grandfather. He was buried in 1839, and five generations of Lotts have been buried not far from his grave.

The Lott who defeated my grandpa was distant kin, probably a fifth cousin or something like that. After the election, I told him, "This is when you know you have too many Lotts."

He roared with laughter and whispered, "I guess I was the one too many."

In a sense, I grew up with politics—a toddler who was taken to political rallies even before he had much understanding of what these gatherings were all about. But I also was a quick study: by the time I was seven or eight, I was eager to soak up everything I could. Those early political conversations among the family politicians were fascinating. They mostly focused their attention on local offices, such as assessor, sheriff, supervisor of roads, and school board member; they were the men—and they were all men in those days—who affected the very life of the county on a daily basis. As they began to exchange real confidences—the good stuff—I'd hunker down in the shadows at the edge of the house and concentrate on the names and histories they recited. It was Rural

Politics 101. They knew which stretches of roads had been kept up properly, which sheriff's candidate had an uncomfortable secret, and which schools had been degraded to an embarrassment.

Occasionally a disagreement would break out in the family, and Grandpa would declare an end to the uneasy grumbling and make the decisions. In the end, he picked the politicians to get the family's support. But my grandfather expected a lot in return for his vote. And he expected those candidates he supported to make good on their promises. They almost always did, whether it was reciprocal support for Lott candidates or money for a particular road project or help for certain constituent groups.

For the most part, however, electioneering in our house was a rather calm affair. I remember only one political argument between my mom and dad. That erupted during the 1952 presidential campaign, when Governor Adlai Stevenson, Democrat of Illinois, challenged General Dwight David Eisenhower, the Republican candidate. It wasn't that Dad was high on Adlai, or a very passionate campaigner. It was just that Stevenson was the Democrat, and Dad had spent a lifetime voting for his party's official choice, regardless of the candidate's political shortcomings and personal characteristics. In 1952, Mother liked Ike, probably because her brother Arnie had served in Europe under his leadership and even fought in the Battle of the Bulge. Mom and Dad got into it, and our dinner-table discussions suddenly grew invigorating and intense. When they split the family vote on Election Day, it gave me a new take on politics. People could be as close as Mom and Dad and still disagree mightily about the viability of a candidate.

After Ike was inaugurated, my own perspective began to change. At the end of my sixth grade year in 1953, Dad signed on permanently with Ingalls Shipbuilders, employed first as a night watchman and later as a pipe fitter. In the early fall, we picked up and moved south to Pascagoula, the Gulf Coast city where Ingalls built ships. For a country boy not quite twelve years old, it was another world.

Pascagoula had a rich history as a European settlement—stretching back to 1669, when Pierre Lemoyne D'Iberville first claimed the area on behalf of Louis XIV of France. The British occupied the area from 1763 to 1781, when the Spanish Bourbons took over. They held sway until June 7, 1798, when Pascagoula and the surrounding territory became part of the United States. Less than two decades later, on December 10, 1817, Mississippi became a state.

When we arrived there nearly 150 years later, you could feel the energy as soon as you drove into town. The local economy was booming with thriving seafood and timber industries, making it one of the most diversified economies in Mississippi at the time. There were about thirteen thousand people living in the small town—a community that wound its way along the Gulf Coast and through the Piney Woods that included marshes and vast stretches of sandy loam. (Pascagoula—"bread eaters" in the language of its Native Americans—was known as the "Singing River" city because the Pascagoula Indians that inhabited the place chanted as they drowned themselves in the waters of the river rather than submit to a fierce tribal enemy, the Biloxi Indians.)

There weren't a lot of rich people in Pascagoula, but there wasn't much poverty either. What impressed me as a youngster was the almost classless society I encountered when I enrolled in Pascagoula Junior High School as a seventh grader. It was definitely at odds with what I felt at other schools in Grenada. As a first grader at Grenada Elementary School, I had met kids from all backgrounds—incredibly rich, desperately poor, and points in between. That variety, in the hands of children, was grist for a kind of caste system: Kids knew their station in life, determined in large measure by their financial circumstances. In Pascagoula, because everyone was more or less the same, I took to it immediately; I was the new kid, a novelty, and that helped as I followed my natural instincts and got into a wide variety of activities—basketball, band, acting, music, and various leadership positions.

Despite Pascagoula's economic diversity, ultimately it seemed as though every penny anyone made there came from the Ingalls Shipyard, either directly or indirectly. Many of the dads of kids in my school worked at the yard; some of the moms did, too. If you were a hospital administrator, you depended on the yard. If you were a dentist, such as my future father-in-law Dr. Perry Thompson, your patients came from the shipyard. I thought that was the way things should be, the way they needed to be. But as I found out over the years, this was not the way it was in most towns.

We moved into a four-room home built as part of the U.S. Navy housing projects during the shipbuilding boom years of World War II. About a quarter of the families lived in these compact, durable subdivisions, which still form a substantial part of Pascagoula's residential neighborhoods today. The homes had a living room, a kitchen with room for a dinette table, a small bath, and two bedrooms. My dad later enclosed the front porch and enlarged the living room.

Church was an anchor in my life. When I was growing up in Pascagoula, half of the community was Catholic. Everybody else belonged to an ecumenical mix that included Baptist, Methodist, Presbyterian, Lutheran, and Episcopalian parishes. We even had some Christian Arabs from Lebanon and Syria, adding to the melting-pot flavor of my new hometown. With my parents, I became a member of the Pascagoula First Baptist Church, the religious institution that remains a source of strength to Tricia and me to this day. Mother attended church regularly and participated in church activities, but Dad never felt comfortable going. There were a lot of respected men at that church, and they tried to help my dad. One of them always would take me to the annual father-and-son banquet in lieu of my father, which was a kind gesture. Earl McKee, a State Farm Insurance agent, taught me Sunday School. Church filled a lot of voids for me, and these men—who served almost as surrogate fathers—were an important part of it. Many of them remained close friends throughout the years. McKee, for example, was campaign finance chairman in my home county when I ran for Congress the first time.

When I became one of the 1,575 students at Pascagoula High School, I waded into activities and student politics with a burst of energy that seemed perfectly natural to me. By the time I was a senior, I'd been on the student council for three years, served as "principal" on career day, starred in a handful of student productions, played the tuba in the marching band, and founded a school quartet that ignited my unquenchable love of music. I had a hunger to get things done and an early can-do way to get them done—whether it was organizing the senior prom or guiding the Drama Club.

I never stopped to analyze my success. You don't at that age. But in retrospect, I believe that my campaigns succeeded because I enthusiastically and sincerely developed friendships throughout the student body. Gaylen Roberts, who became my friend in the seventh grade and who was still at my side when I graduated from the University of Mississippi, told me recently that I was one of the few people he knew who neither saw nor recognized any cliques. "They were there, Trent," he said, "But they were invisible to you."

Nobody called me a politician in that teenage training ground for America's politicians. But I guess I was.

I also became one of a quartet of inseparable friends who included Mickey Schneider, the Presbyterian minister's son; Henry

Skelton, the Baptist preacher's son; and Gaylen, who played the tuba next to me in the band and was the center on the basketball team. During the slow weekends and lazy summers of the Mississippi Gulf Coast, we'd gather at one of our houses and talk through the problems of the world—a game I called "mental calisthenics." I remember one all-night discussion with Gaylen about predestination, which he believed in as a Methodist and which I didn't as a Baptist. We talked six hours and still did not reach agreement. Gaylen recently reminded me that we sat in front of the high school one night and catalogued what specifically was wrong with Washington, D.C. We made a vow then and there to work after college to fix what was wrong.

Starting in high school, I had a number of jobs—partly to maintain the car my parents helped me purchase my sophomore year. I buzzed around town delivering cleaning. I was a champion burger flipper at the Frost Top. I mopped the floor of the Singing River Hospital, and I delivered furniture for the store my parents ran. Dad had started working at the Market Street Furniture Company and became the manager; mother was the bookkeeper and secretary. Someone else owned the store, but my parents essentially ran it, which proved to be too much responsibility for my father. Eventually, it all fell apart for him.

I developed good friendships at work with two local African Americans. One of them was James Betts, the student body president of the segregated Carver High School; he and I delivered furniture together. On one spring afternoon, I carried a doll lamp to his girlfriend and he carried one to Tricia Thompson. Tricia was this cute sophomore when I was a senior in high school, and I'd gotten to know her because she played flute in the band. I offered her rides home from band practice, flirted with her a bit, and even kissed her once or twice. But there was nothing to it: I was going steady with someone else, and she, after all, was a kid compared with a high-school upperclassman.

By my third year in high school, I already knew I wanted to study law. I had toyed with the idea of pharmacy school, because my dad's brother, Yancey Lott, was a pharmacist. But even then, as a teenager, the courthouse and the law held a fascination for me. That was where I wanted to be. The only real issue was where I would go to college and law school—but the more I thought about it, in my waning high school days, the more it wasn't much of an issue after all.

# 3

# THE LEGACY OF OLE MISS

I tackled the chore of choosing a college as if it was a geometry problem. Most of my questions and requirements focused on the strength of a university's law school. How many top-flight Southern attorneys had the school produced? How much attention was given to colloquial law—those quirks and tics that complicated Mississippi's rural legal system? The one thing I knew for certain was that I expected to practice law in my home state for the rest of my life.

My final choices were Tulane University in New Orleans and the University of Mississippi, located in Oxford in the northern part of the state, about seventy-five miles from Memphis, Tennessee. Tulane had plenty to recommend it—a magnificent campus in an exciting big city and the reputation of attracting some of the best professors in America. But its law-school curriculum was based on the Napoleonic Code—*Code Napoleon*—that, in turn, was based on Roman law written during the reign of the Emperor Justinian. Napoleon simply codified it into the civil laws of France and made it easier to read.

Mississippi's codes originated in English common law, which was revamped and tailored to the needs of the colonies not long before the American Revolution. "Ole Miss" made more sense in my practical mind: It seemed only natural to study a form of law that was practiced in my own state. But it was more than that: I wanted a Southern school with demonstrated success in my home state—one that nurtured young law school graduates and provided a support system as well. I prepared to head for Ole Miss, and another universe entirely. With cool and dispassionate precision, I had selected the university for its law school curriculum—but long before I ever got to graduate school, this wonderful place won my heart as well.

From my first day on campus as an undergraduate in September 1959, I was in the thrall of the colorful pageant that is Ole Miss. The campus itself was exhilarating and beautiful. I got a lump in my throat the first time I drove onto campus as a freshman. It was surrounded on all sides by Oxford; both the town (founded in 1834) and the campus (dedicated in 1849) were living examples of antebellum architecture, with many public and private buildings featuring deeply columned porches and fired brick walls. I instinctively felt the history that suffused the place. The founders of Ole Miss had preserved fingers of forest that nestled between buildings and formed walkways and gathering spots—one of them was the Grove, where alumni and students greeted each other at homecoming and other campus celebrations.

Rush already was under way when I got there, and the sororities and fraternities were putting on a dressy show. The brand new Miss America was an Ole Miss student, Mary Ann Mobley, who was a member of Chi Omega. The fraternities were flooded with a record one thousand boys going through rush week.

During the summer between high school and college, some of the Ole Miss boys from Pascagoula came by my house and started to talk up fraternities. I'd gone to Oxford for some rush parties during the summer, but in reality I didn't know much about fraternities—what they were and what they did, how to get into them, and whether I could afford one. But I decided to go through rush, and as I settled into my dorm room I heard plenty of talk about fraternity life in the halls.

Fraternity and sorority row was south and west of the campus—a domain of magnolia trees and azaleas, traditional lines of Doric columns, balconies built for late night serenades, and tradition that stretched back to the 1920s, when the Greek system conquered the social life of the university.

Rush lived up to its name. I was figuratively poked and prodded by determined members from almost a score of fraternities. They dissected my leadership pedigree from Pascagoula, grilled me about my academic record and aspirations, rated my social skills, and probed deeply for any sort of talent that would help their organizations. I must have passed their tests, because many of them kept after me and three fraternities in particular—Alpha Tau Omega, Sigma Chi, and Sigma Nu—pressed me especially hard to join. I had gravitated toward Sigma Nu since my first day in rush, during one of those "cattle call" receptions used by the fraternities to examine the new crop of potential members en masse. Founded in 1861 at the Virginia Military Institute, Sigma Nu was an organization grounded in old Southern tradition, and its 160 members seemed unusually close and particularly attuned to the principles of honor, brotherhood, and religion outlined in their national charter. I didn't ask anyone's advice; it just seemed the right thing to do. Along with forty others, I pledged Sigma Nu.

On pledge night, clutching our Sigma Nu bids in our hands, Gaylen Roberts and I discovered a welcoming band of brothers who defied fraternity stereotypes. At Ole Miss, you could often point out a typical member of Phi Delta Theta (rich kids from planter families) or a Sigma Alpha Epsilon (preppie types) or a Sigma Chi (serious and religious). But the members of Sigma Nu were diverse enough in their personal characteristics to defy easy typecasting. There were scions of planter families from the Delta, sons of Mississippi attorneys and physicians, star athletes on scholarships, children of blue collar workers, kids who were the first in their families to attend college, and "legacies"—the offspring or close relatives of previous fraternity members. They all crowded around us in the chapter room. Fledgling political alliances and social connections formed instantly and lasted a lifetime. Most of my closest friends, even today, go back to those days at Ole Miss and Sigma Nu.

Two fairly unexpected events in my life at Sigma Nu helped to influence much that was to follow. The first occurred naturally as pledge night wore down and Gaylen Roberts sat down at the chapter room piano and began playing one of the pop tunes from our old Pascagoula High quartet. He began humming, and I slowly wandered over to join him. But two other pledges beat me to his side.

One was a personable fellow named Allen Pepper, from a patrician family in the town of Belzoni, in the heart of the Mississippi Delta. His natural resonance blended with that of Roberts. But just as they stumbled to perfect pitch, Gaylen felt a hand on his shoulder and heard a booming tenor voice in his ear. The tenor was Guy Hovis, a striking young man from Tupelo, the town in Mississippi where Elvis Presley was born. A high school baseball and basketball star, Guy was clearly destined to be a star vocalist—something he proved later as a mainstay on *The Lawrence Welk Show*.

My singing voice, which ranges from baritone to deep bass, completed the distinct and harmonious style of what amounted to a rump musical group. The four of us decided then and there that this could be the start of something big. The next night we began to rehearse seriously, with Gaylen beginning to arrange a repertoire of songs that included fraternity anthems, occasional touches of Four Freshmen–type popular tunes, and some Christian music. In short order, we started performing at Sigma Nu parties and other functions, but it wasn't long before we leaped to the wider Ole Miss stage and even beyond. In the spring of 1960, Ole Miss Chancellor J. D. Williams asked us to open the program of a major college benefit. We happily accepted the honor and used the opportunity to reintroduce our group: From that day forward, we were known as the Chancellors.

We took our music anywhere we found an appreciative audience. We could be heard on a nice spring day in the Quad, at fraternity "pinning" ceremonies, on the field during halftime at Ole Miss football games, and at Sigma Nu national functions. We sang further afield, in Pittsburgh and in Virginia and in Memphis—not bad for someone who hadn't been north of Memphis but once in his life. One time, we even pitched up at the legendary Memphis recording studio of Sam Phillips and serenaded the identical black microphone that Elvis used to start his career a few years earlier. The result was a 45-rpm "extended play" two-record set that eventually was remastered into an audiocassette and a compact disc that the fraternity sold by the hundreds in its fund-raising drives. The Chancellors, in short, put us in the campus spotlight for four years, and helped to forge unique and vibrant identities for each of us.

A second propitious incident at Sigma Nu also contributed to my emergence as a big man on campus. It occurred early in my first year, when I ambled into the fraternity chapter room one afternoon after classes and found Roy Williams—an "active" and a campus political insider—waiting for me.

"Stand at attention, Pledge Lott," he boomed out.

"Yes, sir, thank you for reminding me."

"Pledge Lott, you will report to the athletic field next Tuesday morning to try out for freshman cheerleader."

A mild look of dismay must have crossed my face, because Williams repeated his directive in more forceful terms: "You will be there, Pledge Lott, and you *will* do your best to make that freshman squad."

"Yes sir, Mr. Williams, sir," I answered. He sounded like a Marine drill sergeant and I responded like a raw recruit, but that's the way it was in fraternities in those days. Pledges were little more than lowly plebes, subject to mild hazing and riotous initiation rituals, and a command was inviolate. So the following Tuesday, I was on the Ole Miss football field with Guy Hovis, who had received the same message, scrambling to learn the basics of leading cheers. Cheerleading at Ole Miss in the 1950s was far from the intricate and graceful athleticism you see today. We were a bit gangly and awkward then, focused less on coordinated moves than on boisterous displays designed to rouse the crowd and produce the wild roars that were so much a part of the Ole Miss football season.

What surprised me, though, was that some of the yelling and applause was for me. When I made the cheerleading squad, I was introduced as the new guy with the megaphone, and in the process I became instantly recognized. By the time I was a junior, I'd been elected "head cheerleader"—the guy who led the team onto the field just before the start of the game. The booming music of the marching band, and the resonance of the University Men's Chorus, created a wall of sound that stirred hearts and quickened pulses, my own included. In more practical terms, cheerleading before 35,000 students and alumni conferred a statewide identity—and that in turn proved to be a valuable commodity as I began my campus political career. (In fact, Ole Miss was to prove to be a fine launching pad for my career beyond the campus. In the 1950s, all of the governors and statewide officials were graduates of the University of Mississippi. There was a statewide network that continued through my time at the university and beyond. Many of the students I met there went on to be lawyers I worked with or against later on when I practiced law.)

I climbed the political ladder at Ole Miss according to a rough plan that built on my status as a cheerleader, my offices as Sigma Nu commander—equivalent of president—and president of the Inter-fraternity Council, and the key positions I held in a half dozen associations and scholastic fraternities. In May 1962, near the end of my junior year, I ran for student body president. My roommate and campaign manager, Allen Pepper (now a federal judge for the Northern District of Mississippi), mapped out a vast Sigma Nu–based effort that involved leaflets, banners, and visits to every dorm and fraternity and sorority house on campus.

Nobody gave me much of a chance. I was active on campus, all right, but I was a junior; my opponent already was vice president of the student body and a first-year law student. Many of the bigger fraternities were aligned against us because Sigma Nu had a strong, emerging identity that threatened them. They even supported candidates from smaller houses in a frantic drive to prevent a Sigma Nu from taking the top student-government spot, and the powerful perks that went along with it.

So I ventured out on my own to dormitories, independent student clubs, and even apartments—anywhere I could find a crowd of students willing to listen to me. I formed this disparate group into one of the first true "coalition campaigns" in the history of Ole Miss politics. In effect, my base of support came from campus independents—the non-fraternity and non-sorority people—plus the smaller fraternities and perhaps half the sororities. In high school, I had built a large network of students through my enthusiastic participation in clubs and associations. Now I was trying to do the same thing in college, going beyond the Greek system to involve the broader campus in my drive for Ole Miss student body president.

The effort boosted me to a surprisingly strong showing in the primary—within a few votes of my runoff opponent, Dick Wilson, a vital student leader from Jackson, Mississippi. Wilson was a member of the large, respected fraternity Kappa Alpha. The KAs had decided to mount the campaign for their man with an appeal to the big fraternities. But down in the game rooms of fraternities large and small, the Greeks were seriously divided between Wilson and me. Campus wisdom and trend lines shifted like the wind as Wilson and I bounced up and down, always within a few points of each other. The *Daily Mississippian* said the race was "too close to call."

There were a couple of weeks between the primary and the runoff, and I thought we used the time well. While Pepper papered the campus with my name and likeness and marshaled the Sigma Nu troops in impressive numbers to promote my candidacy at fraternity and sorority houses, I concentrated almost exclusively on retail politics, trying to reach the maximum number of independents in dorm rooms and apartments scattered all over the campus. Early on the morning of the election, Allen came back to our room at Sigma Nu with a smile on his face. "I think we've moved out in front," he said confidently. "Trent Lott is now the man to beat."

Later in the day, a right-wing organization on campus known as the Rebel Underground Network made it clear that they believed it was my election to lose. And they wanted in on it. Shortly before two o'clock that afternoon, Allen received a call on our fraternity pay phone from a man who ordered: "Get me Trent Lott's campaign manager. There's something he needs to hear."

Pepper identified himself as my campaign manager.

"I represent the Rebel Underground Network, and we have a proposition that he won't be able to turn down," the man said to Allen. "Now I want you and your candidate—just the two of you—to meet us in the parking lot of Kiamie's Restaurant after 9 P.M." That was when this drive-in and campus hangout closed.

Pepper hung up the phone. He was stunned. The Rebel Underground Network, a disreputable, segregationist organization, operated in the shadows of Ole Miss. Nobody really knew or cared who its members were or how many of them there were. For more than a year they'd been lurking about, painting objectionable signs on University walls and otherwise spreading their messages of racial hatred through anonymous telephone calls. Ole Miss was segregated at the time, and the Rebels wanted to keep it that way.

It was by then no secret that James Meredith was attempting to break the color barrier at Ole Miss. For more than six months, the Rebels had been publishing a small, three-page newspaper dubbed the *Rebel Crier*, filling it with ungrammatical and crude calls for white supremacy. It specialized in bullyboy write-ups predicting the violence that would surely come to Mississippi if the state should proceed to integrate its colleges and universities. Fortunately, both the organization and its "flyer" (for it was really no more than that) had been regarded as crude jokes. Students attending early morning classes laughed when they stumbled upon groups of Rebels trying to distribute the *Crier* just as the campus was coming to life. Nobody took them seriously.

However, Allen felt we had no choice but to meet them in the drive-in parking lot. "Look, Trent," he said. "They can't do us any good, but they could do us a lot of harm. Of course you realize we stand a good chance of getting our teeth knocked out." I nodded reluctantly.

Pepper prepared for everything, even rounding up a handful of Sigma Nu jocks and stashing them in the undergrowth that surrounded Kiamie's. They weren't only there for our protection: Allen wanted observers to document that we weren't violating the University's election statutes. Though we couldn't even guess what they wanted, we weren't going to be lured into any sort of a trap.

Allen and I showed up promptly, just past nine, and posted ourselves side by side under one of the restaurant's parking lights. Several minutes later a nondescript young man sidled over, introduced himself, and outlined what he insisted was an offer we couldn't afford to refuse. "We've figured out that you are going to win, Mr. Lott, and the Rebel Underground wants to strike a deal," the wiry little guy said. "You pick a small number of our members for your student body cabinet from our roster—we'll supply the names—and we'll leave you alone."

Pepper erupted in anger. He hated all forms of dirty politics, whether it was on the state level or this little election for student body president. "What do you mean you'll leave us alone?" Allen shouted. "What can you do to us?"

I put a reassuring hand on his shoulder: "This is nothing, Allen. We'll get this over right away. Just let me handle it."

"What do you *really* want?" I asked the little guy.

"Well, Lott, if you don't agree right here to appoint our members, we're going to race out of here and work all night on a special edition of the *Rebel Crier* that will carry a front-page headline giving you our unconditional endorsement for student body president."

We'd be damned by faint praise. And if I won, it would help to get my administration as student body president off to an uncertain start.

"Good," I answered. "Go ahead. I'm not making any deal with you or with anyone else. Go on! Publish your paper."

"It will kill you," he warned. "Before dawn we're going to take a plane up and flood the campus with these leaflets just as the students head for classes."

I waved him off, chuckling at the thought of an old biplane dropping leaflets all over the quad with a grinning picture of me on the cover. "I can't stop you," I yelled back over my shoulder. "But I'm sure not making any deal with you." He disappeared as quickly as he had materialized just as our Sigma Nu boys emerged from the underbrush with a dozen questions.

It turned out the members of the Rebel Underground were playing both sides. In a more discreet meeting with my opponent, Dick Wilson, the rebels demanded "major representation" in Wilson's cabinet. Wilson was less emphatic than I had been. "Look," he bluffed, "I will look over any of your cabinet candidates if you'd like to send me a list. That's all I can do." Dick told me later that the rebels seemed satisfied and quickly scattered.

Wilson also confided that there was indeed a mimeographed leaflet produced in the wake of the meetings, and that the members of the Rebel Underground had flooded the dorms with them. Dick even remembered the headline that just might have defeated me: THE TROOPERS ARE SUPPORTING TRENT LOTT BECAUSE TRENT LOTT IS A TROOPER. I guess that's what these boys called themselves—troopers. But I sure wasn't one of them.

No one ever mentioned seeing a biplane.

I don't know if that leaflet played even the smallest part in the election outcome, and I never heard from them—or of them—again. Oh, yes, I lost the election by sixty votes.

The activities of the Rebel Underground were warning signs that a different day was dawning at Ole Miss. Race had become a regular topic of conversation among students, and integration began finding quiet corners of support. But no one could foresee the explosive events to come.

*    *    *

The sting of defeat was offset by other challenges, and moments of personal heartbreak and emotional fulfillment in my life soon put everything back in proper perspective.

Midway through my time at Ole Miss, I was home for a long holiday when I noticed that my parents were arguing more, sometimes lapsing into periods of painful silence that lasted the better part of several days. When I was younger, I'd slept in a small bedroom next to my parents' room, and I often heard my mother crying at night—sometimes night after night for weeks. Now, I realized how selfish I had been to insist that they remain married when they were obviously so miserable in each other's company. The pressure of running the furniture business had plainly increased the stress on my dad, and he was starting to cave in. He was a handsome guy, with a great personality in many ways. People took to him, and he worked hard. But he had only a ninth grade education and had a bit of an inferiority complex, particularly vis-à-vis my mother, who had her teaching certificate. The drinking, if anything, had gotten worse. It was all too much for him.

The moment had come, on this visit, to confront what I had previously avoided. Over dinner one night, as I sat across from Mom and Dad, I said, "If you guys just can't make it, then divorce may be the only answer." They both looked at me with relief in their eyes, but neither made a move for a while.

Several weeks later, when I was back in school, Mom called to let me know that she and Dad had filed for divorce. I'd certainly been expecting it, but the reality still hit me in the gut and knocked the breath out of me. I was devastated. As a child I had convinced myself that their marriage would last forever. I was an adult now, but that didn't diminish my bitter disappointment over the outcome.

I sagged against my desk, with Allen Pepper watching from across our fraternity house room. Having heard my side of the conversation, he knew I was deeply hurt. Finally, he got up, walked over, and held out his hands: "Trent, do you want to pray?"

We prayed together for several minutes.

"You were really torn up," Allen told me later. "Glad I was there to help." So was I. It was an enduring example of what bound us together as fraternity brothers—and, more than that, a gesture that bound us together as friends for life.

About that time, Tricia Thompson came into my life again. I had known her, it seemed, almost all my life. Back before we met, my mom, who was teaching at Tricia's grade school, decided that this was the girl for me. "She's perfect," Mom said. One afternoon when I was running track and had to head past the grammar school as part of practice, Mom pointed out Tricia. She was bubbly and cute, but she was two years younger than I was—a lowly sixth grader—so I ran on by. And there were those times in high school after band practice, but that was the extent of it.

Then one summer evening after my sophomore year at Ole Miss, I grabbed some buddies and went to the movies at the Ritz Theater in downtown Pascagoula. Tricia, now a high school graduate, was in line for the snack bar. I noticed her instantly; she'd cut her hair and had become a beauty queen—knockout good looking. By then I had broken up with my longtime girlfriend, so I called Tricia for a date. She said she was busy. I called her again and got the same line: *I'm busy.* I called yet again, and it was the same story. *Look,* I told her, *this is the third time I've called. I'm not calling again.* She broke her date and we went out. The rest is history.

We dated that summer, and then she went off to college at Belhaven, a Presbyterian-affiliated school in Jackson. We continued to date occasionally, then regularly, then exclusively—especially after she came to Ole Miss for her sophomore year. So we were at college together when integration came to the University of Mississippi.

Eight months before the start of my senior year, twenty-nine-year-old Air Force veteran James Meredith—with heavy political backing—applied to all-white Ole Miss in a move that, if successful, would force full integration of the state's educational system.

Our state's self-proclaimed segregationist governor, Ross Barnett, refused Meredith's application and wrote him that he was not welcome at Ole Miss. Meredith announced that he would appeal to the registrar of the university, a man bound to uphold the civil rights laws. But Barnett quickly jimmied the rules, took over as registrar, and rejected Meredith's application a second time.

Meredith found the courts to be much friendlier. It was a classic battle between the state courts and the federal system. The crucial decision came on June 25, 1962, when the U.S. Fifth Circuit Court of Appeals ruled that Meredith had been rejected solely because of his race. Then the judges on the circuit court split, allowing one of them, Judge B. F. Cameron, to issue stays against the full court action.

After another four weeks of battle in Mississippi's state court system, the matter was sent to the United States Supreme Court. On September 10, Justice Hugo Black set aside the stays and ordered Governor Barnett and the Chancellor of Ole Miss to admit Meredith for the fall semester.

Although it seems impossible to believe now, Meredith's imminent enrollment at Ole Miss was not a dominant issue on campus in the immediate days after Justice Black's order. The *Daily Mississippian* wrote very little on the subject in mid-September, and it rarely came up as a topic of conversation at frat house dinners or over coffee in the student union. Most students assumed, I think, that this would be a fairly benign event—that Meredith would walk through the registrar's door at the proper time, purchase his books, and head off to class. The silence on the subject was deafening. Allen Pepper got it right when he said that it seemed as if the Meredith drama was taking place behind a gauze curtain. You could almost see the ramifications, but not quite.

I confess that I was in the ranks of the clueless. I believed then that segregation was wrong and that it was cruel, but we were living in a world our ancestors had created for us. And segregation was an ugly part of that world. My fleeting experience with the ugliness of the Rebel Underground should have given me pause, but it didn't.

For all the apparent apathy, however, some student leaders at Ole Miss believed that Meredith would confront a great deal of hostility and a very tense campus. Shortly after Judge Black's decision, Dick Wilson, president of the student body, had summoned top student leaders to a summit conference; I attended because I was then president of the Inter-fraternity Council. Everyone pledged to nip any signs of violence in the bud. But none of us really thought there would be bloodshed. "This is a school of Southern ladies and gentlemen," Wilson said. "I don't think Ole Miss students are going to deal in cruelty."

After our discussions, I wasn't so sure. But I also believed that the inherent idealism and honor of the Greek system would keep fraternity and sorority members out of the fray. Allen Pepper told me one night: "You know, Trent, all of us have strong spiritual backgrounds: the federal government doesn't have to worry about us."

As September wore on, we inevitably focused on other matters—school work, of course, and our championship football team. Then, two weeks before Ole Miss's big game with the University of Kentucky, Barnett went on statewide television and radio to protest Meredith's enrollment and lay down a gauntlet: "We will not surrender to the evil and illegal forces of tyranny," he said. "No, we will not." Twice, Barnett would block Meredith's attempts to register at Ole Miss; Lieutenant Governor Paul Johnson would block his third attempt.

We expected Meredith simply to appear on campus one morning—after a rushed registration in the predawn hours. That was the only course of action that made any sense. Throughout September, there were rumors that he already was on campus, or that he would be arriving the next day. And Chancellor J. D. Williams hinted that Meredith would be hustled through a back door of the Lyceum Building, where the registrar's office was, to emerge through the front door as a full-fledged student. In fact, Meredith the mystery man hadn't been within ten yards of the campus all summer and early fall. Federal officials were holding him back, fearful of an outbreak of violence.

Early in the last week of September, stronger rumors than usual suggested that this was the weekend. But as Saturday approached, there were no signs of approaching trauma. So we journeyed off to the big game against Kentucky in high spirits. But the minute Tricia and I arrived at the stadium in Jackson on that evening—Saturday, September 29—we could feel that something was up. Governor Barnett was ensconced in a private block of seats, surrounded by some of the most conservative politicians in the state.

A last-minute addition to the program noted that Barnett intended to make a halftime speech, followed by the University of Mississippi Men's Chorus, which was to introduce the new state song. Somehow, the governor had convinced the Ole Miss Board of Trustees to convert his personal campaign song, "Roll With Ross," into "Go Mississippi"—a strange bit of musical nepotism that bound Barnett even closer to Ole Miss and its future.

At halftime, the governor's emotional speech carried Barnett and a large part of the audience to the brink of tears. After briefly mentioning with disdain the "integration at our beloved state university," he threw his arms skyward and boomed out: "I love this state; I love its people; and I love my country."

Some in the audience accepted Barnett's words as a battle cry, or at least a gesture of defiance. I was mystified by his melodramatic performance. It hadn't seemed like a battle cry to me. It sounded more like the ramblings of a politician wishing to turn back the clock. But Barnett wasn't appealing to the audience in the stadium; he was focused instead on the millions of Southerners tuned into the radio and television stations broadcasting the game.

But nothing happened that Saturday. Since most of us were remaining overnight in Jackson, I telephoned the Sigma Nu house back in Oxford and was relieved by reports that the campus was deserted and battened down for the night. It turned out to be the calm before the storm.

It's about 170 miles from Jackson to Oxford, and the roads were unusually crowded as we headed back to campus early Sunday afternoon. It seemed that an inordinate number of trucks and a majority of the passenger cars were ignoring the speed limit. Tricia had been watching the traffic build from a trickle to a flood of vehicles as we neared Oxford. "Trent," she said, "an awful lot of these cars have Texas, Louisiana, and Oklahoma license plates." I switched on the radio, seeking guidance on negotiating the now-crazy roads leading to Oxford and Ole Miss.

Many of the stations were fanning the flames by broadcasting pieces of Barnett's speech. The governor himself was reinforcing his position in phone-in interviews with radio stations. "If we don't save our state, nobody will," he told a Biloxi disc jockey.

"Are you asking Mississippians to join the crowds down in Oxford?" asked the announcer.

"I'm not in a position to do that," Barnett answered quietly. "People just have to follow their consciences and their hearts." That was a fairly transparent code, an indirect way of urging people to do what they could to protest the integration of Ole Miss.

We got our first real look at what would become the "Battle at Oxford" as we drove past the tiny city airstrip. The planes had been moved to the side to make room for a sprawling army camp that included a sea of tents, trucks full of weapons, armored personnel carriers, and even battle tanks. Far in the back was a fleet of ambulances; army medics were setting up tents that would serve as a field hospital.

Tricia turned to me: "Trent, Oxford is such a tiny town. It's not even equipped to handle all of these people, much less the National Guard and the military." We learned later that President Kennedy had ordered the United States Army Corps of Engineers to build a facility large enough to hold fifteen thousand soldiers and Marines.

I was much more concerned with returning Tricia to her dorm so I could get back to the Sigma Nu house to make decisions only the fraternity commander can make. When we got there, we saw a scattering of exploded tear gas canisters around Barnard, Tricia's dorm, which was by then protected by campus police. As the evening of violence unfolded, her dorm would become a kind of safe house for students anxious to avoid the dangers outside.

It took me forty-five minutes to get back to Sigma Nu—a journey that usually took about ten minutes. The Lyceum, to my absolute shock, was surrounded by a ring of helmeted soldiers. It was still fairly early in the evening. Inside the fraternity house I sensed panic, uncertainty, and confusion among the members. As I moved from one group to another, from room to room, it was clear that I had to quiet things down, as well as remind my fraternity brothers of the stakes we faced. "This is not a panty raid," I emphasized. "This is a serious matter that could only have serious repercussions for anyone who participates in the night ahead."

Privately, my emotions were more complicated. It's certainly true that I didn't want any of my fraternity brothers hurt or compromised in any way. But I also didn't want to add any credence to the efforts of the troublemakers and hoodlums who were trying to turn back the clock. Integration was steamrolling through the South. Its time had come. I didn't want anyone in our house entangled in a violent and foolish nostalgia for segregation.

We set about battening down the fraternity house. I asked the brothers already there to stay put. And I dispatched runners to retrieve other Sigma Nus from their dorms and apartments. By 9 P.M., when the nastiness in the Lyceum began in earnest, 136 Sigma Nus were inside our fraternity house. And I saw that they stayed there until noon the next day—after Meredith had quietly and politely registered as an Ole Miss student.

During those tumultuous hours, Sigma Nus monitored the dramatic events using their transistor radios. In the chapter room it was standing room only, with boys jostling each other to watch the fleeting television pictures of the international event unfolding only a mile and a half away.

As "missing" Sigma Nus straggled in, we heard some harrowing tales from members who'd been caught in the storm. One young freshman, returning from a date, had his car rushed as he circled Oxford, fighting for a way back home. Finally, he made it to a distant suburban area and slept in his battered car.

Gaylen Roberts didn't show up until Monday, when he ambled through the door with some bags of donuts in his hands. On Sunday night he'd left to help a friend retrieve his car from a parking lot near the Lyceum. U.S. Marshals greeted them as they stepped up to the car. They were escorted to the basement of the Lyceum and locked up with seventy-five other students. "It's for your own good," said one of the marshals. "The way things are heating up, I doubt if you could get back to your fraternity in any case."

My roommate, Allen Pepper, found himself in a tear-gas fog as he tried to pick up his date—a freshman girl he'd met only once before. He arrived at her dorm a few minutes early and sat down in the reception room to watch the evening news. Halfway through the newscast, the screen went blank and President Kennedy's face appeared on camera. In a national telecast, he appealed directly to Ole Miss students. "Please, help keep the peace."

"You have a great tradition to uphold there at Ole Miss," the president said. "It's a tradition of honor and courage won on the field of battle and on the gridiron. You are men of patriotism and integrity. The most effective means of upholding law and order lies with you—the students of the University of Mississippi. It lies within your courage to accept these laws with which you disagree as well as those you agree with. Remember, the eyes of the nation and the world are upon you—and the honor of your university hangs in the balance."

Less than five minutes later, a barrage of tear gas canisters rolled down the slopes surrounding the dorm. "I had to leave," Pepper told me. "You couldn't breathe in there. That attack was uncalled for." On his complicated drive back to Sigma Nu, Allen ran into a state policeman guarding a walking trail. Pepper pleaded with him to do something about the tear gas flooding into the girls' dorms. But the man just scowled. "Why don't you call up your friend Bobby Kennedy and have him do something about it?"

At the end of the day, not one Sigma Nu was implicated in the violence, which left two persons dead and twenty-nine marshals wounded by gunfire.

My mission had been accomplished, but I felt anger in my heart over the way the federal government had invaded Ole Miss to accomplish something that could have been handled peacefully and administratively.

Ole Miss was a different school from then on. And our innocence was gone.

# 4

# A POLITICAL EDUCATION

L ife at Ole Miss was enjoyable for Tricia, but by the end of her sophomore year she decided she wanted to go to dental hygiene school. She was, after all, the daughter of a dentist. She was accepted at the University of Tennessee Dental School in Memphis, and spent the next two years there. We were engaged by the fall of 1963, after I started at the University of Mississippi Law School. I gave her an engagement ring at "the Point," a spot on the beach in Pascagoula just a hundred yards from where our home is today. It was a beautiful night, with the moon shining on the water, and we watched the submarines come in—or at least that was how we described it in the years that followed.

It was not an easy time for either of us. Tricia was in Memphis and I was in Oxford. After I started law school that summer, the money ran out; my parents, after their divorce, could no longer help. So I went to work full time as a recruiter for the Ole Miss Office of Placement and Financial Aid, and returned to law school part time. I would travel the state the first part of the week for my job, then go to law classes later in the week. I'd see Tricia on weekends. Sometimes, I worried that we wouldn't make it. But we did.

Tricia and I were married two days after Christmas, on December 27, 1964, at the First Presbyterian Church, surrounded by friends and family. Our bridesmaids and groomsmen were all friends from high school and Ole Miss—except for the best man, my dad. It was a short wedding, seventeen minutes, and simple. The reception afterward was in the church parlor, but I never got there. My Sigma Nu brothers grabbed me and took me to the beach seawall, where they chained me to a blinking light, sprayed me with red paint, and left. Some time later, Tricia's older brother, Perry, arrived and unchained me.

Our honeymoon consisted of one night at the Broadwater Hotel in Biloxi and four days in New Orleans. I had three hundred dollars for this beginning to our marriage, and we made it do.

I continued to work part time until the summer of 1965, when I went back to full-time student status at the law school. By that time, of course, Vietnam was front and center, the civil rights movement was hot, and the national debates on both were at high-decibel levels. Ole Miss brought down several professors from Yale Law School to teach us constitutional law and, in particular, the intricacies of the new civil rights legislation. They were young and personable; we would eat with them in the cafeteria, drink beer in the evening, and discuss the issues of the day. But they also were liberal and had an attitude problem. They were at Ole Miss, they felt, to lead these poor, barefoot Southern boys out of the wilderness. And they were not sympathetic to countervailing points of view. I had a friend who argued with these professors in his written work, and he got lousy grades. I decided not to provoke them and got decent grades.

What those young professors did was to create a backlash. Instead of making us more liberal, they helped to create a generation of thoughtful, issue-oriented conservatives who grew up to run Mississippi politics. People like Thad Cochran, the current senior senator from Mississippi. And Haley Barbour, our governor. And, well, Trent Lott.

I had no intention of becoming a politician. Campus politics had been fun, and I liked courting—and counting—votes. But I'd decided to become an attorney in my junior year in high school. That was my dream. When I was working as an Ole Miss recruiter and as the traveling representative for the alumni association, "you oughta go into politics" was a refrain I heard frequently. But I'd taken on those jobs to pay for my law degree. I had become a serious player at the law school, where I was president of Phi Alpha Delta legal fraternity, a student body officer, and, with my partner, winner of the school's first-year moot court competition.

I was serious about the law school curriculum, and hunkered down to master the basic tenets of the legal system. And my grades showed it.

Tricia counted on me becoming an attorney and settling down with her in Pascagoula. That was her dream for me, and she worked as a dental hygienist to help pay the Ole Miss tuition. She didn't want me to become a politician, and expressed that quite forcefully even before politics finally sought me out.

Not long after graduation, I joined Pascagoula's prestigious law firm, Bryan and Gordon, and hit the ground running, hoping to season myself as quickly as possible. We bought our first house in a nice middle-class neighborhood. Some of my Sigma Nu buddies, who are still in my life, described the house as a love nest—an allusion to Tricia's and my devotion to each other.

On a late winter Saturday in 1968, I was at my law office, totally engrossed in writing a brief for the Mississippi Supreme Court. Tricia was home with our young son, Chet, and I had the suite of offices pretty much to myself. It was an intricate and complicated brief; I'd come in early and planned to stay an hour or two, but as the clock clicked past noon, I was still there. That's enough for a Saturday, I thought, and began to think about leaving. I was prowling through a logjam of sentences when the phone rang. I looked down at the flashing buttons and saw that the call was on my private line.

Naturally, I thought it was Tricia.

"Hi," I said jauntily, "Don't worry, I'm not going to be here all day."

A booming voice answered me.

"Trent Lott, this is Congressman Colmer. Have you got a minute?"

"Sure, of course," I said, mystified as to why one of Mississippi's most respected legislators had me tracked down on a Saturday afternoon. At the time, William Colmer had represented the state's Fifth Congressional District for thirty-four years. He was a legend—not only in coastal Mississippi but in Washington as well. He was chairman of the House Rules Committee, and had been an inside adviser to Presidents Roosevelt, Truman, and Eisenhower.

Colmer also was one of a score of Democrats who briefly bolted from the party after presidential nominee Harry Truman adopted an aggressive civil rights stance as part of his platform. Strom Thurmond raised millions in campaign funds and fielded a roster of candidates who called themselves Dixiecrats. Colmer was one of those who supported the Dixiecrats—and supported Thurmond's bid for president at the top of their ticket. Governor Fielding Wright of Mississippi was Thurmond's vice presidential running mate.

Though the Dixiecrats became little more than a footnote in America's political history, they carried South Carolina, Alabama, Mississippi, and Louisiana in the 1948 presidential election, winning margins of up to 80 percent in the all-white electorates of those states.

By the time I got the phone call from Colmer, the Dixiecrats were also little more than a footnote in *his* career. He'd been too busy fielding progressive legislation to benefit his home state. Like Strom Thurmond, he was well past his firebrand days, and had become more moderate on civil rights issues as each year passed. He had worked tirelessly to improve Mississippi's standard of living, bringing new roads, better flood control channels, deeper shipping lanes, and a burst of new industry to his home state. But I knew little of this history when Congressman Colmer approached me. "I'd like you to come over and talk with me," he said. "This afternoon." For a young attorney on the first rung of the ladder, this was a command performance. "I'll be right down," I said as I hung up the receiver and sprinted across the room for my coat.

The congressman lived on Pascagoula's Gulf shore, and when he was in town—which was infrequently—he'd be out fishing. He greeted me at his back door, a tall, spare man who still had a full head of red hair. We had coffee and made small talk—about my achievements at Ole Miss, about the bright future for my law practice, and about Tricia, whom Colmer considered "the best catch on the Gulf Coast." He was preaching to the choir.

Then he turned serious: "Trent, I'd like you to come to Washington and become my administrative assistant. And I'm going to need you up there pretty quick. My old AA just told me he's decided to retire." I was overwhelmed by the suddenness and the sincerity of the offer, and flattered by his confidence in me since I was both young and inexperienced. There was a lengthy pause. Congressman Colmer was expecting an instant "yes," and when he didn't get it, his eyes locked on mine.

"Sir, I know a lot about campus politics but nothing about the demands of Washington," I told him. "I need some time to think about it and to discuss it with Tricia and the senior members of the law firm."

"Sure, son," he said. "But I think you are the man for the job and that this is the job for you."

There had been a political precedent for this. Shortly after I returned to Pascagoula and got into my law office, I received a telephone call from a young attorney I'd known well at Ole Miss. "A lot of us have been talking," he said. "And we think you should run for Congress in the fall of 1968."

"Thanks for the vote of confidence," I said idly. "But it really is too soon for me." And it was. I had no money to speak of, no experience to speak of, and a wife and a new son to support. My bosses were top-drawer attorneys, and they were giving me the chance to learn the law while working side by side with them. And, only half-jokingly, Tricia announced she'd expected to marry a successful Mississippi lawyer, not a congressman whose pay was in the moderate five figures. So I turned the guys down.

But I did campaign aggressively for Congressman John Bell Williams for governor of Mississippi. In fact, I became his youth chairman and organized groups of young men and women for his appearances. I was an advance man for what turned out to be a successful gubernatorial campaign. Once again, I had tumbled onto a road where I could meet the best and the brightest in the Mississippi political world. That was the experience Colmer recognized, and thought could be turned to good use as his administrative assistant.

Pascagoula was safe and secure for me. I was in one of Mississippi's top law firms; I was president of the local Jaycees; all of our family roots were in this small city by the Gulf. I told Rex Gordon, a senior partner in the firm, that I'd had a political offer. Without consulting anyone, he offered me a nifty pay raise and an immediate junior partnership. I decided to stay put.

Then I learned that Josh Morse, dean of the Ole Miss Law School, had personally recommended me for the job with Colmer. That gave me pause. If the dean had that much confidence in me, maybe I should go. I was back on the fence. But when it came time to phone Congressman Colmer, I backed off again. Tricia finally made up my mind for me. At dinner one night, she looked up and said, "Look, let's go for a couple of years. It'll be fun for a while, and then we can pack up and come home." She helped put the offer in perspective. I also realized that even a couple of years in Washington would help my law career when I returned to Mississippi.

In May 1968, I drove Tricia and Chet to Washington, D.C., in our 1968 Pontiac. We were anxious to see the monuments and to experience the grandeur of the nation's capital. We didn't bring furniture, only what we could get in the car. But we got off the freeway and drove straight into a war zone. The student protests against the Vietnam War were gathering power and supporters at a frightening rate. Some fifty thousand protesters filled the streets. There were Special Forces personnel high up on the Capitol dome, and all streets leading to the White House were cordoned off by both soldiers and policemen.

Tricia was wide-eyed. Back in Mississippi, the state's basic conservatism had turned back most signs of the hippie movement. Whatever fatigues were on display in our state belonged to the men and women from the Gulf Coast's military bases.

We found a one-bedroom apartment far in southwest D.C., filled it with rented furniture, and I reported to Congressman Colmer's offices for what I expected to be a relatively brief education in the intricacies of the United States Congress.

When I first arrived at Congressman Colmer's office in the Capitol, I was struck by its simplicity and by the absence of memorabilia from his four decades in office. I was also surprised at the small staff—six staffers in his congressional office, and five to help with his work on the Rules Committee. Compare that to the twenty or so that staff the average congressional offices today, and seventy for the Rules Committee.

Colmer threw me into the churning political waters of Congress immediately. I ran his office, supervised the drafting of legislation, handled the press, and often represented him at national political events. The congressman, by then seventy-eight years old, also relied on me to carry his message back to the cities, towns, and communities of Mississippi's Fifth District, where I soon became a well-known figure.

I learned quickly how much power resided within the Rules Committee. I learned that Colmer, as chairman, could have a bill "pigeonholed" with a single telephone call. I would invoke his name, and the measure would just disappear for good—as if it had never been introduced. Such was the power of the old postwar Congress. I have never again witnessed that much power, in all my years of leadership in both the House and Senate.

Despite the depth of that power and Colmer's length of service, hostile Democrats had begun ganging up on him not long before I came to Washington. Colmer was well respected on both sides of the aisle. But as I grew to know him better, I began to notice that his closest cronies were Republicans—politicians such as House Minority Leader Gerald Ford, Republican Whip Les Arends of Illinois, and H. Allen Smith of California, the ranking member of the Rules Committee. It seemed to me that Colmer was a bona fide Republican in the guise of a Southern Democrat. His philosophy was clearly Republican. He was for a strong national defense and states' rights; he hated deficit spending and high taxes. And he often said that you can count on federal control following the federal dollar. That partly explained his unbending opposition to federal aid for education.

He was a courteous and humble man, without a cruel bone in his body, and he was always generous in sharing his knowledge of public policy and the rules and folkways of the House. Our working days often would end at five-thirty or so. I'd fix him an Old Grand-Dad bourbon and Coke, he'd fire up one of the cheap cigars he loved, and we'd talk in his cozy inner office. His anecdotes taught me much about principle and about flexibility. Once, John McCormack, the Speaker of the House, wanted Colmer to do something that he didn't want to do, so Colmer just left town and went home to Mississippi. Then he reversed position on the issue. In one of our "fireside chats" in his office, he explained why. "Well, when you're riding a bronco and about to get thrown, it's smart to get off first." I could translate easily enough: He knew he was going to lose anyway, so he conceded the point, didn't cross his speaker, and lived to fight another day.

In one of our conversations, I confronted him with my theory about his political preferences. "You're more of a Republican than a Democrat," I blurted out. He put down his glass of bourbon—his only drink of the day—and looked out the window for a minute or two. "Hmm, maybe you're right, Trent," he finally said. "But it is far too late for me to change now. For one thing, I can't put the chairmanship of the Rules Committee at risk. The people of Mississippi earned that position—and its power—by keeping me here all of these years."

I wasn't tied to the Democratic Party in any way. I was just the newest staffer on the block. So I began to reassess my own political philosophy—patterns of thinking handed down by scores of politically active ancestors. I had made friends with Democratic staff members but also with Republicans, probably more of the latter. I was an original founder of a bipartisan, bicameral organization called the Conservative Luncheon Club—another clue that I was slowly slipping over to the other side. Its members included both Republican senators from Nebraska, Carl Curtis and Roman Hruska; GOP Representative Phil Crane of Illinois; Dick Moe, assistant to Vice President Spiro Agnew; Ralph Vinovich, administrative assistant to Republican Representative Bob Michel of

Illinois; the scholar and budding columnist George Will; and Paul Weyrich and Ed Feulner, two conservative minds who would help to found the Heritage Foundation think tank in 1973.

At the height of my personal dissatisfaction with the Democratic Party, Gene Ainsworth and I strolled over to the Senate side for a luncheon given by the Young Burros Club—a club for Democratic senatorial staffers. The key speakers were Lawrence O'Brien, chairman of the Democratic National Committee, and Representative Ray Blanton of Tennessee.

The presentations were tediously long and filled with boilerplate Democratic rhetoric. On the walk back, I elbowed Ainsworth and whispered, "I don't agree with a single word I heard today. Gene, I'm not a Democrat!"

That was the day I crossed the Rubicon and became a Republican.


In December 1971, Tricia and I had been in Washington for three and a half years, longer than we originally had expected. Colmer was eighty-one, but it didn't look as if he planned to retire. I hadn't severed my relationship with the law firm back in Pascagoula. It was time, we thought, to go home.

When I told Colmer, he turned out to have a surprise of his own: After four decades in the House, he told me, he was thinking of retiring. But he hadn't made up his mind quite yet, and asked me to stay until he did. "Of course," I said. He had been so kind to me; there was no way I could refuse.

In February 1972 Colmer announced his retirement, and Tricia and I began making plans to move back to Pascagoula. *Not so fast,* I began to think. I hadn't believed that elective politics was for me, but that thinking had begun to change over those first few years in Washington. And try as I might, I couldn't escape the feeling that this was part of God's plan for me. Without really admitting it to myself, I had been idly considering a run to succeed Colmer as the congressman from the Fifth District. I was barely thirty years old then, but I had been given enormous responsibility and access by my mentor. I'd made speeches on Colmer's behalf when he was too tired or disinclined to give them himself. I knew his organization and all his money people. And I had a political presence in the district from all the time I had spent there at his behest.

Even so, if I was to run, I wanted to do it on my terms. I wanted to run as a Republican in a district that was only 8 percent Republican. As usual, I leaned heavily on Tricia. I wouldn't do it without her blessing and her analysis. She immediately said: "Take a chance. Let's go for it." From then on, our discussions were no longer about whether I should run, they zeroed in on the question: *If I'm going to run as a Republican, can I win?* Tricia was terrific. "I guess we'll find out whether or not a Republican can take this district," she said. At that point, we had two children—our daughter, Tyler, was born in 1970—and Tricia was working part time as a dental hygienist. We didn't have a lot of money, so in my book it took guts for Tricia to commit to the uncertainty of an uphill run.

When I told Colmer, he smiled: "I admire you for your courage, Trent, but I fear you are embarking on a hopeless crusade." My heart sank. When I told my mother, she sank back into her chair and said, "Oh, my God." I held steady. If voters were confronted with a candidate, they deserved to know his beliefs. They needed to know that he was a Republican, not a Republican disguised as a Southern Democrat. Besides, as I quipped to my neighbors, Dr. Paul Moore and his wife, Jean, "most voters in the Fifth District *are* Republicans; they just don't know it yet."

I have a basic philosophy of government that I want to make crystal clear before I ask for someone's vote. And it's in line with Republican beliefs. I believe the best government is the least government—the government that is the closest to the people. I believe in fiscal responsibility and in a strong national defense. And I have priorities—the highest being my family. I also feel very strongly about my faith, but I don't wear it on my sleeve. Anyone who knows me understands that family, loyalty, faith, and friends guide my life. That is what drives me on every front. And that was, quite simply, what I offered the Fifth District voters back in 1972.

It wasn't that easy, of course. I had to mount a heck of a campaign—from the beginning. Ten candidates qualified for the Democratic primary, competing for 107,000 votes. And leading the pack was an energetic, media-handsome Mississippi State Senator named Ben Stone from Gulfport.

To the surprise of many, I had three primary opponents: Paul Grady, the mayor of Hattiesburg; former Mississippi Republican finance chairman Buddy Klumb; and Karl Mertz, a Gulf Coast gadfly with little chance of winning. However, Mertz could and did prove disruptive—confusing the issues and distracting the electorate.

I withdrew the five thousand dollars Tricia and I had in savings, and got about nineteen thousand dollars in campaign donations from civic and business leaders in the district. My bag of tricks included an echo of those words to my neighbor, a slogan remembered to this day: "The voters in here are really Republican to the core; they just don't know it yet." A more serious and effective slogan anchored the campaign and tagged me as a veteran of the wars on Capitol Hill. Referring to my Colmer years, our banners, bumper stickers, and newspaper ads carried this tagline: "Experience Means a Lott in Congress." Corny, but straight to the point.

I stressed my experience with Colmer every chance I got; he was a genuine legend in the Fifth. And I spoon-fed them a heavy dose of how liberal the Democrats were in Washington. Judging from the faces in the crowds, I could tell that liberalism was about as popular as castor oil before breakfast. At one campaign stop at a Methodist campground, I shouted out: "Do we really want Hubert Humphrey and Ben Stone running things in our capital?" My words were greeted with silence. But one after another, the worshippers began to nod their heads "no"—a fine compliment from tent revivalists.

I used some of the funds we had to purchase a few television ads, but I basically used the money to stump the district—from the shrimp docks on the Gulf to the piney woods, from Biloxi mansions to four-room houses situated on the banks of Mississippi bayous.

My first confidence builder was a convincing win in the Republican primary. In fact, 70 percent of the 11,345 Republicans voters cast ballots for me—a happy statistic, but an election-night pittance compared with the hundred-thousand-plus Democratic voters who were up for grabs.

I was well aware that fewer than one in ten people in the district identified themselves as Republicans. I even blurted out on a local radio show that I had "never met a Fifth District Republican in my life." A feeble joke, but it highlighted my dilemma. Not only did I need to capture all of the GOP voters; I had to corral at least 40 percent of the district Democrats—the same folks who had presented my opponent, Ben Stone, with a landslide when he first ran for state senator.

The savvy political thinking went this way when it came to my candidacy: We've got this sharp young man from Colmer's office, but the victory is going to Gulfport's Ben Stone. As the fall campaign season approached, I was hoping for a miracle of sorts. With a wave of his much-used political wand and a few choice words, my former boss William Colmer could easily have anointed me as his heir apparent, or at least the front-runner. But the man back at the Capitol remained stoic and silent.

Maybe it was his message to me that I needed to roll up my sleeves and mount a grassroots campaign that covered every town and settlement in the coastal district. There was no guidebook for this task. Given Colmer's political longevity, there had not been a truly contested Fifth District congressional race in decades.

I expected little or no help from the Republican National Committee. The Democrats had taken the state for granted since the Roosevelt administration, and the Republicans ignored it. They didn't even bother to campaign—not even in hot presidential balloting. For all intents and purposes, it was a one-party state. The Nixon reelection campaign was about to change all of that. But the results wouldn't come until election night.

With my five thousand dollars in savings emptied by the primary, I scurried back to Colmer and ran the campaign from his congressional office in Washington. I couldn't afford to do it any other way. But evidence poured in that I was making some headway—despite my absence from the political playing field. By mid-September, I found out that polls showed Stone and me in a tie. About that time, I began running spots to build up my name; it was necessary despite the profile I had built working for Colmer.

By fall, Stone began running attack ads, the most prominent of which sneered: "Trent Lott isn't a Republican. He's just a quitter." I don't think the negative campaigning won Stone many votes. But it helped me a little. The ads made Tricia so angry that she dropped her original plan to remain on the sidelines and joined me on the campaign trail.

My key campaign staff held a meeting in early October to decide whether to run our own, competing ads. "Don't respond," said Colmer, when I sought his guidance. "Go ahead with your positive ads and ignore him." Despite his enthusiasm and advice, Congressman Colmer still hadn't given me his blessing.

So I threw myself into a grassroots campaign that would keep me traveling constantly until four days before the election. I appeared unannounced in the parking lots of urban shopping centers; I visited town councils that were so far from navigable roads that we needed a four-wheel-drive vehicle to get there. And before it was over, I passed out 150,000 leaflets.

I haunted the site of any reasonable gathering place—bake sales, greased pig races, barbershops. But above all, I wandered down the main streets of a hundred towns and villages, shaking hands as I went. I listened to complaints, kissed babies (of course), and took copious notes about things that needed attention in the district.

In late fall, as we were rushing head-on toward Election Day, I hired a prop airplane, pasted my logo on its side, and calculated a flight plan that would hit most major stops in the district. The success of this airborne jaunt gained quite a bit of class when my Sigma Nu buddy, Guy Hovis, decided to come to Mississippi and sing at my rallies. He'd gotten permission to take off a few days from the grueling *Lawrence Welk* schedule to help me. As a bonus he brought along his new wife, Ralna English, a brown-haired beauty who was one of Welk's top stars.

We took off from the Gulfport Airfield—Tricia, me and my copious notes, Ralna, and Guy with his guitar, the only music we could afford. By combining politics with entertainment, we drew people from in front of their television sets, away from fishing trips and meetings. We frequently emptied the offices of the town we were visiting: Ralna and Guy were so well known that the bosses were as anxious to see them as the employees.

The formula targeted our ideal audience. Once Guy and Ralna had energized the crowd with their repertoire, which included a fair number of gospel songs, I pulled out my speech and chatted for about fifteen minutes. Then we jumped back into the plane and were off again. No matter the venue, we offered the full presentation—often in the living room of single-family houses.

But there was glitz as well. We played before five hundred people at a bowl just above the Gulf in Biloxi, and filled auditoriums in several towns. Often we played outdoors. And once, Ralna, Guy, and I climbed two stories to the top of an air-conditioning tower, where the singers brought down the house with "Put Your Hand in the Hand."

Back in Pascagoula, I found I'd lost about eighteen pounds and was as tanned as a surfer. Election Day was only nine days away.

But Congressman Colmer still kept his silence. Finally, a Gulfport attorney supporting me, Thomas N. Roberts, asked him why he hadn't endorsed either Stone or Lott. On November 1, 1972, Colmer finally replied: "The people have been very generous to me over the past twenty elections. I do not feel it is incumbent on me to try to tell them how to vote; however, as for myself, I shall vote for that patriotic young American Trent Lott." Use this anyway you wish, he concluded.

I had it in newspaper ads within hours. With that endorsement and the expectation of a Nixon landslide in the district, I felt the tide turning in my favor. On Election Day, the incumbent president took 80 percent of the vote in my district. I received 56.3 percent of the vote, against the toughest opponent I have had in all my nine campaigns.

The Monday after the election I was back in Washington on the congressman's payroll. I spent the next two months closing out Mr. Colmer's office and sending his papers to the University of Southern Mississippi. In those days, nobody paid much attention to the irony of a Republican successor closing out a Democrat's office. It all felt quite natural.

I couldn't wait to get onto the floor of the House of Representatives. I expected it to be *Mr. Smith Goes to Washington*. But I hadn't digested the fact that I would be the greenhorn in a body that was rich in experienced congressmen—and all of them out to protect their turf.

# 5

# A HOUSE BECOMES A HOME

During my first week as a congressman, I stood behind my chair in the last row of the chamber and watched the powerful representatives gathered near the speaker's rostrum. You could almost taste the power exuded by the leaders at the front of the hall. I sat down in my chair and leaned back, wondering how long it would take me to travel the fifty yards between my seat and the heart of the action. Stuck back there with the other freshmen, I hadn't had such little clout in an organization since my days as a pledge in Sigma Nu. But this was big-time intellectual hazing. The leadership kept their congressional rookies in the political boondocks, where they introduced few bills, held no powerful committee chairmanships, and got virtually no time on the floor. There are no instant stars in the House of Representatives. So I sat back and closely followed and absorbed all of the procedures, turning the daily pageant of Congress into a graduate course. When power finally came my way, I intended to be ready for it.

*    *    *

I got a taste of the rarified air that congressmen occasionally experience when President Richard Nixon staged a particularly beautiful Christmas gala for congressmen and their wives. The meal consisted of four courses and was served at elaborately decorated tables. The formal dining room of the White House was a sea of sparkling white lights, dominated by an enormous Christmas tree. Shortly before the banquet began, an ice storm blew into Washington, bringing splashes of snow and hard-blown sleet. At one point, I looked out and noticed that water drizzling from the ice was trickling down the magnolia trees, causing a shimmering effect on the banquet tables. I thought to myself: "Here I am, sitting in the White House having dinner with the president of the United States." For the son of a pipe fitter and a schoolteacher from little Pascagoula, Mississippi, it was pretty heady stuff.

Despite what I considered to be ineffectual rumblings about Watergate, 1973 had been a good year for me as well. I was a mere thirty-two years old when I was sworn in, the second youngest member of the House of Representatives. But my up-close work as Bill Colmer's chief aide, and the contacts I'd made, gave me an insider's edge. I found that the experience *did* make a difference—a major difference that separated me from the other freshmen. For one thing, I didn't have to learn my way around a difficult and quirky branch of government. And I'd already worked and briefly socialized with minority leader Gerald R. Ford—who would soon be moving up to bigger things in the government—and I was also familiar to House Republican whip Les Arends. I immediately landed two top committee assignments: Judiciary, with all of its power and controversy, and Merchant Marine and Fisheries, which would advance my efforts to protect the vast Gulf coastline and fishing industries back in Mississippi.

But I received my biggest boost when the choosy Republicans who ran the Chowder and Marching Society tapped me as one of five new members. It was a singular honor, since forty-seven Republican freshmen joined the House in 1973—many of them riding Nixon's landslide to victory. Joining me in the freshman class were Jim Martin of North Carolina, Dave Treen of Louisiana, Bud Shuster of Pennsylvania, and Claire Bergner of California.

Chowder and Marching was not unlike a secret society. It was founded in 1947 by a group of freshman Republicans in the House that included Richard Nixon of California, Thruston B. Morton of Kentucky, Glenn Davis of Wisconsin, Norris Cotton of New Hampshire, John Lodge of Connecticut, Kenneth Keating of New York, and Caleb Boggs of Delaware. In 1949, a freshman named Gerald Ford was recruited and came aboard. The club set as its initial goal to lobby against what the members considered to be an outrageously funded veterans bill. They were so successful that they transformed themselves into a permanent band to bond and advance the Republican agenda.

Once tapped, a Chowder man became a member for life in or out of the House, in or out of power. The society met every Wednesday afternoon at 5 P.M. to plot strategies and size up candidates. Food and drink fueled the camaraderie, as well as the staying power of the sessions.

No matter how high its members ascended, they still seemed to nurture their personal allegiance to the society. For instance, both Nixon and Ford hosted meetings of Chowder and Marching in the White House. Through Chowder and Marching, I developed friendships with Dave Treen of Louisiana and Jim Martin of North Carolina, who later became governors of their states. I also became close to Bill Archer of Texas and Jack Kemp of New York.

*   *   *

Then Watergate heated up. The news coverage of the burglary didn't impress me. It seemed typical of the liberal press, which was always out to bag another Republican leader. I was convinced it was partisan politics as usual. But I was soon at the center of the controversy.

The Judiciary Committee was made up of thirty-six lawyers, including some of the most liberal Democrats in Congress—men like Peter Rodino of New Jersey and Don Edwards of California. They and others were just dying to get an investigation going. We brushed it off as long as we could. But by spring of 1974, the committee, worn down by conflict and savaged by the press, voted to begin an investigation.

It was an excruciating dilemma for me. Here I was, for the first time in Congress, sitting on the Judiciary Committee, about to conduct hearings on the impeachment of a president I respected greatly. I was horrified by the prospect and intended to be a very aggressive defender. I was a stalwart and partisan Republican, and I saw Nixon as a victim of politics and the press. So I persuaded fourteen freshman congressmen to sign a letter in support of the president.

I also publicly defended Vice President Spiro Agnew early in the state kickback scandal that eventually brought him down. One Sunday I was shocked to pick up the *Washington Post* and read that columnist George Will blamed my misguided support as a "typical [example of] southern visceral sympathy for lost causes."

Objectivity, even simple fairness, was hard to come by. The Republican Judiciary leaders, including California's Chuck Wiggins, who was Nixon's official defender on the committee, assigned me to defend the president against the charge that he had taken improper tax breaks for donating his papers. Having represented

Colmer against precisely the same charge, I knew Nixon was innocent. That potential article of impeachment was easily defeated by a committee vote.

Throughout the weeks of early summer, the media and the Democrats continued to cry for Nixon's impeachment for obstruction of justice. The president's enemies claimed he had used the FBI and CIA to cover up the White House's role in the Watergate break-in. However, as far as I could see, there was no evidence of wrongdoing or cover-up. By then everyone was aware of the Oval Office tapes, first revealed during the Senate Watergate hearings in the summer of 1973, but no specific tapes to date had involved the president in staging a cover-up or obstructing justice. By this point, I had voted three times against impeachment charges.

But then one day, during a Chowder and Marching meeting, I was approached by Jerry Ford. By this time Ford had been nominated as vice president by Nixon and confirmed by the Congress. Discreetly, he leaned over and told me not to go so far out on a limb for the president. I was speechless. What did he know that I and other Judiciary Committee members didn't?

Before Ford's warning could sink in, there was a lull in the investigation, and I took Tricia, Chet, and Tyler to Destin Beach in Florida for our annual vacation. While we frolicked in the Gulf of Mexico, President Nixon's most damning tapes became public. On Wednesday, July 31, the president's lawyer, James St. Clair, was given the transcripts of three conversations held on June 23, 1972, between Nixon and his top aide, Chief of Staff H. R. "Bob" Haldeman. The transcripts showed that just six days after the Watergate "burglary"—really an effort to bug the offices of the Democratic National Committee—Nixon was aware that his campaign director, former Attorney General John Mitchell, and two former White House consultants, E. Howard Hunt and G. Gordon Liddy, were involved.

"The FBI is not under control," Haldeman told Nixon, "and agents are tracing money found on the burglars to Nixon's re-election committee," which Mitchell headed.

Nixon immediately proposed a series of actions that clearly constituted a cover-up. His first suggestion to Haldeman, according to the transcripts, was that each campaign contributor whose check was traced to the burglary by the FBI should claim that the burglars had approached him independently for the money. Haldeman vetoed that suggestion: "That would just involve more and more people all the time."

Haldeman then relayed a suggestion from Mitchell and White House counsel John Dean that the CIA should be asked to tell the FBI to "stay the hell out of this" because the FBI probe would expose secret CIA operations. The president asked Haldeman about the FBI: "You seem to think the thing to do is get them to stop," he said. "All right, fine, I understand it all. We won't second-guess Mitchell and the rest."

In subsequent discussions, the transcripts showed, Nixon ordered Haldeman to call in CIA Director Richard Helms and Deputy CIA Director Vernon Walters and get them to tell Acting FBI Director L. Patrick Gray to "lay off" his investigation of the Watergate burglary money. On tape, Nixon suggested that Haldeman could "claim the president believes that such an investigation would open the whole Bay of Pigs thing again." Of the five burglars, three were men born in Cuba and another apparently had been involved in training Cubans in exile for some sort of covert activity against Castro's dictatorship.

These few paragraphs, which garnered blockbuster coverage when they were revealed, would become the "smoking guns" of Watergate. White House staffers began a frantic effort to locate the president's seven main supporters on the Judiciary Committee—all of whom were still voting against impeachment—to warn them of the new taped disclosures. With the committee deliberations in recess, however, the members were scattered all over the country, and it took some doing to track us down.

Presidential staff member Gene Ainsworth located me at the Holiday Inn in Destin, Florida. Gene had worked for Congressman Sonny Montgomery, a Mississippi Democrat, but not long after our shared experience at the "Young Burros" meeting, he had become a Republican.

It was early on a Saturday afternoon—a thoroughly unexpected call. I could tell by Gene's voice that he was shook up over something. He didn't go into great detail: "We need to meet; I have something to show you that can't wait," he said tersely.

"When and where?" I asked him.

"Late today in Washington," he said. "As soon as you can get here."

A quick check of available flights indicated that I could meet him late that evening at Baltimore-Washington International Airport, a much-used gateway to Washington, D.C., during the 1970s.

Ainsworth remembers pacing away the hours until my flight arrived shortly before 11 P.M. He told me later that, because I'd been such a vocal and persuasive champion of Nixon's, he didn't want me to get caught short by the revelations that were shaking the White House and the entire administration. He met me at the gate and we retreated to a small coffee bar, where the documents could be spread out before me. It took me some time to piece together a full picture of the president's actions because of the disjointed nature of the transcriptions. But I soon saw that this was the real deal—indisputable evidence of a cover-up involving the president of the United States.

I sat and stared at the transcriptions for several minutes. I was just sick to my stomach. A short time later I began drafting a statement that I would now vote for impeachment of the president on the grounds that he had "obstructed justice." It was one of the hardest things I've ever had to do. Three days later, on August 8, 1974, Nixon resigned. As his televised speech played out, I was in my office, my head in my hands. I couldn't look at the screen. This was a constitutional crisis, and I had contributed to it.

Perhaps it should never have reached that point. It was the classic case of the cover-up—obstruction of justice—being worse than the crime itself, and the press pursued it with a vengeance. We would have impeached him in the House, and in a subsequent trial the Senate would have voted successfully to remove him from office. In his final act, Nixon did the right and honorable thing. But his resignation didn't make it any easier for those of us who had supported and looked up to him.

Nixon's disgrace was a watershed for me. It took me three months to get over the trauma of his near-impeachment and resignation. Of all the challenges you can experience in Congress, already—in the second year of my first term—I had seen the worst. From then on, I was honed for battle. But there was another side to it. I was thirty-three years old and sitting on the Judiciary Committee of the nationally televised Nixon impeachment hearings. And however painful the experience may have been, there was no denying that this exposure helped me advance rapidly within the leadership. I was named to the Rules Committee in 1974 and would add to my credentials as the decade went on. But advancement only brought into sharper relief the dilemma I would soon face as the first election of the post-Nixon era approached.

# 6

# THE REVOLUTION IN WAITING

The presidential election of 1976 between Jerry Ford and Jimmy Carter was unquestionably the toughest of my political career. Don't get me wrong: I had gotten to know Representative Jerry Ford of Michigan in my years with Congressman Colmer—they were good friends—and had come to admire his leadership of the Republicans in the House. Ford was one of the first Republicans to urge me to run for Congress. In those days, there weren't that many leadership political action committees, but I did receive a contribution from the campaign funds of Minority Leader Gerald R. Ford. He was, in short, a fine man and a strong Republican.

But during the early 1970s, I found myself increasingly attracted to the conservative and charismatic governor of California, Ronald Wilson Reagan. In fact, my fascination with Reagan had begun even earlier: His speech at the 1964 Republican convention had been an inspiration, and its core message was still having a galvanizing impact on me a decade later. It was there, with the nomination of Arizona senator Barry Goldwater for president, that the conservative movement in America had flowered for the first time. A decade later, Reagan was the movement's most exciting standard bearer. He had shown real leadership and courage during his two terms as governor of California—taking on the liberal University of California system, for example—and on November 20, 1975, he announced his candidacy for the GOP presidential nomination.

My philosophical instincts drove me to Reagan's corner of the ring, a place crowded with many of my key friends and supporters in Mississippi. But it wasn't that simple. Ford had come into the Oval Office at the worst possible moment—after the resignation of a president—and I felt he had done a good job in many ways. He didn't come to the office with a mandate; in fact, he inherited a mess. But he stepped in with humility, honesty, and determination. He took on the triple evils of deficits, high interest rates, and inflation. Most of all, in the post-Watergate, post-Vietnam era, he helped to reestablish the people's faith in their national institutions. He was careful about ethics in government. He vetoed hundreds of excessive spending bills passed by Congress.

Still, Republicans were deeply split. In Mississippi, a huge fight was brewing, with the folks who had built the party dividing into warring camps. Clarke Reed of Greenville, one of the founders of the modern Republican Party in Mississippi, became the leader of the Ford forces. Other longtime leaders, such as Billy Monger, James Moye, Victor Mavar, and Wirt Yeager, were with Reagan. Even my most trusted aide over the preceding four years, Tommy Anderson, was an avid Reagan supporter.

While my colleague in the House, Thad Cochran, and I held back for a while, it was clear that Thad was leaning toward Ford. My heart, however, belonged to Reagan. The day of reckoning came when we were both invited to fly down to Mississippi with President Ford for a brief campaign stop. Ford pushed us to come off the plane with him in Jackson and endorse his candidacy. I remember my hesitation. But in the end he was the president, and he had done a good job, if not an exciting one. I thought he deserved a chance to win a term on his own. So I came off the plane with Thad, and we announced our support for President Ford's election to a full, four-year term.

I was not very happy with my decision, and many of my friends in the district back home were not pleased either. I couldn't bring myself to actively work against Reagan, so I sat out the rest of the primary season and didn't even go to the 1976 GOP convention in Kansas City. Tommy Anderson went as a delegate in my place and supported Reagan.

As history recorded it, the Mississippi delegation went 17–16 for Ford on a procedural vote that gave the nomination to the incumbent. I was in shock at how it all turned out, and I have often wondered whether the outcome would have been different had I gone to Kansas City and supported Reagan. When he spoke to the convention that final night, I was truly inspired. The context was the Cold War, of course, and Reagan talked about the critical importance of freedom and the need to preserve it despite the tensions caused by the nuclear arms race.

After the convention, I went to work trying to help the Ford campaign. It would be tough to carry the South with a moderate Michigan Republican over a Southern Baptist Democrat, but given some of Georgia governor Jimmy Carter's liberal positions, I thought we might pull it off. I recall arguing with Mel Laird, Ford's defense secretary and a former congressman from Wisconsin, that we could carry Mississippi; he didn't believe it. I told him and the president himself that Ford would have to come to the Deep South to have any chance.

To my surprise, Ford did: He decided to make a big swing to Louisiana and Mississippi. The president boarded a river boat and made stops along the Mississippi River, with former Democratic congressmen on board to offer support. He then drove the length of the Mississippi Gulf Coast, stopping at Bay St. Louis, Gulfport, Biloxi, and Pascagoula. The final stop included some heavy support from Southern stalwarts—former Congressman Colmer, Congressman Jack Edwards of Mobile, and Paul "Bear" Bryant, the legendary football coach for the University of Alabama Crimson Tide. I rode in the car with Ford all the way. It was a thrilling experience riding down the azalea-lined Pascagoula Street with the president of the United States and waving to my friends, teachers, neighbors, and former classmates.

Ford's entourage from Washington for the Mississippi trip included his chief of staff, a young fellow about nine months my senior by the name of Dick Cheney. It was one of my first contacts with the future congressman, defense secretary, and vice president, and I remember thinking he was friendly and very efficient in his work.

Meantime, I was campaigning to defeat my own opponent, Gerald Blessey, by as wide a margin as possible. In the end, I got 69 percent of the vote and President Ford carried my congressional district by ten thousand votes. It wasn't enough: The rest of Mississippi went for Carter by twenty thousand votes. Still, losing close in my home state was something of an achievement for Ford. Nationally, it was a close race. Carter edged Ford in the popular vote, 40.8 million to 39.1 million, and won in the electoral college by 297 to 240—with Reagan getting a single electoral vote in a split West Virginia ballot. If Ford had carried Mississippi and Ohio, with thirty-two electoral votes between them, he would have won a full four-year term.

Why didn't he pull it off? There inevitably were dozens of reasons. Remember that on September 8, 1974, a month after the resignation, Ford had pardoned Nixon of any and all crimes he may have committed while in office. It was the right thing to do, and it took great courage. We had to get the Watergate nightmare behind us, and the pardon was a big step in doing so. But it caused a firestorm in the media and among Democrats, and the residual bitterness lingered into 1976. There is no way to tell for certain, of course, but you can make a strong case that the pardon, in the tight election of 1976, probably determined Ford's fate.

When the new Congress convened with Jimmy Carter in the White House, I was concerned about what would happen. The new president seemed sincere, unassuming, and pleasant in my personal contacts with him. He even called on me to ask the blessing at a breakfast meeting he had with some House Republicans. He was our president, and I tried to support him when I could—working with his staff on some budget issues, for example, and on a postal reform bill. But I really wondered if he was up to the job. He had brought a cadre of people with him from back home, which was fine—up to a point. But he didn't bring enough people into his administration who were familiar with the rough and tumble of politics in the nation's capital—people who understood Washington even if they weren't *of* Washington.

We had picked up a few seats in the House in the 1976 election and we gained some more in 1978, by which time we were beginning to smell blood. The economy wasn't doing well, with soaring gasoline prices and rising inflation, and the Iran situation had become a disaster—first with the overthrow of the Shah, then with the seizure of the U.S. embassy in Tehran in November 1979, and finally with the tragically botched rescue mission that cost the lives of eight U.S. Marines. I knew it was over for Carter when he spoke to the nation about a "crisis of the spirit in our country"—an address many called his "malaise" speech, even though he didn't use that word in it. Carter was all negative. The man who would run against him, Ronald Reagan, was the eternal optimist—the man who foresaw morning again in America.

I had considered a run for the Senate in 1978 when my state's senior senator, Jim Eastland, who had served since 1941, announced that he would not seek reelection. We even had a poll done that showed I had a good chance of winning the seat. At the time, though, I just didn't feel ready to go to the Senate. I had just defeated Blessey, who would take my House seat if I gave it up. Besides, I was enjoying my growing clout on the House Rules Committee and had a shot at moving into the leadership. I decided not to run. My colleague, Thad Cochran, ran instead and won. That fall I was elected chairman of the Republican Conference Research Committee, the party's fifth highest leadership position.

By early 1979, after the Republican victors of November 1978 were sworn in, the House was full of future national leaders: Bill Archer of Texas, Bob Livingston and Dave Treen of Louisiana, Jack Kemp of New York, Dan Quayle and Dan Coats of Indiana, Jim Martin of North Carolina, Carroll Campbell of South Carolina, Don Sundquist of Tennessee, Connie Mack of Florida, Dick Cheney of Wyoming, and Newt Gingrich of Georgia. And, yes, Trent Lott of Mississippi.

We had no real sense that we were at the beginning of a period of profound change, no sense of what would happen over the next two decades. But among the members of this group of talented people, there was a feeling of exhilaration. We had youth and we were brimming with ideas. Kemp was causing us to think beyond budget deficits and to focus on opportunities to create economic growth. We were trying to reach out to unions and minorities with new approaches to public policy. And then there was Newt Gingrich, who brought inspired language to bear on these ideas and plans that made them resonate with voters across the land. We didn't quite know it at the time, but the Reagan Revolution was staffed and ready to go.

# 7

# THE REAGAN YEARS

The Neshoba County Fairgrounds near Philadelphia, Mississippi, were full to bursting on the hot summer day in 1980 when I brought Ronald and Nancy Reagan there to campaign in my home state for the first time. As Mississippi chairman for Reagan's presidential campaign, I'd waged a stirring battle to bring the candidate to this century-old event, which was colloquially known as "the South's biggest political house party." It wasn't an easy victory. The future president's men found all sorts of reasons to keep Reagan out of Mississippi—not least the fact that three civil rights workers had been murdered near there in the early summer of 1964.

But the most frequent refrain was the old political prejudice that a California Republican couldn't win in Mississippi. I knew better, and had said so after I became part of Reagan's House of Representatives steering committee back in the spring. Finally, I had the luck to speak with Reagan myself. "Governor, you *can* cover the South and Mississippi," I told him. "Just come out to this one event—this is the biggest such event in the South." He gave me a quick okay, and that was it.

But when I began to plan the appearance, I ran into trouble again. I wanted to present Reagan with one of Mississippi's most famous rocking chairs—one from the line made by master furniture craftsman Greg Harkins of Vaughn, Mississippi. But again there were moans from the campaign: *A rocking chair,* the staff cried in horror. *That would make him seem like an old man!* Born in 1911, Reagan was sixty-nine years old in that election year; there was nothing the campaign wanted less than to raise the looming age issue.

But once he was at the fair and reacting to the booming applause from the Southern crowds, Governor Reagan graciously accepted the chair from Greg. Then he took ownership of the moment—dropping jauntily down into the rocker, grabbing Nancy with one hand, and pulling her into his lap. The television cameras whirred and the news cameras clicked as campaign photographers got the photo op of the week—a younger-than-springtime candidate putting the moves on his lovely bride. When the images appeared across the country the next morning, the weight of Reagan's age as a factor in the contest had lightened considerably.

Our national convention was in Detroit, which worried me at first. As the center of the American automobile industry, it was a big union town, and we were regarded—wrongly in my view—as antiunion. How would we be received? With enormous warmth, it turned out. Detroit put out the red carpet for us and made us feel right at home. I had a few difficult moments with the Mississippi delegation, which I headed. When it was announced that Reagan had selected George Herbert Walker Bush as his running mate, we almost had a revolt. Some in my delegation insisted that because we hadn't backed Bush in the primary, he shouldn't be on the ticket with Reagan. I had to take some of our boys to the back of Cobo Hall—my woodshed for the occasion—and educate them in the political facts of life. We picked our man, I told them, and that's Reagan. We have faith in him. Now he's made his choice, and we've got to support him, whether we like the choice or not. To underscore the point, I represented our delegation in casting our state's ballots for the vice presidential nominee, and allowed someone else the honor of casting our ballots for Reagan.

The outcome of the election was stunning. Reagan's tight-knit campaign organization in the House helped to register victories for the governor in scores of congressional districts across America, including my own, and set the way for a tight bond between House members and the incoming president. In his landslide victory, Reagan won the popular vote by ten percentage points and got nearly ten electoral college ballots for every one cast for Jimmy Carter—489 versus 49. My exhortation to Reagan that he could win the South proved prescient: He carried Mississippi by nearly twelve thousand votes, and took every other Southern state save Carter's own Georgia. The Senate changed hands, putting Republicans in control, and we picked up thirty-four seats in the House, narrowing the Democrats' majority considerably.

The conservative revolution didn't begin with Reagan. But it had grown since Barry Goldwater, and gained strength through the 1970s. Now, with Reagan's election and the dramatic changes in the Congress, you could feel the political ground shift. We were preparing to run up a string of unprecedented legislative victories, and to shape history in the process. My role in helping to achieve those successes was considerable, I believe, because I was about to transform the way my party, then in the minority, did business in the House.

After the 1980 election, Bob Michel, then GOP whip, was elected minority leader by his Republican colleagues, succeeding John Rhodes of Arizona. When I learned that Michel was moving up to become Republican leader, I hesitated at first. I wasn't sure the whip's position was where I wanted to go—and in practical terms, I wasn't sure I could win. My opponent would be Representative Bud Shuster of Pennsylvania, a pal from the Chowder and Marching Society. Bud held the number four House leadership position: chairman of the Republican Policy Committee, one rung above my spot as head of the Republican Conference Research Committee. In the end, I decided to take Bud on—not because I thought Bud would do a bad job, but because I thought I could do a better one.

In my time in Washington, I'd learned a lot about Congress—a set of lessons that began in Congressman William Colmer's office, and grew crisper and clearer when I stepped into his shoes on Capitol Hill. The art of government, I had learned, involved equal parts patience, persistence, and persuasion. In short, it was just like herding cats. By now I knew that mixing with other House members was in my blood; it tickled me to try to convince them to vote my way. Whip and I seemed a natural match.

It wasn't an easy race; I beat Shuster by only seven votes. The *Congressional Quarterly* calculated my victory this way: "Congressman Lott hasn't had the time to earn as many enemies as Shuster." *The Almanac of American Politics* characterized my opponent as "too activist to be a major House leader." After the vote, Shuster and I met on the floor and shook hands. Over the years, he proved remarkably helpful as we tried to mold together a voting majority on the House floor.

If groups such as the Conservative Opportunity Society, formed by Newt Gingrich a few years earlier, and the Chowder and Marching Society provided the heart and soul of our House-bound insurrection, then my rebuilt and reorganized whip machine provided the force that turned voting patterns inside out. The voting realities of the House of Representatives when I took over as whip were bad enough to make a Republican cry foul!

There were 192 members of the GOP and 242 Democrats, with one independent. In addition, five of our members were liberal congressmen who usually could be counted on to vote with the Democrats. Though the numbers varied during the Reagan years, I generally had to persuade a bare minimum of thirty Democrats to vote with us in order to reach the magic number of 218. But things were rarely that good. Because of absences and the liberal Republicans who would "flake off," I usually needed forty Democrats to win.

To pass the Reagan agenda—particularly the foundation legislation for what became known as Reaganomics—I recruited a young and gung-ho team of seventeen deputy whips and carefully trained them to wring votes out of the frostiest of Democrats. But first we took our targets apart and put them back together again. We psychoanalyzed them and studied their congressional lives to the nth degree. We identified their friends and enemies, located their key supporters back home, tracked their voting records back to the day they'd first set foot in the House, and put their political philosophies under a microscope.

Amazingly, ours was the first truly organized whip organization in congressional history—a machine that soon became an innovative new tool for the Reagan administration. Besides my chief deputy whip, Representative David Emery of Maine, I had four regional whips and three or four deputy whips for each region. It was organized on paper—including the Democratic targets—like a battle group of Napoleon's army. The standout Republicans in the organization included such people as Ed Madigan of Illinois, Olympia Snowe of Maine, Bob Livingston of Louisiana, Tom DeLay of Texas, and Jon Kyl of Arizona.

Tom Loeffler of Texas, only a sophomore in the House, also was a key part of the team. His sole job was to work with Democrats such as Sonny Montgomery of Mississippi, John Breaux of

Louisiana, and Phil Gramm and Charlie Stenholm of Texas. Most of them became reliable "boll weevils" in the early 1980s. In Reagan-era slang, the boll weevil Democrats from the cotton states frequently supported the Republican president and voted for his programs. A lot of them backed the Reagan agenda religiously because their constituents had voted for the president.

My chief deputy, Dave Emery, was something of a computer whiz, and he skillfully programmed every member of the House of Representatives into our database. Every scrap of information available was fed into these profiles, including career voting records, members' propensity to vote with their party and their leaders, and their ratings by various organizations—left, right, and center. Most of the information from such journals as the *American Almanac of Politics* and from organizations as diverse as American Constitutional Action and the American Conservative Union on the right and the American Civil Liberties Union and the Sierra Club on the left were added to the files.

How members did in their congressional elections became part of the mix, and in some cases offered good ammunition. For instance, if I came upon a Democrat who only won 50.4 percent of the vote back home, I knew we needed to be very careful—you let him go or you put even more pressure on him, depending on how much you needed him. If I found a representative who got 67 percent of the vote, on the other hand, I might ask myself: Why is this guy so worried about one vote affecting his reelection? It gave us valuable information to use on that member.

I kept the computer in the small whip room just off the floor. Any of us in the whip operation could dash in and, say, call up a given congressman from Pennsylvania, and look at his voting records, the names of his big contributors and supporters, or the economic strength of his district—how much of it depended on manufacturing, on agriculture, on defense spending. For instance, when we were trying to pass the bill to allow President Reagan to post Pershing cruise missiles in Western Europe, we learned that some key backers of three local congressmen had graduated from the U.S. Military Academy at West Point. We talked these pro-defense, pro-Reagan politicos into calling the local representatives they had bankrolled and talking them into voting with us. Those three votes were crucial: We won by only four.

The final, key vote came from Congressman Pat Roberts of Kansas. Pulling up his computer printout, I saw that he was a solid voter with us on Reaganomics issues and social issues. But he had repeatedly shown concern about the money we were spending on defense. When you looked at his voting patterns and the makeup of his district, there was no reason he shouldn't have been with us. So I hiked over to his office. "Pat, you could be the key for the party on this issue. Your vote might be the deciding one." He resisted, but as I left his office I had the feeling—based upon what the computer told us—that he would be with us. And he was.

As effective as this computer-generated politicking was, my human army—battle ready congressional troops who could be deployed onto the floor in a matter of minutes—probably had more to do with my reputation for success during eight years of triumphs. During key votes, I haunted the whip office, usually hunkered down over my massive chart that showed each member, with notes that indicated how and when he came on and off the floor, and sometimes who his best buddies were.

I was already armed with the most complete dossier to be assembled on the bill in question. From the minute legislators began drafting these bills, I saw to it that I got regular reports—often annotated by the drafters—that kept coming until the legislation was ready for presentation in its final form. My paper trail often included everything that had been written about the bill, and early opinions from the committees involved.

It was key that I knew more about a given piece of legislation than the voters on the floor, and at least as much as both the supporters and detractors who would soon clash in combat. Then I could set the floor in motion in a political pageant that often transfixed everyone. This required organized and craftily trained troops—often from both sides of the aisle.

My maneuvers acquired nicknames that were folksy and sometimes sophomoric. But these titles belied the sophisticated function of each raid, for that's what these were—calculated raids onto the floor in search of votes.

The "Buddy System," perhaps the simplest weapon in my arsenal, was a way to put a key trooper in play without attracting much attention. Whenever I identified someone who was going to be a shaky voter on a particular bill, I enlisted a friend who was close to the congressman to slip down and sit with him on the floor. It was like a warm, friendly hand on the shoulder. But it also allowed one of us to work this jittery player all through the voting process. It was more effective than you might imagine: after all, everybody likes backup.

Similarly, I had a small corps of "bell cows." We recruited these congressmen by identifying the natural leaders among various voting groups (the bell wearers) that inevitably ally together in any session of Congress. Then I publicly tagged these front men so that the other followers had no trouble pursuing them to the desired outcome in the roll call vote—much as a rancher bells the lead cow so the herd can follow.

Then there was the elaborate technique I labeled the "Chinese Water Torture." This maneuver, which could involve whole groups of representatives, was the opposite of simple techniques like the "buddy system." It was based on intricate knowledge of a member's pattern on the floor: what door they used to enter the chamber, which aisles they followed to their seat, who they chatted with along the way, and the amount of time they spent doing so.

As usual, I stood just outside the whip's office at the back of the chamber—the perfect vantage point to spot a voter who was not with us but who certainly should be. I would already have assembled a series of people—a ranking member, a colleague from his home state, personal friends, and fellow committee members. Then I would flood him with this vote-getter squad—one at a time. Often the members themselves weren't aware what they were doing, that they were part of a larger plan, but I had it carefully orchestrated.

The representatives I'd selected were people I was certain had the power to work on the wayward voter. So it became a little more like intimidation than my other techniques. The people who had the greatest influence on this guy would hit him repeatedly during the vote. Quite often it worked.

When I needed a quick analysis of an upcoming vote—quicker even than the computer—I formed an emergency response team of nine "in the know" congressmen. Numbering eight Republicans and one Democrat, they each served as a proxy for thirty members based on a variety of reasons—philosophy, region, propensity to vote with the Republican line. I would ask them for an instant prediction of an upcoming vote. Their forecasts were uncannily accurate, enough so that they remained a staple of my organization for my entire eight years as whip.

I also had a blue-ribbon panel of Democrats who were unofficial members of the team. They included Sonny Montgomery of Mississippi, Buddy Roemer of Louisiana, and Charlie Stenholm and Phil Gramm of Texas. I could go to them and get their estimates of how many Democrats we were going to get on an individual vote.

To give the whip organization additional direction, I hired voting consultant Robert Bauman, a former member of Congress from Maryland who had been a superstar vote-getter on the floor of the House. He wrote a whip guide for me and conducted a thirty-day whip school for my incoming team members. The symposium imparted secrets that strengthened our arsenal.

Bauman was on the manifest for sixty days specifically to train my people. But even his temporary employment generated controversy. He had been forced to leave Congress the previous year because it was revealed that he was gay and had cruised a Maryland area bar seeking sexual encounters. He was married to a wonderful lady and had a daughter. Bauman was devastated when he left Congress and had no income—a desperate man who needed a bridge to the rest of his life. He was an expert on the House rules and we needed a teacher on the subject, so I hired him for that limited purpose.

His hiring made news, and soon I was being criticized by pastors back in my home district. When I called one of them to discuss what I had done, he accused me of promoting the homosexual agenda, which I denied as I explained my narrow objectives. Besides, I reminded him, God teaches us to be forgiving and understanding and reach out to all his people in need. There was silence on the other end of the line; I heard nothing further from the pastor on the issue after that.

For eight years, my master plan for the whip organization worked remarkably well, producing the desired results 95 percent of the time. When you look at the Republican vote on key issues during the 1980s, we lost very few votes—even though we were in the minority the whole time. And we almost never lost a key contest.

During those eight years, my party's high-water mark was 196 Republican votes in the House of Representatives; it went as low as 178. The Democrats never had less than 239 votes—and even when they had 257, we were still beating them on the major issues.

The first critical vote came on the Gramm-Latta Budget Act in 1981. A cornerstone of Reaganomics, Gramm-Latta aimed to cut federal spending by approximately eighty billion dollars.

A professor with a doctorate in economics, Phil Gramm had real authority on the subject; he staked his reputation on the vote, and he lobbied his fellow Democrats endlessly to join him, particularly those from the South. We saw to it that the bill also carried the name of Delbert L. Latta of Ohio, the ranking Republican on the budget committee. His sponsorship allowed the Conservative Democratic Forum, led by Gramm's Texas colleague Charlie Stenholm, to sell the issue as bipartisan.

The voting was tough and close. Throughout its history, the House had traditionally been reluctant to cut federal spending. To show how high the stakes were, the speaker of the House, Democrat Thomas P. "Tip" O'Neill of Massachusetts, left the speaker's chair, slowly made his way to the side of Democrat Sam Hall of Texas, and softly badgered Hall to vote against the bill. Then O'Neill returned to the Speaker's chair.

I felt the outcome to the nation was important enough for me to break a rule, so I went right over to the Democratic side of the aisle and stood right next to Hall. It was an unprecedented move. I leaned down toward him, "Sam," I said softly. "This is a chance for you to make history. Do the right thing to control federal spending."

Nothing happened for a few seconds. Then Congressman Hall took out his card, and without a glance at Speaker O'Neill he voted with us.

In the end, we lost five Republicans on the bill, including Jim Jeffords of Vermont and Claudine Schneider of Rhode Island. But we got sixty-three Democrats to vote with us, and that was enough to carry the day.

Gramm, known as "the prophet of free enterprise," was martyred by vengeful Democrats over this vote. They moved to strip him of his committee assignments, and promised to campaign against him in Texas.

Later he came to my office. "Trent, I'm going to switch parties," he said. "I'm flying to Texas, announcing that I'm resigning from office, and running for reelection as a Republican."

I pleaded with him not to resign; it would be far simpler to stay in office, but announce that he was changing parties, as others with far less justification than Gramm had done. "Nope," he said, "I'm going to do this in the open, before the people who elected me."

"Phil, I admire you for this decision," I replied, and wished him well. Gramm resigned his seat on January 5, 1983. In a special election less than six weeks later, he was reelected as a Republican.

Next up was the Hance-Conable bill to cut taxes. It provided for a three-year program of tax cuts—5 percent in year one, 10 percent per year in years two and three, beginning with the start of the federal government's fiscal year—October 1, 1981. This measure was easier, but it required us to deploy all the whip teams, and to pool information with White House operatives, allowing them to run a campaign that paralleled ours.

On July 27, President Reagan made an impassioned televised plea for the bill, asking people to let their representatives hear from them. Letters and phone calls flooded Congress. Representative Carroll Hubbard Jr., a Democrat from Kentucky, received 500 calls, 480 of them supporting Reagan. Hubbard voted for the measure. The White House worked closely with me on this issue, using my computerized data to guide Reagan in bargaining one-on-one with individual congressmen we had recommended. The president told his staffers that I treated each vote as if "it were a lost lamb that had to be corralled"—a quote that appeared the next day in the *Washington Post*. It would be repeated so often that it became a temporary part of my legend. Reagan also quoted me as saying "Everybody else is getting theirs, it's time we got ours"—a line that reportedly made Reagan laugh out loud when he heard it.

But the White House wasn't laughing in the hours before final voting on Hance-Conable: I was certain we would win, but the president spent the afternoon of June 29 sitting by his phone, holding his breath. He needn't have worried: When it was over, forty-eight Democrats had joined all the House Republicans but one to approve the tax bill, 238 to 195. Reagan phoned me the next morning: "I'm mighty grateful for this, Trent. You've done it for us again." The president wrote this in his diary that night: "This on top of the budget victory is the greatest political win in half a century."

He would make similar calls praising me with each victory we shared. I don't know if someone handed him a card with my name on it each time, but he was extraordinarily gracious.

M y whip organization was never so effective as during the se- ries of bills and spending plans we enacted to rebuild the weakened military establishment of the United States. The military had been allowed to languish through almost nine years of inaction—since the beginnings of Watergate. Repairing the damage had been one of Reagan's campaign promises, and I told him that we were of one mind on the issue. I repeatedly put the revamped whip machine at his disposal for an unprecedented series of bills—beginning, properly, with massive pay raises across the board, but particularly aimed at the backbone of the military: America's noncommissioned officers.

The NCOs' salaries had become pitifully outdated, and many of them had been reduced to cost-of-living measures that were, frankly, a joke. Some noncommissioned officers in Germany and other parts of Western Europe were living on food stamps; their wives were taking any available jobs to shore up family income.

Our first legislative package provided a 19 percent salary increase across the board, skewed away from the generals and colonels and toward the lower ranks. We didn't have much difficulty passing this omnibus bill. Even Democrats found themselves in a tough spot voting against a pay raise for NCOs who were often living at the poverty level. The generals, by the way, loved it. More than one later approached me to say, "Tell President Reagan for me that he has made such a huge difference on the morale of our soldiers. It is just incalculable."

We followed that with significant defense spending on new weapons systems, cruise missiles, modern battle tanks, and the next generation of ships. It was a huge buildup of military spending—massive enough that it would eventually break the back of the Soviet Union. In the end, they could not keep up with us. Standing before the Brandenburg Gate on June 12, 1987, Reagan called for Mikhail Gorbachev to "tear down this wall." By the end of the decade, the Berlin Wall was history—and so, in just a few years, was the Soviet Union.

The Reagan years were times of excitement and change. We added about three dozen new members to our Republican ranks in the House because of the 1980 Reagan victory. These were outstanding people, many of them men and women of exceptional courage. Some of the votes on the agenda were tough, but they didn't blink. The press started calling them "Reagan Robots" because of their faithful support of the president's agenda. But they weren't robots; they simply believed in what President Reagan stood for. And sometimes, it cost them.

I recall one especially difficult vote involving a Social Security–related issue. In 1980, we had elected two Republicans from West Virginia, and I knew it wouldn't be easy for them to keep their seats the next time around. One of them, Mick Staton, had followed the Democrats' party line on the issue and voted "yes." As the vote continued, I eased to the back of the chamber where Mick was standing and asked him straightaway: "Are you sure you're doing the right thing on this vote? It might really hurt your reelection effort."

He turned toward me: "It might. But I didn't come here to get reelected; I came here to make a difference." But he wouldn't have much chance to make the impact he wanted: Staton lost his seat in 1982, along with twenty-five others in his class.

The House Republican leaders met with President Reagan often—usually on Tuesdays at 9 A.M.—but it could be tough to get out of our offices and through the impossible traffic to the White House at that hour. In compensation, the president had his signature jelly beans waiting for us on the Cabinet Room table. He usually made a few remarks, reading the cue cards with perfection. As amiable as Reagan was, he rarely made any truly personal comments to any of us. But he listened a lot, and made sure we kept our eyes on the major issue of the week.

The first thing to drive a wedge between my streamlined whip organization and the Reagan administration surfaced in early 1985 when the president proposed a budget that included major tax increases in the guise of tax reform. It seemed to be a step backward from Reaganomics and from the gains we'd made in Gramm-Latta and Hance-Conable. At least many conservative leaders, including Jack Kemp, saw it that way.

As I studied the budget proposal carefully, I found I agreed with the critics. It looked as if I might have to use the power of the whip to defeat a bill the president wanted—a strict and jarring departure from what had been a smooth working arrangement between the Republican leadership in the House and the White House.

At a highly charged meeting at the White House one morning, the president launched into a sales pitch for his budget concept. But I was unmoved. "Mr. President," I said, "I don't agree that this is some sort of tax reform. I just think it's another tax increase. I don't think it's the right thing for the country. It's not what I came here to do, and I don't think it's what you came here to do."

He seemed to ignore my views; he just kept talking and talking, until his chief of staff, Jim Baker, joined in, pushing me to "help round up votes." Uncomfortable minutes passed. I wasn't moving an inch. Finally, the president stopped and turned toward me. "Well, Trent, if I can't count on my whip, who can I count on?"

I leaned back in my chair and thought about that. Here I am, Trent Lott, born in Grenada, Mississippi, son of a shipyard worker, sitting here in the Oval Office with the most powerful man in the world, telling him I can't help him when I'm in the elected leadership of his party.

But still we sat.

Finally, I leaned forward. "I'll do it," I said, more eagerly than I'd expected—knowing full well that it would be the biggest legislative mistake of my years as whip, and the worst vote I had yet cast in the House.

I let him talk me into it, because of my admiration for him and because of the leadership responsibility that was inherent to my elected office. I knew it was wrong. The president's advisers were pushing a series of tax increases on the real estate industry as tax reform. "We have cut tax rates and capital gains," Reagan told me. "And now we have this unfair tax code with loopholes for real estate and industry." (The closing of this so-called loophole would almost crush Houston, Texas. After the bill passed, the real estate market there collapsed.)

In my opinion, the bill wasn't really about real estate at all; it was a manifestation of Reagan's old worries about the deficit. But in the end I put aside all my misgivings, cranked up the whip organization and passed it—but without the key support of Jack Kemp, who served as our conscience for this sort of thing.

I still regret it.

Not so long afterward, I found myself in a rare, head-to-head confrontation with President Reagan over proposed import tariffs on textile goods—a bill that aided an industry already struggling in the United States. Mass-produced goods from abroad were making a dent in an indigenous American business whose roots stretched back a century. The proposed tariffs would help protect this industry—including two textile plants in my district, which would benefit directly.

I informed the administration, which opposed the bill, that my support for the legislation prevented me from performing my whip duties, causing me to pass the task to other members of the team. The same was true for Tom Loeffler, then my chief deputy whip. We both recused ourselves. Still, the bill passed, only to be promptly vetoed by the president. I did lead the drive to override the president's veto in an exhaustive campaign, and we managed to get 276 votes—71 Republicans and 205 Democrats. But it takes two-thirds of the votes to override a president, and our tally of 276–149 fell eight votes short.

During these years, the Republican majority in the Senate and the decidedly Democratic majority in the House caused occasional strains between the two chambers. The worst of these conflicts involved Social Security and a modest deficit-reduction proposal. In mid-1985, the Senate was considering a bill that, among other things, would abolish the program's cost-of-living adjustment for one calendar year. Flat-lining benefits for Social Security recipients in 1986 would result in a cut of 4 percent in real terms, assuming the Reagan administration's inflation forecast for the year was accurate. The bill passed by the narrowest of margins, with the Republican leadership in the Senate even rousing California's Pete Wilson from his hospital bed, where he was recovering from an appendectomy. Pete entered the Senate chamber in a wheelchair for the late-night vote and got a standing ovation. Even so, it took a tie-breaking vote cast by Vice President George H. W. Bush for us to prevail, 50 to 49.

In retrospect, it was a truly courageous step. But we in the House thought it was a devastating political vote. Social Security is known as "third rail of American politics" for a very good reason: Touching it can figuratively kill a candidate running for reelection.

At a meeting with Don Regan, who became the president's chief of staff when Jim Baker left to become Treasury Secretary, a group of us made our case against the bill. Somewhat to our surprise, President Reagan pulled the rug out from under the Senate bill and warned strongly against it. For years afterward, New Mexico senator Pete Domenici reminded me of how bad a deal this vote was for Senate Republicans, all but four of whom embraced it. Maybe it wasn't the deciding issue, but the Republicans in the Senate did lose the majority in the 1986 elections.

Throughout the Reagan years, Newt Gingrich of Georgia was beginning to make his presence known in the House. Gingrich, a brainy and articulate former history professor, had entered the House in January 1979 as if he was prepared to go eight rounds with the heavyweight champion. As soon as he arrived, he began stirring the pot. His first step was to make us aware that the words we chose to use in the public square had an impact on our status as a national party. If we were always negative and focused on such issues as the control of government spending, he said, we were sending the wrong message. He hammered away at us to talk about what we were *for:* that we stood for hope, for growth, for opportunity. We New Age Republicans had a different way of doing things. We wanted more emphasis on providing incentives for growth, inclusion, and improving education. Newt would host sessions to talk about these distinctions, bringing in outside experts to help make the point.

One move that helped us make our point was Reagan's proposal to create a separate Department of Education, giving it its own status and freeing it from the intellectual poverty and social politics of the sprawling Department of Health, Education and Welfare, which was renamed the Department of Health and Human Services.

Perhaps because of our backgrounds in education or educational issues, Newt, Senator Thad Cochran of Mississippi, and I all supported the new Education Department. Most Republicans in the House did not. Congressman Dan Quayle of Indiana gave us a particularly hard time about it. "Trent, it's just going to create another huge bureaucracy," he warned me. "It'll become another tool for the teacher's unions."

I didn't agree, and I joined only four other Republicans in voting for it. But the bill passed, and Reagan signed it into law.

Times were changing, and Newt continued to push the envelope. He formed a group called the Conservative Opportunity Society, which included, among others, Bob Walker of Pennsylvania and Connie Mack of Florida. I was in the group—well, sort of— but I spent a lot of my time there just keeping an eye on Newt's guys. The leadership was concerned that they would rise up on some issue and cause problems. But mostly they were a positive force that kept the leadership under pressure to do the right thing.

The Gingrich crowd also created a publicity bonanza by carefully and diligently using C-Span, cable television's twenty-four-hour, all-seeing eye on Congress. Newt realized early on that the snooze network was capable of creating indelible images that could in turn be fashioned into unforgettable media events—whether beneficial or devastating to those involved. From those deadly hours-long monologues, sound bites could be plucked that were potent enough to lead the morning newscasts the next day.

In addition to C-Span's direct audience, already numbering in the millions, the major networks—at first just NBC, ABC, and CBS and later including CNN and Fox—joined most of America's major daily newspapers in monitoring the channel around the clock, foraging for those few bright words to wake up the country's news coverage.

Later, in the late 1990s, Gingrich saw that the exploding Internet, with its thousands of political and quasi-news sites, was using C-Span as a basic news source. Without staffs or news services to rely on, the guys running the websites were usually dependent on the established media for their data and essential quotes.

To capitalize on the advantages C-Span offered, Gingrich and his principal lieutenants—Mack, Walker, and Jon Kyl of Arizona—found an obscure rule that allowed them to go to the floor of the House of Representatives after hours and speak for an hour on any subject. Of course, this rule would have been worthless without the sudden reality of this eye on Congress. They used it with sensational skill; headlines and "news breaks" followed until the Democrats—media-oriented as they are—began complaining that this was a misuse of House privileges. One who took this particularly to heart was House Speaker Tip O'Neill. His childish dissatisfaction with the Gingrich forces—and an unusual incident that occurred because of it—gave me an opportunity to make a point about the House rules that made me grateful for my years on the Rules Committee, a body most congressmen underestimate at their peril.

Late one afternoon, O'Neill turned his gavel over to fellow congressman Joe Mobley of Massachusetts and hiked down to the microphoned podium from which the regular members speak. From his first words, he blasted Gingrich and his corpsmen for what he called their "shameless use of C-Span." With his tone and language, I saw at once that O'Neill was in violation of the statutes barring one member from impugning the integrity of another member—in this case, the speaker of the House against one of his members in good standing. Sitting next to me was congressional staffer Bill Pitts, who worked for Minority Leader Bob Michel and who happened to be an expert parliamentarian.

I turned to Pitts with an inquisitive look. He nodded back: "Yep, he's out of order." I rose and directed my remarks to Mobley, then the acting speaker: "Mr. Speaker, I demand that the speaker's words be taken down." With that, all action on the floor of the House stops automatically. The words were taken down and handed to the Parliamentarian. I knew we had O'Neill. The chamber grew as quiet as a church. Mobley had to rule that his colleague, the speaker of the House of Representatives, was out of order. That ruling brought a swift and difficult punishment: O'Neill was immediately barred from the floor for the rest of the day. He couldn't utter another word.

I let the Democrats stew for a couple of minutes, then moved that the speaker's words be expunged and that the House resume its normal business. O'Neill was off the hook. But I'd made a couple of points. Not only did I know the House rules, but I was willing to use them—even against the speaker. That was all there was to it, but the incident got a good deal of press coverage. The speaker, to his credit, never mentioned it to me, and as the years went on he would continue to treat me with respect. That was typical of his way of doing business. Tip didn't hold grudges.

But it was a time for unusual confrontations and, just as often, unusual and creative solutions to decades-old problems of lawmaking.

By 1987, with Reagan late in his second term and Congress totally controlled by Democrats, it had become almost impossible to negotiate a federal budget. The Senate majority finally made the legal process so difficult that we couldn't get a budget passed through normal means. The bureaucratic snarl brought everything to a standstill.

And that's how the legendary "Gang of 19" was born. The Gang was drawn from all the layers of the executive and legislative branches—from my whip operation, the minority leadership, and congressional budget experts from both parties, to the movers and shakers in the Office of Management and Budget, the White House, and the Treasury Department. We took this list of financial all-stars and hit the road on a closed-to-all-comers tour, pitching up at meetings in Georgetown mansions, obscure suites of rooms in the White House, and the out-of-the-way Montgomery Room in the House of Representatives. One meeting took place over breakfast in the spacious sunroom of Treasury Secretary Jim Baker's suburban home. Our assignations appeared on no printed schedules, and we sped in and out of the locales in our private cars—leaving no trail of the government's omnipresent chauffeured vehicles or fancy departmental limousines. Our only means of identification were stacks of T-shirts with "Gang of 19" printed on the back.

Those T-shirts typified one of the strangest budget negotiations in American history—a combination drama and comedy that has never been repeated. In addition to Jim Baker and me, the participants included Democrat Bill Gray of the House Budget Committee; Senator Lloyd Bentsen of Texas, representing the Finance Committee; Mississippi Senator John Stennis of Appropriations; and House Minority Leader Bob Michel.

The issues were tough. How do you control spending? Can you touch Social Security? What about tax increases or cuts? Baker, who presided over this strange caravan of meetings, was just trying to get a deal, but the positions of congressional Republicans and Democrats were miles apart.

At one point, the conversation drifted toward Social Security reforms—benefit cuts, if you will. I listened for a while and then blew up the discussion, both privately and publicly. I wasn't going to let the Democrats trap us on that one. The result was that the Republicans appeared to be protecting Social Security in the discussions.

As the weeks went by, little progress was made in the talks. We stalled over and over again, despite the freshness of our morning meetings. Then came Black Monday: On October 19, 1987, the stock market crashed, with the Dow Jones Industrial Average plunging 508 points, or nearly 23 percent—the worst one-day collapse in history. It scared all of us. And suddenly there was a stern focus on the issues. An agreement was reached less then ten days later, and the budget passed easily.

By then, however, the steam was going out of the Reagan Revolution, if not from the House insurrectionists who had embraced and nurtured it. President Reagan seemed to be losing focus, and refused to veto *any* appropriations bills. I remember urging him to do so in one of our last White House meetings. His administration's inattention to fiscal matters may have been due to other factors, especially the rising Iran-Contra issue. The media was transfixed by two questions: What did Reagan know about the Iran-Contra plan, and who was to blame? I never received satisfactory answers to those questions. All I knew was that the issue was a serious distraction, especially after it led to congressional hearings. Oliver North testified and Secretary of Defense Casper Weinberger took the fall for it. President George H. W. Bush later pardoned him—appropriately, I felt.

The Reagan White House was waiting out its term in office. During one visit to the Oval Office, I remember speaking to President Reagan, and he looked at me as if he didn't know who I was—though I'd been with him hundreds of times. I had no details, of course, but I knew he was having memory problems: His troubles had obviously begun.

On Capitol Hill, the House of Representatives I had enjoyed for so long was becoming more and more partisan. Speaker Jim Wright, who took over for Tip O'Neill in January 1987, was not running the House with an iron hand—or much of a hand at all. It was grating on me, especially as the give-and-take atmosphere that had made me so effective there vanished. One night there was a close vote; in fact, it ended in a tie with all normal time expired. The speaker held the vote open for twenty-five minutes while the Democrats frantically tried to switch votes. No luck. Then they sent for Congressman Jim Chapman of Texas, who had earlier repaired to his office.

The unfairness of it all caused me to lose control. At one point, I became so angry that I pounded the rostrum in the well of the House until it bent. We demanded "regular order" for the vote to be closed. Nobody replied, and the clock kept running. Chapman finally showed up and changed his vote.

I was deeply embarrassed by such brazen behavior. Maybe it was time for me to leave the House. I had been whip for eight years—the full span of the Reagan administration. It was time for me to move up, I thought, or move out. But Bob Michel showed no sign of leaving his post as House minority leader, and I could not bring myself to run against him. While I thought Bob was too pliable in dealing with the Democrats, I respected him and would not challenge him for his leadership position.

In Mississippi, Senator John Stennis's term was ending. The last decade or two had been hard on him: he had been shot by robbers, had his leg amputated, and had suffered an extreme bout of double pneumonia. By now he was in his eighties and in poor health.

In the fall of 1987, he announced his retirement. A couple of weeks later, I announced that I would seek his seat in 1988.

I was leaving behind not only the House, but a historic whip organization we had built there. After I won the Senate race, Dick Cheney was elected to be my successor in the role of whip. A few weeks later, though, he was chosen by the first President Bush to become Secretary of Defense. Ed Madigan and Newt Gingrich ran for whip. Newt won by one vote. And another era in the House was born.

# 8

# HAIR: AN ISSUE FOR OUR TIME

In early February 1988, my son, Chet, and I hiked into the wilds surrounding Black Creek. We were dressed in jeans and rough jackets to ward off the chill. When we reached the water's edge, we paused, waiting for a camera crew to break through the undergrowth that stretched as far as the eye could see on both sides of the creek. It did my heart good to see the water following its untamed course—protected forever by our scenic river statutes.

A sturdy canoe was slid into the water, grasped firmly by a group of production assistants. Chet and I hopped in and paddled the canoe out into the mild currents of Black Creek, as the film crew from Baltimore's Bob Goodman and Associates set up their equipment on the river bank.

As the camera focused on both of us, Chet dipped a paddle in the water, looked toward the lens, and said he was proud of his dad for saving this isolated creek by having it designated as a "wild and scenic site." Then we pulled the canoe up the bank, I threw my arm over his shoulder, and we slowly walked up the hill and out of camera range.

The ad was on the air within two weeks, competing for airtime with the TV spots of my Democratic opponents—Mississippi congressman Wayne Dowdy and secretary of state Dick Molpus. They were locked in a tough primary to determine who would face me in the general election for Stennis's seat in the U.S. Senate. The ad soon caused a sensation. There was no Republican primary, and the opposite camps weren't expecting me to hit the airwaves until the early summer at least. But the environmental spot was just one of three that peppered the state's television stations as the Democratic primary reached its height.

Just a week earlier, I had received a call from my political adviser, a little-known New York consultant named Dick Morris. Morris was eager to suggest how we might be able to win the senatorial election in the spring. "Let's start our ads now during *their* primary," he said. "I've got a potent trio of ideas." His strategy appealed to me: I like to be out of the gate first. And though it wasn't clear to the Democrats until fall, I believe those early ads did lock up the Senate race for me in February. Designed to establish my image early—and to preempt the attack ads we knew they would throw at us—the campaign cost $160,000, but it was money well spent.

For instance, an intelligence source within the Dowdy campaign alerted us early on that the Democrat was planning to portray me as an intractable enemy of the Social Security program. Armed with that knowledge, we hit the airwaves first with a strong ad outlining my support for Social Security, and defused the issue.

In the same way, since we knew that environmental groups would put me on their "Dirty Dozen" list, we filmed the Black Creek spot to inoculate me on the issue.

Then we learned that Dowdy was preparing to light into me over public works—despite my record of obtaining new and improved roads for Mississippi. To counter the attack, we filmed a spot at a road construction site. In the ad, I pulled up to the site in a red pickup truck, and stepped out wearing one of my worn red plaid shirts, khaki pants, and boots. I turned to the camera: "I know how to get money for projects like this because I've done it before as a congressman. And, in fact, I obtained the funds for 'Bloody 98' highway as a House member." (Mississippi voters got the reference: "Bloody 98" was the local nickname for a thirty-mile stretch of Highway 98 between Hattiesburg and Beaumont. The route had been a hilly and narrow two-lane road that carried heavy truck traffic, including big log carriers, and caused too many fatal accidents. The federal money we procured didn't flatten the hills, but it widened the highway, and paid for other safety improvements that reduced the body count on Bloody 98.)

It wasn't long before I realized the impact of this highway spot: With its image of me as a regular Mississippi guy in a truck, it drove the other side nuts. They even challenged my wardrobe. "Trent Lott doesn't even own a plaid shirt," a spokesman for one of the opposition campaigns told a Jackson newspaper reporter. "And where did he get that red truck? He sure doesn't drive it around Washington." (In fact, the truck belonged to my father-in-law, Dr. Perry Thompson.)

That shot was the first sign that they were going to try and portray me as an over-dressed elitist—a country-club Republican.

"We don't have to take this," Dick Morris insisted. "We have to show them that, while you wear a suit to Congress, you're the same unassuming guy from Pascagoula who weeds his yard on the weekends in khaki cutoffs and T-shirts—the local guy who went to Pascagoula High and married your college sweetheart."

At that time, we didn't know how far Wayne Dowdy—who won the primary—would take his character attack. I was prepared, however, to combat his strengths and solid achievements. Dowdy was a hometown boy from McComb, a city in southwest

Mississippi. A graduate of the Jackson School of Law, he first practiced law in his hometown, where he was soon elected city judge and mayor in the 1970s and early 1980s. He was elected as a Democrat to the Ninety-Seventh Congress, and reelected to three succeeding Congresses. A tall fellow with thick curly hair, Dowdy even bore a vague resemblance to Abraham Lincoln.

I got ready for a stiff fight. I put together a blue-ribbon campaign team headed by Tom Anderson, who had served as my chief of staff before going on to become U.S. ambassador to Barbados. General Mickey Walker, former adjutant general of the Mississippi National Guard, was my campaign committee chairman. Billy Mounger, formerly Mississippi finance chairman of the Republican Party, was finance chairman. Ed Goeas did the polling.

But perhaps the key ingredient was Dick Morris. Born and raised in Brooklyn, Morris had learned politics in the rough-and-tumble arena of the American Northeast. But over the years he had gained some valuable experience in the South, and had used his considerable talents to elect some prominent figures. Morris had managed Bill Clinton's first and third campaigns for governor of Arkansas, both successful, and he also had helped to put Buddy Roemer into the Louisiana governor's mansion. And through his involvement in the gubernatorial campaign of Bill Allain in 1983, and the Senate campaign of former governor William Winter in 1984, he had mastered the complexities and the quirks of Mississippi politics.

The campaign he helped direct for me in 1988 was unique in several ways. First, it was the year when the Republican Party recognized that it could take the state for the first time. The party made my election a top priority, starting with a rally for me at the 1988 GOP convention in New Orleans. After the August convention, George H. W. Bush's brother, William, and Governor Carroll Campbell of South Carolina descended on Mississippi to campaign.

President Reagan, in his final months in office, came down for "An Evening with Ronald Reagan," which sold out at $2,000 a couple. The president also taped a commercial in which he said. "I know Trent Lott as one of the most important leaders in the country on issues vital to all Americans."

Jack Kemp headlined a fund-raiser in Jackson, drawing a sell-out crowd of seven hundred. Finally, a flying team of U.S. senators—Bob Kasten of Wisconsin, John McCain of Arizona, Bob Dole of Kansas, John Warner of Virginia, and Don Nickles of Oklahoma—trooped in for a tour of select cities. Their clout paid off: I jumped five points in the polls.

The ad blitzes, newspaper reports, high-profile appearances, and debates all ended up focusing on the Dowdy campaign's relentless attempt to paint me as a Republican elitist, an insider who had forsaken his Mississippi roots. But the gritty battle fought in towns across the state—at community picnics, at revival meetings, and in sun-drenched parking lots—dealt with better highways, more jobs, civil rights, and the one real question: Who was really more qualified to be the new senator from Mississippi?

Out in the heat and the dust, speeding from town to town, it was easy to see that I was winning that battle. I could tell from the looks on the faces of the Mississippi voters and the firmness of their handshakes. I was outworking Representative Dowdy mercilessly, and it was paying off.

I designed a series of sweeps that took me to every corner of the state—from the breakwater at Gulfport to the rural settlements near our northern border with Tennessee. With military precision, Tricia and I visited as many as six cities a day, using a relay of vehicles and a staggered schedule. My famous singing buddy, Guy Hovis, and my talented son, Chet, traveled in the first car with an advance man. They hit the crowds first, jumping up on makeshift stages and singing patriotic and gospel songs. Tricia and I and a press person arrived just as Chet and Hovis finished their last number and jumped in the car to head for the next town. We began backing out of the crowd during question-and-answer sessions as a backup team of campaigners passed out literature and took names and addresses. As we sped to our next stop, I organized the business cards people had shoved into my hands, and started writing personal messages on specially printed picture postcards. I mailed them at the first post office box I spotted in the next town.

By late October, the press was estimating that our campaign stops were almost doubling Dowdy's. We were still rolling the day before the election.

The one thing we didn't expect was the battle over my image, which started with the complaints over the highway ad and continued with what seemed a harmless campaign tactic from the Democrats. In June, Dowdy began opening his speeches by saying, "Sorry, folks, my hair isn't as neat as Trent Lott's. I don't have that much time." It wasn't much of a line, but it got a few chuckles before Dowdy moved on. Slowly, though, his attacks became more severe: "Wouldn't you like to mess up Congressman Lott's hair?" he goaded one campaign gathering in Jackson.

"Maybe it's not real," cried one of the Dowdy supporters.

By July, signs were beginning to appear at Dowdy rallies deriding my neatly cropped, tightly brushed hair. One sign said: TRENT LOTT'S HAIR IS TOO SLICK; SO IS HE. Several banners simply featured silhouette profiles of my locks and Dowdy's unruly curls. MESS UP LOTT'S HAIR. VOTE FOR WAYNE DOWDY, read another message.

The fracas soon spilled over into the press. Editorial cartoonists at several Mississippi newspapers focused on the so-called hair issue, with various caricatures of my well-kept style.

It's hard to believe anyone would take such name-calling seriously, but a spokesman for the Dowdy campaign told reporters that all the talk about hairstyles was dead serious. "Research has shown us that Congressman Lott is vulnerable to the 'too slick' labels being tossed around. His hair is merely a symbol of that," the spokesman said. "We believe that Lott's slick appearance suggests a class identification with Washington cocktail parties and afternoons on the golf course." The message was clear: They were portraying me as a man who had abandoned his roots to join the elite class.

My campaign manager Tim Carpenter was incensed. "Trent doesn't even know how to hold a golf club," he protested, "yet he's getting beaten up for being a country club Republican." I was dumbfounded. My roots were as blue-collar as anyone's. I had struggled financially myself. I didn't recognize the portrait they were painting. Country clubs? I was a stranger there.

But I soon realized that I could weather the hair issue—and in short order I was turning the tables on Dowdy. When we appeared together in Biloxi before the Mississippi Bar Association, he again apologized for his unruly hair while glancing slyly at the top of my head. I pulled a new comb out of my suit pocket and handed it to him. "This is gratis, Wayne," I chuckled. When his complaints continued, I took another good-natured jibe at Dowdy's tousled locks: "I think the good ole boy look is on its way out." The laughter convinced me that I was escaping from Dowdy's trap.

Then he hit below the belt.

In a fiery speech at the Neshoba County Fair, Dowdy suddenly roared out: "Before we cut services to senior citizens in Mississippi, let's cut Trent Lott's chauffeur, George Awkward." Recognizing the name from radio commercials, the Dowdy enthusiasts began chanting, "Let's cut George. Let's cut George."

Dowdy continued: "Let's don't cut money for roads in Mississippi. Let's tell the chauffeurs like George to hit the road."

His media people quickly fanned the flames with a big television campaign that opened only days later. The ad spot showed a guy riding in the back seat of a chauffeur-driven limousine. It drove past a group of elderly people at the mailbox getting their Social Security checks. When the long black limo sped by, the checks went swirling in the wind. The voiceover intoned, "Don't cut Social Security. Cut Trent Lott's chauffeur, George Awkward."

The ad got noticed. Columnist Sid Salter, who was syndicated throughout Mississippi, declared, "This appears to be a frivolous issue on the surface. But it's something Trent Lott better dispose of quickly." Salter was right: It was a very effective commercial. It was also a clever manipulation of the truth. George Awkward was no chauffeur; he was a U.S. Capitol police officer and bodyguard, assigned to me because of my leadership status as House Republican whip.

But George Awkward also was an African American, and the Dowdy campaign was playing into an almost racist stereotype— equating "black" with "chauffeur." The spot wasn't fair to me, but that was par for the course. What really rankled was that it wasn't fair to this brave public servant.

Morris and our other strategists mobilized to counter the ad, brainstorming ideas in search of the right response.

Several days after the Dowdy commercials debuted, I got into the car with George to go to work and found a $100 check on the seat.

"What's this?" I asked George.

"Mr. Lott, I'm sorry that I'm being used against you. I want to help."

I handed the check back. "Don't worry about it, George. But I appreciate your concern."

When I told Tommy Anderson and Dick Morris about Awkward's moving gesture, though, Morris saw an opportunity. "Wait a minute," he said. "This may be the answer."

We drove George to the Goodman office in Baltimore and positioned him in front of a flag, with his coat off and his gun prominently visible. Looking into the camera, he described his background as a highly experienced lawman—first with the Washington, D.C., police department, later for the U.S. Capitol.

Then the security officer glared at the camera and said: "And I'm nobody's chauffeur, Mr. Dowdy. Got it?"

The ad had an immediate effect. My campaign headquarters was flooded with calls of support, and my poll numbers among black voters rose about 20 percent. Dowdy was forced to pull his spot. And later ours won a national award for best response ad.

By the final weeks of the campaign, even Dowdy acknowledged to reporters that our fieldwork was swamping his. But he had one last gasp. He bounded back briefly with an ingenious fifteen-second spot on Social Security. "Trent Lott voted to cut your Social Security," it said. "For more information, call this number." When we called the number, we got an audio reading of some pages from the *Congressional Record*. Though the message made no sense, my poll numbers dropped four points, to 56 percent. We had to do something fast.

Dick Morris and company enlisted my mother, a retired schoolteacher. "I'm Iona Lott, Trent Lott's mother," she said. "I depend upon Social Security, and I can tell you my son would never cut my Social Security benefits." The fire was out.

On election night, I discovered that Dowdy was not quite the threat to me the press had made him out to be. I took 54 percent of the vote; Dowdy grabbed only 46 percent. I won by a landslide in my home Fifth District, where I racked up a two-to-one margin. My statewide strength held him to small winning margins in the three districts he carried. I trailed Dowdy by a mere ten thousand votes in the predominantly black Second District.

I had made strong efforts to win black voters over to the Republican column, and ended up with a surprising 13 percent from a block that had been voting 95 percent Democratic just five years earlier. Jackson businessman Les Range, who led the crusade to get black Mississippians to vote for a Gulf Coast congressman, had hoped for 15 percent. But I was ecstatic with our result. It was the start of a slow march of African Americans into the Republican ranks.

On victory night, we had a huge crowd at the Ramada Inn in Jackson, the state capital. All the family was there—Tricia, Chet, Tyler, my mother, Tricia's dad (Dr. Perry Thompson), her five brothers and sisters, plus friends, college fraternity brothers, long-time Republicans, and moss-backed Democrats. We had a great party. George H. W. Bush won that night as well. But when I got up to speak, I announced that we had a special guest named George, "And it's not George Bush."

George Awkward walked up on stage, and the crowd went wild.

I couldn't sleep that night, I was so excited. I got up at 5:30 in the morning, went downtown, and waved thank you to workers as they drove to work. Later, when I looked at my watch, it was 9 A.M.

I was a very grateful junior senator from Mississippi.

# 9

# SENATORIAL PRIVILEGE

I wandered around the old Senate chamber, trying to drink in the history and pomp of the place—and the people who had populated it before me. It wasn't long after my victory, and I was still full of reverence for the upper house of Congress. Even after two hundred years, the Senate was still known as the "gentleman's club" of the United States government.

Though my adventures on the floor of the House had been exhilarating, I still felt a rush as I prepared to enter the Senate. Wandering amidst the eighteenth-century brocade draperies and gilt-edged ceilings of the old chamber took me back to the earliest days of the institution, formed when a group of distinguished gentlemen banded together for the good of the nation.

Despite Dowdy's ineffective jibes at my so-called country-club image, I chose to arrive at the Senate with a new wardrobe that reflected what I perceived as the seriousness of my new job. From my old sport coats and slacks, I graduated to custom-tailored blue and dark gray suits—dressy enough for a corporate boardroom, dignified enough for the floor of the United States Senate.

In January 1989, I vaulted into the chamber full of ideas, bursting with enthusiasm and eager to hit the ground running. I intended to make an early assault on the leadership, as I had in the House. But this time I had a successful record to back me up: with my work as whip, I had made a name for myself in Washington. After emerging unscathed from a tough and contentious election, after giving up real national power in the House of Representatives, after winning a score of big victories for Ronald Reagan, I expected a warm welcome in the Senate.

Instead I was seated in the back row with the other freshmen, including a handful of friends and confidantes who had come with me from the house. We found ourselves "in storage" as the Senate machinery creaked to life. I use the word "creaked" because that's the way the upper house appeared: as an aloof, sedate organization, set in its ways and distinctly unfriendly to the plebes who entered the chamber after their first Senate election.

For sixteen years, I'd been fighting my way through the trenches of the House of Representatives. Truly the "people's house," the House more closely echoes the character and concerns of American voters. House districts range from 500,000 to 600,000 people, whereas senators can represent up to 35 million people (as in California). Almost by definition, senators are a bit more distant from their constituents. What's more, House members serve two-year terms, which means they always are running for office; that's a sure way to guarantee regular contact with the voters.

From my back-row vantage point, I quickly learned that the Senate was a very different institution from the House. One paradox was that while there were one hundred senators, compared with four hundred and thirty-five House members, many of the senators were themselves distant, all but impossible to befriend.

The Senate also was a confused and disorganized institution. The majority leader was George Mitchell of Maine—a driven bachelor who didn't seem to understand that other senators had families. The schedule was terrible, and there was no certainty. Some days we wouldn't know whether there would be further votes until after nine o'clock in the evening. Sometimes we didn't get home until after ten.

Slowly, though, I began to know and understand my fellow senators. Many of them were lone wolves—courteous enough in conversation, but hardly warm and personable. How do you get elected statewide with that kind of personality? I wondered. The only answer I came up with was that they must do a heck of a job for their constituents.

Many of the senators had become celebrities in the national spotlight. Some of them even became heroes. That list included Republicans Bob Dole of Kansas, John McCain of Arizona, Jesse Helms of North Carolina, and Strom Thurmond of South Carolina. Across the aisle, it included Democrats Ted Kennedy of Massachusetts, John Glenn of Ohio, and Sam Nunn of Georgia. But other senators, it seemed to me, were just marking time.

I soon came to understand an enduring adage: When you first got to the Senate, you wondered how you could be so honored to serve with these great men and women. After a few months, though, you started to wonder how these characters ever got elected. Familiarity bred contempt.

Except for a brief period in the early 1980s, the Democrats had been in control for so long that they had adopted bullyboy tactics to enforce their power. Using their superior numbers, they simply rammed their bills through, blind to the effect bad legislation might have on the future of the Senate. It was a nasty scene on the floor—devoid of courtesy and festering with hate.

I got an unpleasant taste of this early on during the Democratic massacre of former Texas senator John Tower, the first President Bush's nominee for secretary of defense. Tower was perhaps *the* ideal candidate for the post. He'd chaired the Armed Services Committee in the early 1980s and really knew the Pentagon. I'd worked with him on the 1980 Republican platform, and got to know him well during my years of House leadership. I thought his confirmation would be a slam dunk.

Instead it erupted into a donnybrook, as the Democratic caucus launched a campaign of lies, rumor, and innuendo that resulted in weeks of fighting, left the appointment practices of the Senate in tatters, and led to deep public mistrust of the Senate's honesty. The Armed Services Committee ordered an FBI report on Tower and instructed the bureau to make sure it covered his time in the Senate, including his after-hours activities and his drinking with congressional colleagues.

Then the process got downright ugly. The FBI started to investigate senators who had associated with Tower socially; within days, these Tower intimates began giving in to pressure and turning on their former colleague, pulling back the curtain on the private, informal conversations Tower and his colleagues enjoyed after Senate business concluded each day. The Senate was eating its own, its members turning themselves in along with Tower. They spoke freely about what they called "Tower's drinking problems," and about the business they had done together over wine. In all the years of its history, the Senate had always been a close-knit club; these little after-hours sessions were part of its tradition of gentlemanly discretion.

But there was no stopping it. One senator's tales of imbibing after hours only encouraged others to jump in with their contribution to Tower's alleged sins. It became a chorus of tattletales. Still, most of what showed up in the FBI report was a matter of unsubstantiated rumor and gross innuendo. Some of the stories came in over the transom and were slightly bizarre. One had him dancing drunk on top of a piano in Texas.

To my amazement, even his colleague Sam Nunn turned on him. Nunn had served with Tower as ranking Democrat on the Armed Services Committee, and was currently serving as committee chairman; he knew how good a job Tower had done there. What would make a man as powerful and as dignified as Nunn rely on gossip in order to slam his old friend? I still have no answer to that question. John Tower wasn't a teetotaler. Sure he'd take a drink, and he'd been single for several years. But it never got in the way of Senate business. He had always done a flawless job. Sam Nunn had to have known that.

Senate Minority Leader Bob Dole pleaded with his colleagues to stop the witch hunt: "We are crossing a line here," he said. "We are dooming future confirmation hearings to a lower standard— the one that includes lies and rumor held up to be the truth."

My first real speech on the floor of the Senate was in defense of Senator Tower. I lauded his credentials, and warned of the damage we were doing to his reputation and to the Senate itself. It was a coming-of-age act for me, and I struck out on my own to investigate charges made against Tower before the Armed Services Committee. Almost all of the initial allegations against the nominee were discovered to be baseless. But by that time the damage to a good man's reputation had been done.

For instance, Armed Services Committee members were told a story about a Russian ballerina that Tower had supposedly propositioned during a drunken evening in the Soviet Union. "We have all heard this now-famous story," I told the Senate. But the fact that this story was totally baseless was trumped by the very fact that it went public. On February 8 and 9, the committee was close to concluding its work; we could have had a vote before the Senate went into recess for Presidents' Day. Instead, I remember a prominent senator saying, "Now, that is a serious allegation. If there is any evidence, whatsoever, that any of that is true, I want to know about it." At that crucial juncture, when the committee would have recommended that the Senate confirm John Tower as secretary of defense, the committee stopped and said, No, we want this ballerina story investigated. In late February, after the recess, I checked and found there was no truth to the story at all. But this unfounded, hysterical allegation had caused us to hesitate at a critical moment—and cost Tower his nomination.

In my defense of Tower, I offered the committee proof of two more totally unfounded "incidents"—stories that were ultimately disproved, but not before they'd done their damage. The most crucial of these concerned an allegation that Senator Tower had acted out of order during a visit to Bergstrom Air Force Base near Austin, Texas—drinking and acting indiscreetly with a female member of the Air Force. I told the Senate: "So, again, we asked if this was true. In fact I had the media asking me, 'Well, Senator, if you found out he did let his hand slide down in an untoward manner, would that affect you?'" Sure it would, if it were true. But it wasn't. We had no reason to believe this story was credible. Still, it was on the front page of the newspapers, and it caused the members to pause.

I summarized: "I have heard senators on the Armed Services Committee and others outside of this great body, and senators here, talk about perception. It is the accumulation of accusations, even though they may have been proven to be untrue or unfounded or totally hysterical. It is the accumulation of those baseless allegations that seems to have created a perception that Senator John Tower is wrong for secretary of defense. I have to question that. Should we cast such a historical vote on the basis of what we perceive may or may not have been happening? No. I submit that is fundamentally wrong."

Dole followed with an equally fiery speech. "Now I have heard others say, 'Well, this has been around for quite awhile now and we have had so much news on it, and a lot of people back home are opposed to Tower.' Why would they not be? Every night on the nightly news, on every network, on CNN, in every newspaper, there is some rumor, some rumor that somebody has spread and it is repeated on the news. If somebody in my state sees that scurrilous report, they would not be for John Tower either."

The *New York Times* said that the Democrats built a case against his character rather than his competence. The whole truth was much worse: The real problem was that the case they built was unfair and untrue. The result was one of the Senate's most rancorous debates in modern times—and a nomination killed by a largely party-line vote of 53 to 47. It was the country's loss.

Episodes such as the Tower tragedy, and the regular bullying by the Democrats, gave me some pause at first over whether the Senate and I were a good fit. Having been in the leadership of the House for eight years, I was coming from a very different place than the other House members who had been elected to the Senate with me. I'd been on the short list of House leaders who were at the center of things. And then I wasn't. Republican leader Bob Dole gave me some early opportunities, but the process was slow—almost slower than I could stand.

The Senate was the most frustrating place I had ever been in my life. The process was glacial, messy, and unpredictable. All I could do was go along, get along, and start making lists of things I would change in the Senate when I had the opportunity.

But I had a hidden strength that, before long, would begin to shatter the status quo. I could rely on a tight, conservative clique of relatively young senators and former representatives—some who had preceded me to the upper chamber, some who arrived with me, some who soon followed. This group included Judd

Gregg of New Hampshire, Don Nickles of Oklahoma, John Ashcroft of Missouri, Slade Gorton of Washington, Dan Coats of Indiana, Phil Gramm of Texas, John McCain and Jon Kyl of Arizona, Jim McClure of Idaho, and Malcolm Wallop of Wyoming. Some of the "old bulls," like Jesse Helms, Strom Thurmond, and Ted Stevens from Alaska, were helpful from the beginning.

We were conservative, we were hungry, and we intended to make a difference and to eventually capture the leadership. Some journalists called us the "kitchen cabinet." Others described us as the steering committee. Whatever the name, these philosophical buddies would help push me into the leadership and stay with me. The time was right. The Republican leaders under Bob Dole were far more moderate than the Republican Conference as a whole.

Four years into my first term, my committee assignments included Armed Services, Budget, and Energy and Natural Resources. I also served on the Commerce, Science, and Transportation Committee. Then, in 1992, I got the chance to jump onto the bottom rung of the Senate's Republican leadership ladder. When Wisconsin senator Robert Kasten, once known as "Landslide Bob," lost his seat to the liberal Democrat Russ Feingold in a spectacular upset, his defeat opened up the position of secretary to the Republican Conference.

Backed by my former House mates, I ran for the post—the number-four leadership position among Senate Republicans—and won, capturing twenty votes to fourteen for Senator Christopher Bond of Missouri and five for Senator Frank Murkowski of Alaska. My foot was on the ladder at last.

My work with the conference attracted the attention of Bob Dole, who soon began seeking me out for splashy and specialized duties. For example, he wanted to put me on the Ethics Committee, a damnable position because you had to sit in judgment of your colleagues. I joked with Dole that he was trying to finish me as a leader in the Senate before I even got started. But he said he needed someone who commanded respect and was willing to do the job, so I took the assignment.

In 1994, I won reelection over an underfunded Democratic challenger, former Mississippi state senator Ken Harper. My campaign was financially muscular: We spent $2,136,544, compared with the $366,476 my opponent spent. Nationally, we regained the majority in the Senate that year, with an influx of even more conservatives. At the same time, though, Senate Majority Leader Bob Dole's moderate establishment was weakening a bit. New leaders were on the rise, drifting further away from the old leadership. It was time to ascend to the top rungs of Senatorial power.

Bolstered by my steering committee of former House members, I was considering a challenge to Senator Alan K. Simpson, who appeared to be entrenched as Dole's Senate whip. The son of Milward Simpson, who had served Wyoming as governor and as a U.S. senator, Al was a friendly, gregarious, and authentic politician who traded in ranch talk and a limitless repertoire of jokes. He came to the Senate in 1978 after succeeding retiring Republican senator Clifford P. Hansen. During his twelve years as a state legislator, he was active in environmental matters and in the drafting of a state land-use planning law.

Simpson had become a national figure, much applauded for both the intensity and the fairness he displayed during Supreme Court nominee Clarence Thomas's confirmation hearings. When I began hinting that I might challenge him as whip, some people—including a few members of my own kitchen cabinet—urged caution. "Put it off a year or two," one of them said. "He might retire." *No way,* I thought. There was a lot more at stake here than met the eye. I suspected that our majority leader, Bob Dole, was planning to quit the Senate in 1996 to campaign full time for the presidency. Dole was determined to bring down Bill Clinton, and if he succeeded, the Senate whip would be primed to become majority leader.

I wanted to test my thinking on a keen political mind outside my immediate orbit, so I asked Dick Morris to come down to Pascagoula for a chat a few days after the 1994 election. As we sat in rockers on my front porch, looking out at the Gulf, I told him about my tentative plan to take on Simpson. Dick urged me to go for it. His analysis told him I could win, though he figured the race might be tight. Then he told me that his old boss, President Clinton, had contacted him about coming to work at the White House.

"Are you going to do it?" I asked him.

"Yeah, I think so," Morris said.

"Well, I'd prefer you didn't work for any Democrats," I told him with a chuckle. But Clinton was the president, after all, and Morris's relationship with him went back to the late 1970s.

Dick lit up. "This could be great," he said. "You take over the Senate, I'll take over the White House, and we'll pass everything!" We laughed at that. But Dick, as it turned out, was only half joking.

I realized that challenging Simpson was personally risky. I could win it all, or I could lose it all. I'd been in the Senate only six years, and I'd been conference secretary for less than two. If I lost, it would mean a tortuous climb back into the leadership—that is, if I could make the climb at all.

I was also disdainful of the way the whip organization was being operated under Dole. Simpson himself had relatively little to do with going out and getting the votes. By tradition, the whip duties were carried out by the majority leader's staff. It was an informal process. The staff members went from senator to senator trying to learn how the members planned to vote, rather than making the effort to persuade them one way or the other. It was a passive process—nowhere near the organization I'd built up in the House, and hardly good enough. There's a world of difference between a staff member politely inquiring how a senator might vote, and another senator bringing to bear peer and partisan pressure. The Senate whip organization needed a complete overhaul.

Using the conservative group that surrounded me, I conducted informal polls, interviewed key senators, and tried to get a handle on the votes. The early data indicated that I had thirty-two votes going into the election, so I thought I'd probably win by ten. It's important to note that I wasn't so much running against Simpson as against an antiquated way of counting and soliciting votes. In that election, I stood for a new way of doing business.

My son, Chet, had a great deal to do with my race for this key leadership slot. At the Ramada Inn in Jackson, Mississippi, after I'd won reelection, I turned to Chet. "I'm thinking about running against Simpson for whip," I told him.

Chet paused, then asked: "Do you have the votes?"

"I think I can get them," I answered.

"Well," he said, "You've been a whip before. You know how to count the votes. And if you say you've got the votes, I guess you can win."

During the campaign, senators close to me sometimes took their fight to the media. One of them described Simpson as "a tired old conservative, unable to properly manage the whip counting operation and afraid to take bold policy risks." The *National Review* summarized the contest nicely: "Most of all, Lott has positioned himself as the candidate of change versus Simpson's status quo. He believes he can work better with the Gingrich House group and with incoming senators who are House alumni. Citing Olympia Snowe of Maine, who was a deputy whip under him in the House, Lott argued that he knows how to bring along GOP moderates and Democrats. 'In the early Eighties, we had to get 50 House Democrats to pass Reagan's legislation and we got them.'"

I believed my record would help me capture the whip's spot, the second most powerful position in Senate Republican ranks. As a first-term senator, I had voted against the 1990 tax disaster, when the first President Bush violated his no-new-taxes pledge. I had also compiled a solid record favoring growth-oriented tax cuts, domestic budget restraint, a strong military, and tough measures to fight crime. Meantime, I was considering a balanced budget amendment with a tax-limitation provision. And I announced I was prepared to cut welfare and spending. All in all, it was a responsible and strongly conservative set of positions.

Then Dole inserted himself into the race, using his influence in an effort to tug key senators back into Simpson's camp. He worked hard at it. By the time of the vote, I had only twenty-seven guaranteed votes. While the ballots were being tallied, Simpson sauntered over and told me good luck, "no matter who wins." Then he held me in the back of the room until Dole, who was out front, declared the winner.

As I started through the door, I heard the majority leader call my name. I had won by a single vote—but even that narrow victory heralded significant long-term changes in the life of the Senate.

Simpson draped one arm around my shoulder and we moved forward, smiling and comfortable with one another. In the aftermath, he couldn't have been more helpful. He showed me his operation from top to bottom, then tried to educate me about working with Dole. "Don't inundate him with a lot of talk," he said. "Just get the number and the data down, write it on a card, and present it to him." That method proved enormously successful. Whenever I handed Dole the crucial card, he roared into action—confident of the votes he would get.

Once, he wrote "good job" on the bottom of one of the cards, high praise indeed from the majority leader. "This is an outstanding young man and rarin' to go," he told Elizabeth Letchworth, the secretary to the Majority. "Let's make sure he has plenty to do."

\* \* \*

I took on with relish the task of establishing the first modern whip organization in the Senate. I picked a committee of nine, including Chief Deputy Whip Judd Gregg, who proved to be a dynamo. With fewer heads to count and votes to get, I was able to assign each deputy whip to five or six senators—contacts that they monitored closely. It was personal service, and it worked wonders. I molded this approach entirely to serve Bob Dole's needs, and our arrangement was cordial and professional. When he left to run for the presidency, Dole told me: "Thanks. You're a good whip."

When we began together, I told Dole that we were in a tough spot. If we were going to win close votes—with a new majority in the Senate, but a president whose agenda was very different from ours—we'd need much the same whip organization as we had in the House: one that would provide the members with serious listeners, a friendly shoulder, even counseling. The system I established helped us keep track of the senators over the long term; it brought back a level of member-to-member contact that had not been used by Senate Republicans since Ted Stevens of Alaska was whip in the late 1970s and early 1980s. This Senate was a club full of loners, men and women with a very different view of life and politics from that of House members. The Senate glorified the individual, and the individual senator can involve him or herself in the debate on anything that interests him or her. Individuals in the House, for the most part, are out in the cold. My new deputies in the Senate had to get to know their individual charges, and know them well.

We created a whip organization that accommodated the Senate's peculiarities—a full-service vote-getter that would later help forge bold connections to the administrations of both Bill Clinton and George W. Bush. But I would supervise its operation at one remove. I fine-tuned the whip machine through 1995, and had it running smoothly by the spring of 1996. Then my hunch paid off:

Senate Majority Leader Bob Dole announced that he would be resigning to devote his complete attention to the race for president against Bill Clinton.

Compared with my campaign to win the whip position, my ascension to majority leader was swift and painless. I was elected to succeed Dole in a matter of days, beating fellow Mississippian Senator Thad Cochran by a margin of 44–8. The lopsided victory had less to do with Thad than it did with the close-knit group of conservatives around me in the Senate. And it didn't dim Cochran's considerable record of service to Mississippi. Thad ran, I believe, because he was the "senior" senator from Mississippi and felt he was next in line. But from that day forward he was nothing but cooperative and helpful to me. I have sought his counsel many times—as he has done with me.

My ascension was a tribute to the overhaul of the Senate by the steering committee of former House members and other close associates. It was hailed as a "historic transfer of power." University of California political scientist Barbara Sinclair concluded: "This is an amazing change in the Republican Party's ideology. Indeed, it brings the Senate much more in line ideologically with the House." In the House, Gingrich was the new speaker, joined by outspoken conservatives such as Texans Dick Armey, the new majority leader, and Tom DeLay, who got my old job as whip. For the first time in history, the top Republican leaders in both houses of Congress were from the South—the culmination of a political transformation that began when Barry Goldwater ran for president in 1964.

There was an immense amount of work to do. When I came into the leadership, the Senate was completely tied in knots. The Democrats were determined not to let us pass legislation that Bob Dole could take credit for during the presidential election. The minority had really garbled things up. In the forty years that the Republicans were mostly in the minority, they slowly managed to slant the rules in their favor. When we ascended to the majority, the Democrats were in deep denial; they simply couldn't figure out how to function. They were the minority party now, but they couldn't accept the lowered standing, and they didn't know what to do with it.

To bring order to the chaos, I commanded the divided Senate through a team of six to seven of the Republican members. I set a huge nineteenth-century table in front of a bay window in the majority leader's office, and summoned my closest colleagues for advice at least once a day. In a nod to the aged British table we met around, that panel was nicknamed "The Council of Trent." Its core members included Connie Mack of Florida, Judd Gregg of New Hampshire, Dan Coats of Indiana, Slade Gorton of Washington, Spencer Abraham of Michigan, Kay Bailey Hutchison of Texas, and Rick Santorum of Pennsylvania.

In addition to the friendship and comfort these senators provided, there was another great force in my life at this time. Even though Dan Coats and I had supported another candidate for the job, Dr. Lloyd John Ogilvie had been selected as the Senate chaplain in 1995 at the urging of Mark Hatfield of Oregon. His presence and messages had an instant impact on the strength of my faith. Our daughter, Tyler, even noticed a change in my countenance. When I asked her what she meant by that, she said, "I'm not sure, but you seem calmer and more religious in your attitude." I was surprised, and pleased that she noticed. Lloyd's presence and weekly bible and prayer meetings meant a great deal to me, and I know the same was true for other senators and even our staffs.

Early in my tenure as majority leader, the chaplain gave me a copy of his book of daily Bible readings and prayers, *One Quiet Moment,* with an inscription: "To Trent: God's man for such a time as this!—Lloyd." I was amazed at how often that book provided just the right message for the daily challenges ahead. I still read it each morning before I leave for the day—to work or to play.


It had been half a century since the Senate had included fifty-five Republicans. The Senate itself, of course, didn't engineer this leap into the majority. The credit goes largely to Georgia representative Newt Gingrich, a fiery orator and a relentless and angry leader.

Gingrich had been perfecting his combative style since his days as one of the House's backbenchers. As a freshman, he freely offered strategic advice to his party elders, using a crayon to draw scenarios for Republican dominance in Congress. Newt was an irate whirlwind who couldn't or wouldn't stop until his party was back in the majority.

In an early 1994 phone call, Newt, a close colleague of mine in the House, told me he had a plan to catapult the Republicans back into the majority. And he promised to call soon with details of what he called "a foolproof plan." Meanwhile he jumped onto every scandal he could unearth, putting the conduct of his fellow representatives under a microscope. He made hay with both the congressional banking scandal and a handful of sex scandals. And in 1989 it was arguably Newt who brought down House Speaker Jim Wright of Texas, who resigned in the wake of alleged ethics violations that Gingrich had publicized.

Newt's message was simple: The Democrats had been in the majority too long. In one session, borrowing a line from the British historian Lord Acton, he thundered: "Power corrupts and absolute power corrupts absolutely. That has happened to us." Then he haunted his offices, working day and night on a kind of mission statement—a document House Democrats had every reason to fear. When he was done, Gingrich had come up with a strategy to nationalize the 1994 congressional contests to a degree rarely seen in a midterm election.

Just before he released his carefully guarded document, he telephoned me and described an election plan he termed the Contract with America—a promise to bring ten broad issues to floor votes within the first hundred days of the new Congress. The Contract included internal House reforms, such as cutting committees and staff and outlawing proxy voting in committee. But the document also represented a renewal of the basic Reagan agenda— strengthened national security, major cuts in spending, lowered taxes, and reduced regulation of business. In figurative terms, Newt was proposing to destroy the House, then restore its power under a different banner.

In a brilliant political move, Gingrich had the entire Contract reprinted in *Reader's Digest,* on a perforated page you could tear out of the magazine, which was read by millions of voters. To enhance the House Republicans' image further, Gingrich told me he was planning to gather them all together on the front steps of the Capitol. "The media," he told me, "are prepared to cover that assembly intensely."

Then he added: "Trent, why don't you and your fellow Republicans in the Senate join us out there?"

Phil Gramm and I both thought it was a terrific idea, and we both separately approached Bob Dole, who at that time was still Senate majority leader. "We should join them," I told Dole. "We should sign the Contract and join them on the Capitol steps."

"Nah, we don't want to do that," Dole scoffed. I knew where he was coming from: The Senate likes to think of itself as the more mature and deliberative partner in the legislative branch, and its old bulls were bound to dismiss what the young upstarts in the House were doing as foolish grandstanding. So we sat impotently in our offices and watched this remarkable ceremony on television.

I could never have done what Newt did to win the majority. I could never have torn down the institution in order to rebuild it. But it worked beautifully for him. The Republicans had gained fifty-two seats in the 1994 election, with the Gingrich coattails carrying the Senate back into the majority as well. Then, when Senators Richard Shelby of Alabama and Ben Nighthorse Campbell of Colorado switched sides, we reached that magic number of fifty-five.

Now, as the new majority leader, I intended to use this newly minted power to great effect in the Senate. With a single realigning election, the stage suddenly was set for one of the most creative and successful bursts of legislative activity in the history of Congress.

# 10

# TRIAD: PRESIDENT CLINTON, DICK MORRIS, AND ME

In the late spring of 1996, as I was about to assume the most powerful leadership position in the U.S. Senate, Dick Morris suddenly leaped back into my life. And he came bearing a proposition that, at first, sounded both politically dangerous and pragmatically impossible.

Dick's call came the night after I was elevated to majority leader. He reminded me of our conversation on my front porch a year and a half earlier. Since then he had accepted President Bill Clinton's offer, and was now working out of the White House. As Morris told the story, it was a hard invitation to refuse. Clinton had called late one night—not unusual for this president—and told Morris: "I need you." Morris could sense a hint of insecurity in the president's voice. He was up for reelection, and the prospects seemed less than spectacular.

"Come on back," Clinton repeated. "We've got a lot of changes to make." But quietly, the president suggested. At first Morris's new appointment would be kept secret from White

House staffers, who jealously guarded their turf in the West Wing. But by the time of Dick's call to me, his role as Clinton's political strategist was well known.

"I can tell you what one of your biggest problems is," Morris told me. "You're not getting enough done. And the public is aware of that. But I have a plan." Morris's plan centered on two unlikely partners: me and Bill Clinton. "Look," he said in his insistent voice, "I've just become Clinton's most intimate adviser, and you're the majority leader." What Morris proposed was a highly unusual alliance between the president of the United States and the majority leader of the opposing party, with himself serving as clandestine intermediary. It may have been unique in the history of American politics.

Morris's plan was stunning in its audacity. He wanted me to forge a working relationship with Bill Clinton to enact a series of landmark bills that the president would quickly sign into law. As Morris pointed out, both the Republican Senate Conference and Clinton would benefit from this series of legislative coups. Clinton would be seen as a "can-do president" as he headed toward Election Day. And the GOP would get credit for breaking the logjam in Congress, and for sponsoring truly significant legislation. And Morris wasn't talking about everyday bills, though we needed to enact those as well. Instead, he embraced my suggestions for major welfare reform, a balanced budget act, that would include Medicare cuts, and immigration reform.

I believe in action, but I couldn't agree to Morris's proposal on the spot. He was asking me, in effect, to take steps that might well strengthen the president's political position and reelection prospects against the candidate of my own party. I didn't think Bob Dole and his strategists would be terribly happy with me if I consented to work so closely with Clinton.

But there were other factors to consider, and after thinking it over for a day or two I agreed to Dick's unorthodox suggestion.

Why, you might ask? For one thing, I've always had a great enthusiasm for making law—and I believe that that was why my constituents sent me to the Senate in the first place. It seemed to me that if we failed to do these important things, they weren't going to get done—at least anytime soon. Of course I have a set of strong philosophical principles. But what good is an unbending purist position if you don't produce results for the people you care about and your country?

So Morris and I went ahead with this plan, forming a backstairs relationship with the Oval Office that relied on telephone calls with Dick, sometimes at odd hours, and eventually scores of direct conversations between President Clinton and me. I took to calling Morris "Mr. Prime Minister"; he dubbed me HMO—"His Majesty's Opposition."

There was no way I could keep everyone in my camp in the dark. At first I confidentially informed the members of the Council of Trent and a handful of key staffers who needed to know. Others would later be clued in on a need-to-know basis. Before it was over, the entire Republican Senate was involved: So many bills were passing so fast that every able Republican body was a necessity.

For starters, I presented Morris with a rundown of pending legislation and an estimate of what it would take to clear the calendar to make way for these big, focused bills—such as the Welfare Reform Act, which Clinton already had vetoed twice, and the Balanced Budget Act. But first, I told him, we had to get the issue of minimum-wage legislation off the floor so that it didn't block everything. The bill had been stalled in the Senate for months, burdened down by amendments and partisan disagreements. I promised to engineer a fair vote on the minimum wage by itself. If it passed, it passed. "But let me get it off the floor so we can do business," I told Morris. "Let's get some momentum going."

Changes in the minimum wage had become controversial over the years as more and more evidence accumulated of a perverse effect: Mandated increases could actually be job killers, as small businesses operating on very thin margins proved unable to afford them. I carefully guided a revised package to passage, increasing the minimum wage by 90 cents an hour—from $4.25 to $4.75, effective October 1, 1996, and to $5.15 in a second step effective September 1, 1997. At the time, it was considered a substantial increase. But to cushion the pain, I persuaded the Senate to provide bonuses and tax breaks to small businesses to offset losses they might suffer when the wage package was put into effect. We also set out to bring these small operators into the twenty-first century by giving them tax deductions for computerizing their businesses, which would also make them more competitive.

The first major fruits of my backstairs arrangement came with the difficult passage of a health insurance bill co-sponsored by Senator Ted Kennedy, Democrat from Massachusetts, and Nancy Kassebaum, a Republican from Kansas. The Kennedy-Kassebaum bill had become almost hopelessly entangled in a dispute over some very specific clauses. The legislation aimed to provide Americans with portable health insurance—insurance they could carry with them when they moved to new jobs, protecting their coverage despite any preexisting illnesses or injuries. Both the Senate and President Clinton agreed on the basic principle of guaranteeing continuity of insurance.

The bill actually was stalled in the Senate by opposition to a revolutionary Republican concept—medical savings accounts. Newt Gingrich had initiated these MSAs in his Contract with America and had sold Republicans on the idea. MSAs would allow people to put a sum of money aside, tax free, for medical expenses through a system modeled on individual retirement accounts (IRAs). Out of these savings—and the individual could determine the amount—patients would pay all of their health care costs, including whatever form of insurance they contracted. If the costs went over, the holder of an MSA would pay the costs out of his own pocket. If the costs were less, he could keep the difference tax free.

The Democrats and Clinton were unenthusiastic about the idea, to put it mildly. But the bill's sponsors, Kennedy and Kassebaum, had accepted some provision for MSAs as part of the bill. I passed the word through Morris that the Democrats and the president would have to compromise and make room for this unique concept in the final bill.

Morris informed me of the president's concerns. He believed, as Kennedy did, that the MSAs would cream off the healthy and wealthy, who would use their accounts mainly to buy insurance policies against catastrophic health care costs. According to Morris, the president told him: "Dick, this will leave only the old, the sick, and the poor in the traditional fee-for-service insurance. All the healthy people will be in MSAs, keeping their money instead of using it to pay for treating those who are sick."

Clinton told me that he would agree to a small regional trial for the MSAs, but I turned down the offer. The MSA idea was unique to the Republican Conference, and we wanted to be responsible for implementing this revolutionary concept nationwide. Things were getting pretty tense until Dick Morris suggested putting a cap on the number of Americans who could buy into the plan. That seemed workable to me; it was at least a beginning. But this time the president demurred, and we were back where we started.

Morris told me he jumped all over Clinton, accusing him of quibbling over the fine print and spoiling what should be major legislation and a big political win. "Look, Mr. President," he responded. "Health care is your single biggest failed promise in your administration. It is your biggest black eye. If you can get Kennedy-Kassebaum passed, it will get rid of that. Who cares whether the MSA experiment is exactly right? Who cares how many people it covers? The larger point is to give portability to two-hundred fifty million Americans."

The president then began dealing with me directly. He called at 7:30 one morning and said, "I think we can work this out so everyone will be satisfied."

But it was easier said than done. It took weeks of wrangling with Clinton and his legislative affairs director, John Hilley. MSAs continued to be a key stumbling block, and it took some cooperation between two unlikely allies—House Republican Bill Archer of Texas and Senate Democrat Ted Kennedy of Massachusetts—to get the breakthrough we needed. The final deal called for a cap on MSA participants at 700,000, and flexible ground rules regarding the program's operation.

Still, when it was over, it was clear that we had registered a big one. And I took our success as my cue to plunge ahead with a ripe agenda of bills, which would identify the Republican Party as the party of substance and legislative action—an enviable space to occupy as we went into the 1996 elections.

But I was treading on dangerous territory. It wasn't long before Bob Dole and his camp—in the midst of his bid for president—sent word that this sudden and sweet atmosphere of compromise and bipartisan action was in danger of fouling his campaign. But I thought there was more at stake than Dole's chances at winning the White House. Dole wasn't providing as much coattail for other Republicans on the ticket as we had hoped. I told the press that our incumbents were facing the electorate with a paucity of achievements. I also said that we intended to change that—to make sure the electorate got the message that the Republicans in Congress were the folks making things happen on behalf of the nation. But given Dole's concerns and the practical difficulties of going public, I believed success in this enterprise depended on keeping my backstairs connection to the Clinton White House a secret.

We quickly enacted legislation ensuring clean drinking water, even in rural areas, and moved on some environmental-protection measures. Then it was time to dust off an issue close to the Republican Party's heart—welfare reform. We had given Clinton two earlier version of a welfare reform bill, but they had been burdened down with provisions that doomed them to fail. Now I was determined to get a breakthrough.

It wasn't easy. During the frenzied weeks between the drafting of this compromise welfare measure and its approval by a very jittery president, I immersed myself in a diplomatic battle that involved the White House staff, both houses of Congress, my own Republican Conference, and the hardcore conservatives in my own party. First, the White House tried to bring congressional Democrats on board. Senate Republicans and Democrats had been almost totally estranged for the better part of two decades. Compromise just wasn't in their vocabulary. And the Democrats had been fighting welfare reform for at least that long.

Clinton deputized John Hilley, his legislative affairs director, as his emissary to the combative legislative partisans on Capitol Hill. Hilley sent a stern message that, despite Clinton's earlier vetoes, welfare reform was something the president was intent on doing. Faced with this new GOP–White House alliance, the Democrats proved envious and petulant. In the end, it didn't matter; with Morris's help, Clinton, Newt Gingrich, and I engineered all the changes. The Senate Democrats were like a fifth wheel. We didn't need them.

There was little opposition of any kind in the Republican Conference. To us, welfare reform was the Holy Grail of our legislative master plan. The one real question mark that remained was the president himself. Clinton said he wanted to reform the great American welfare universe, but he had also commented once that he would never sign anything that would pull apart the longstanding entitlements game. We figured Morris would face an uphill battle with his boss when the time for a final decision came. But Morris was confident. "Give me a reasonable measure, and I'll get Bill to sign it," Morris told me. "This is crucial to his reelection, and I'll hammer that home."

"But what about Hillary?" I asked.

"She'll be dead set against it from the beginning, and most of the president's staff will back her up. But when I show her that a second term as First Lady may depend on this, I think she'll start listening fast enough."

The prospect of even peripheral participation by Hillary Clinton alarmed me. "Look, Dick," I said. "I'll work secretly with Clinton. I'll face down the objectors in my own party; I'll offer changes even if I know they'll be politically unpopular. But I don't want to deal with the First Lady."

Morris laughed. "Don't worry, I'll handle her."

We moved into marathon work sessions. I discovered right off the bat that our proposals were bold and strong enough that even the protective walls of the old Democratic welfare establishment buckled before them. The welfare system, spawned by the New Deal sixty years earlier and overhauled in the 1960s, had been an abject failure. It had shunted people onto welfare for life, broken apart the African American family unit, encouraged the rise of drug use, and wiped out virtually any hope that people could ever escape from the welfare rolls. It had also generated fraud and encouraged misuse of the billions that flowed into the system like an untamed river.

Less than a month after our sessions began, we unveiled reforms that were startling in their freshness and visionary in their reach. First, we required work in exchange for welfare, and limits on the length of time for which welfare could be collected. We also proposed ending the entitlements for welfare, and substituted a system in which Washington would make block grants that the states could administer. One provision converted welfare centers from pay stations to specialized employment offices that were designed to find jobs for the recipients.

Morris collected the draft of the proposal early one Monday. Then he swung into action. For the next ten days or so, he seemed to be everywhere at once. He operated from his cell phone, calling from his car and from a secret office in the White House that was purposely off the beaten track. Every once in a while he would dash in to see me during lunch hour, or arrange to meet me in my hideaway deep within the Capitol.

His sessions with the president were considerably more complicated to arrange. Morris rarely saw him in the Oval Office, and never in the Clinton living quarters. Most of their serious discussions occurred over the phone, and usually at two or three in the morning when the White House was virtually deserted. Almost nothing was committed to paper.

Surprisingly, President Clinton was happy with the basic provisions of the reform bill we presented him. But he became agitated and angry about canceling the entitlements for welfare. "You can tell Trent that there's no sense canceling the entitlements now, when Texas can pay one hundred eighty dollars a month and another state pays seven hundred. What kind of entitlement is that?" It was true that there was great disparity among the states, but we regarded that as just another symptom of a broken system.

Then the president grumbled, "All Senator Lott cares about are entitlements, entitlements, entitlements. He doesn't care what happens to the people."

But several days later, in an early morning telephone call, Clinton told me he was prepared to accept the revolutionary shift from entitlements to block grants. "I'll sign off on that," he said. I was elated. But then, a few days later, Morris warned me that the president was angry and hurt over the bill's cut off of welfare, Medicaid, Social Security, and food stamps to illegal immigrants. Further, Clinton was railing at the ban in the bill on vouchers for diapers and other child-care necessities.

I bristled. "Mr. Prime Minister," I told Morris, "the president's moving the goalposts. You said he wanted school lunches fixed, and we did that. Then you said he wanted day care. Then he wanted a contingency fund, then the separating out of Medicaid. Now you come back with a whole new set of demands. We have caved in on almost everything, and each time you come back with more, more, more."

I knew how badly the president wanted to sign a welfare reform bill; he needed it to get reelected. If the president refused to sign the bill, he would face the anger of the electorate for stonewalling the issue.

"Why shouldn't illegal immigrants be cut off from benefits?" I asked Morris. "They came here to be self-supporting, and if they're not, do we have the responsibility to pay for them?" Morris forwarded Clinton's impassioned answer: "An immigrant comes here, pays his taxes, works hard and gets hit by a truck, and they want to cut off the disability benefits to his child? Is that fair?" When it came to welfare reform, Morris told me, he could sense a war between the president's head and his heart.

I talked to the president personally several times about the funds for child health and vouchers for child care, and agreed to restore major amounts of funding for these projects. But that didn't seem to assuage him. According to Morris, Clinton was deeply unhappy with the final bill. It left Medicaid to legal immigrants, but the other cutoffs remained.

As Morris reported to me, the president seemed almost to collapse on the other end of the line as they discussed the final bill, his rage spent. He unburdened himself to Morris about the deep emotional pain at the cuts the welfare bill imposed. Then Clinton's political instincts took over. Morris noted that the president knew that all of the political signs pointed "one way and only one way—toward signing." From my conversations with Clinton, I could tell that he felt that work requirements, day-care funding, and time limits were vital to reducing welfare dependency in America.

We knew the president was still under tremendous pressure—that liberal Democrats, Hillary Clinton among them, were hollering at him that he couldn't sign this bill. There were other pressures on Clinton as well. The people running the welfare program were diehard liberals, and they hated what we were doing. We knew the advice the president was getting from them. In fact, two top officials in the Department of Health and Human Services threatened to resign if the president didn't veto the bill.

When it was certain the bill would pass, Morris says, he told the president: "You've got to sign it. This is the best it's going to be. It's needed. It will be well received. It will get people out of poverty and into jobs. You've gotten more money in there for training, education, and child care. Sign it! It will be a huge success for the American people and for people living in poverty." And if you don't, Morris implied, you risk losing the election.

On the Republican side, we weren't free of pressure either. From the campaign trail, Dole let on to his closest Senate associates that he didn't want the issue taken off the table. He was planning to use welfare reform as a major campaign issue in the fall. If Clinton signed, it would neuter the issue—while making Clinton, not Dole, the welfare-reform hero.

I heard Dole's concerns. But I had the Senate and House elections to consider. Passing this bill would add political luster to each and every congressman and senator out on the stump. So we passed it, with the votes in both chambers that were veto-proof. The House passed the bill on Wednesday, July 31, 1996, by a margin of more than three to one—328 to 101.

The next day, Clinton phoned me early to say he was going to sign the legislation. "I'd like to thank you for all the help you've given me," he added. But he continued to grouse about lost millions and provisions that would leave children out in the cold.

That evening the Senate completed its work, approving the measure by nearly four to one: 78 votes for, 21 votes against.

The next night, after he had signed the bill, the president went on *Larry King Live* and praised the reforms as the most significant achievement to date in the war on poverty.

A landmark study of the reforms by the Brookings Institution in 2001 proved him—and us—right. As the study revealed, the national welfare caseload had declined by well over 50 percent from its peak in 1995. The number of recipients on the rolls had declined for five consecutive years—the largest number ever. The study noted: "The typical state now has much more money per family left on welfare. Plus, Child Care Block Grant cash has increased from $3,500 to almost $8,000."

The detailed Brookings study showed that child poverty overall, and among African American families in particular, had declined as well. In fact, black child poverty declined more in 1997, 1998, and 1999 than in any previous years. Overall child poverty also declined substantially, and by 1999 it was at its lowest level since 1979.

Studies of mothers who had left welfare as a result of the reform bill found that from 60 to 75 percent had been employed for "major periods of time" since their last welfare checks. Because of their employment, these single-mother families had seen their total income increase annually by about nine hundred dollars—even though their welfare and food stamps had been eliminated.

In addition, the Brookings study noted, "most states have dramatically revamped their welfare programs. No longer are local offices simply check-writing operations; now they also are programs that help people prepare for and find jobs."

The continuing reforms will remain a tribute to an extraordinary effort that would never have occurred without my backstairs relationship with President Bill Clinton.

We moved on to other projects—initiatives that weren't sexy enough to bring out the full-force paparazzi, but were important nonetheless. My successful immigration reform bill was one of these, but many conservatives jumped all over it. It was a unique bit of work. Instead of going after the illegal immigrants crossing our borders daily, I concentrated on the benefits the legal immigrants received, aiming to whittle that down. But it was a difficult bill, and I had to compromise to ensure its passage. The final legislation wasn't as conservative as I would have liked, but I considered it a starting point. Instead of clinging to ideology at the expense of success, I followed my own dictum and went for results.

Then came the chemical weapons ban. Clinton was already floating one version of a ratification bill when I received an extraordinary conference call from former presidents George Bush and Gerald Ford and General Colin Powell, asking us to move forward on the chemical weapons treaty. But the Republican Conference didn't want to do it. Senator Jesse Helms, then chairman of the Foreign Relations Committee, was adamantly against the bill. He and others felt that it would undermine our sovereignty if we allowed outsiders to check on what we were doing in this area; they also thought we needed to keep such weapons in our arsenal.

I had some reservations myself, but I also felt the opponents were overreacting and that we had to approve this treaty—especially in the context of today's world. So I convened the Council of Trent. "Okay, guys," I told them, "you may not like it, but I think this is something we have to do. I need your help; I need you to be for it, and go out and push it on Congress." They were reluctant, but they did as they were told. On April 24, 1997, the Senate ratified the Chemical Weapons Convention by a vote of 74 to 26. I got more than half of my Republican colleagues to join all forty-five Democrats in approving it, exceeding the necessary two-thirds majority specified in the Constitution for ratification of international treaties.

My relationship with Dick Morris underwent a painful transformation in the late summer of 1996 when tabloid cameras captured him in an adulterous affair at the Jefferson Hotel in Washington. The scandal forced Clinton to sever the ties with his longtime consultant, just as the three of us had begun preparing the ground for the far-reaching, ambitious 1997 Balanced Budget Act. The proposal had languished in the Senate for months, going absolutely nowhere.

As a parting shot, Morris had ignited Clinton's interest in considering balanced-budget legislation. Still, both Morris and I realized it might be a hard sell—both at the White House and on Capitol Hill. The proposal involved major Medicare reform, including limits on payments to providers, and would restructure government spending in ways that were far from easy to execute. At first the president was afraid of it, worried in particular about the impact it would have on his own party. But the proposal came with a future political bonus. The way we'd structured the measure, it would almost certainly lower the deficit. Morris pointed to the historic credit Clinton would receive for balancing the budget, creating cash surpluses, and lowering the national debt—something no president, including several Republicans, had managed to do since 1969.

Though the liberal press would later say that Trent Lott, Newt Gingrich, and Dick Morris forced the budget deal on President Clinton, the reality was far different. With Morris out of commission, I dealt personally with the president on this issue. And despite opposition from some of his aides and Democratic leaders in Congress, he was intrigued from the start.

Though the Medicare cuts caused the greatest concern, the prospect of cuts throughout the vast federal government was soon jangling the nerves of department heads. In fact, the atmosphere surrounding this budget was highly contentious. Some of the Democrats' most potent allies opposed it with all of their strength. And we took it on the chin as well. Some of our natural conservative allies thought it was a terrible deal because it didn't make even deeper cuts.

Fortunately, Clinton's staff, especially Treasury Secretary Robert Rubin and Chief of Staff Leon Panetta, joined the battle on our side. In the meantime, Gingrich and I stoked the reformist fires of our own troops. Once again, the Democrats were pretty much out of the loop.

It was a tough deal, one that took eight weeks of negotiations. The president and I must have spoken a score of times as we tugged and shoved this bill through the Congress. Our greatest victory came in a package of tax cuts that we had proposed, aimed at stimulating economic growth.

President Clinton agreed to sign the measure. But then, on signature day, he suddenly stalled. In a series of communiqués, we dared him to sign the bill—or not. Late that afternoon, I gathered several key people in my office, including Gingrich, House Budget Chairman John Kasich of Ohio, and Senators Pete Domenici of New Mexico and Connie Mack of Florida. It was getting late, and I hadn't heard a word from Clinton or Panetta. I told my chief of staff, Dave Hoppe, to telephone the White House. The president, we learned, was in his helicopter headed for Baltimore. No one seemed to know whether the Balanced Budget Act of 1997 had been signed.

Hoppe called Clinton's legislative affairs director. "What's going on?" Hoppe asked Hilley, who was driving to New England. "He's going to sign. He's going to sign," Hilley assured my guy.

"But John," Hoppe protested, "we have had no official word."

Ten minutes later Clinton called me: "Trent. We've got the deal." The act not only produced a balanced budget, but generated $50 billion in unencumbered revenues that could be applied to the national debt. It was the final victory in this strange and historic secret arrangement between the majority leader of the Senate and the president of the United States.

# 11

# THE TOBACCO WARS

My back channel to the White House remained wide open after the 1996 election. Only now my principal intermediary was Erskine Bowles, who had replaced Leon Panetta as chief of staff. President Clinton and I still talked, regularly and irregularly and at all times of the day and night, even in the wee hours of the morning. Topic A for us in the early part of 1997 was a stunning tobacco initiative. The idea was to make the cigarette industry pay for its transgressions against the nation's health. Clinton, to put it mildly, was enthusiastic about the enterprise. I had some doubts, given my antipathy toward the excesses of plaintiff's attorneys. But my concerns about teenage smoking had convinced me to play a part in this historic move.

Before it was over, I played almost more roles than I could count in what started as a dramatic initiative, then became a melodrama, then a farce, and finally a tragedy. I served as a CEO-style diplomat to longtime contacts in the tobacco world, bringing them together with their traditional enemies—plaintiff's lawyers—and keeping them in the mix when things got rough. I played cheerful political optimist to the White House gang, seeking full Democratic backing for an unprecedented assault on the health costs cigarettes were imposing on the federal budget. And I was a guarded Senate majority leader, keeping the Republicans with me in backing action that would drastically affect the GOP-friendly tobacco moguls.

Finally, and most important, I was an eager partisan, anticipating a package of tobacco settlements and legislation that would become the most important achievement in the history of American health.

Instead I was eventually forced to engineer the bill's collapse and death, after it was corrupted by naked and crass politics and the greed of the public health community. A project that began with great promise went up in smoke.

The modern crusade against tobacco had all begun in May 1993, in the three-room office of a Mississippi attorney named Mike Lewis—a friend and Ole Miss classmate of both Mississippi Attorney General Mike Moore and a prominent plaintiff's attorney, Dick Scruggs, who also happened to be my brother-in-law.

Lewis had just come back from visiting his secretary's mom— a visit that was also a farewell, as she was near death from heart disease brought on by thirty-five years of chain smoking. She was uninsured and had sold her car, her house, and, finally, all her jewelry to pay as much as she could of the massive medical costs. But those funds were long gone, leaving her destitute. As a consequence, Mississippi's Medicaid system paid out more than a million dollars to cover the medical expenses in a program bolstered by matching funds from the federal government.

A day earlier, Lewis's secretary had asked him: "Why can't we sue the cigarette companies over this? They got Mom early. She was smoking at the age of twelve."

"No point in even trying," Lewis answered. "Dying smokers and their families have filed two hundred suits like your mom's in the South alone. But juries have always ruled that smokers bear the responsibility for lighting up in the first place."

As he pondered the impossibility of seeking individual damages, he got the spark of an idea. Instead of individual dying smokers, why couldn't the state of Mississippi sue the companies? After all, its overloaded Medicaid program bore the costs of caring for the patients involved. When Lewis passed along his idea to his two Ole Miss classmates, Moore and Scruggs, they decided to take the initial idea one step further. To square off against the industry's notoriously tenacious legal defenses, the state should subcontract to private attorneys skilled in plaintiff's law. "We spent a year trying to think as diabolically as the tobacco industry," Scruggs told me one night. "This is a public relations and political war as much as it is a legal fight."

As he elaborated, I knew immediately that this was a way to deny the industry its traditional defense—that the smokers themselves voluntarily consumed tobacco. I also realized that the battle would end up in the laps of Congress and the White House, because it would inevitably result in regulatory changes. And when it did, I warned Dick Scruggs, he'd better be aware of tobacco's lobbying power—and beware the armies of "experts" the industry can muster to bolster its position before Congress.

Scruggs believed the plan would keep the cases in Mississippi. He wanted that insular advantage, since it would make the big city lawyers operate in a judicial universe they had rarely encountered. For years, Big Tobacco's attorneys had pushed and shoved the legal system to ensure that the trials were conducted in federal district courts. Federal trial judges had a far dimmer view of plaintiff's lawsuits, tossing out thousands of personal injury cases.

Dick already had represented Mississippi in a suit to pay for the cost of removing asbestos from state buildings, with enormous success. In the years that followed, he had been exploring ways to take on the tobacco industry, but he had yet to move on any of them. Now, as a plaintiff's lawyer, he realized that he would have to use some of his millions to bankroll the tobacco suit he had planned with Moore. It was later estimated that my brother-in-law paid out $5 million to cover the costs of his tobacco litigation campaign.

Mike Moore was passionate about moving forward: "I'm like Saint George—I want to slay those dragons," he told me. "It doesn't make any sense to legally attack the industry one smoker at a time. Even if we won all the cases, the industry is so wealthy that they could go on losing forever." Instead, he said, the state could raise the stakes to hundreds of millions, or even billions, of dollars. "This is serious litigation in anyone's book," Moore said. "A state suing for the costs of Medicaid could shake up the tobacco industry for the first time."

Moore and Scruggs spent nine months meeting with health professionals, retired tobacco executives, and others in a search for evidence locked away in the industry vaults—or in the minds of its attorneys and scientists. The search focused on finding talkative tobacco managers or chatty former employees who might have grown disillusioned with their companies over the years.

On May 23, 1994, in a shabby Chancery courthouse set in a former grocery store in Pascagoula, the state of Mississippi became the first in the nation to file suit against the industry. A day later, Moore and Scruggs took off in Dick's jet to recruit other attorneys to their cause. Before long, the tobacco industry's solidarity began to show signs of breaking down. During lunch in the fall of 1995, Scruggs phoned to tell me that one of the tobacco companies was about to cave in and settle with Mississippi and four other states that had followed its lead. Liggett Group Inc. was only the fifth largest company, with a 5 percent share of the market. "But they're breaking ranks, Trent," Dick said. "That break will cause panic, rattling all of the much larger firms." He believed that Bennett S. LeBow, a corporate raider who acquired Liggett in 1986, had gutted the venerable company and was relieved to settle.

In one of my regular telephone calls with President Clinton, I mentioned the progress being made in Mississippi, and noted that one firm was about to desert Big Tobacco's circled wagons. The president was excited—so excited that he held a press conference the next day. "This is a major breakthrough," he said. "This is the first crack in the stone wall of denial." The president's interest in the tobacco lawsuits made an impression on me, and I kept an open channel on the subject through Erskine Bowles.

In its settlement offer, Liggett agreed to acknowledge publicly that "cigarette smoking causes disease and is highly addictive." The company also agreed to splash these statements across its packaging—in larger type and in brighter colors than the small warnings already required. In addition, company officials released all documents relating to the issues of smoking and health. And finally, they acceded to permanent monitoring by the Food and Drug Administration.

The Liggett settlement convinced me that whatever agreements the states finally reached with tobacco were going to require congressional action—major legislation to convert the industry's concessions into law and regulations and to oversee the payments. At first I wasn't sure how I would handle that, considering my familial and other ties to Dick Scruggs. But I began to investigate what might be needed from Capitol Hill and the White House. During conversations with Scruggs and Moore, I suggested to them that enthusiasm for tobacco litigation and legislation was muted at best. Congress might pass such legislation, but it figured to be mighty close.

So I put Scruggs together with my old ally, Dick Morris, whose stint in the White House was still in the future. Having done some work for Scruggs on the asbestos lawsuits, Morris eagerly signed on for the new battle, and within a matter of days he was out in the field to gauge voter approval of various tobacco litigation issues. His polling over the ensuing months, in Mississippi and nationally, was illuminating.

Confirmed smokers, he found, were always pro-tobacco. Smokers who had fought and given up smoking were always anti-tobacco. People who had never smoked were divided evenly in their views of the industry. But Morris's results showed that, above all, people agreed on one thing: They were ferociously intent on stopping American kids from taking that all-important first puff. And they were deeply suspicious of the tobacco companies, which, they believed, actively targeted kids in their advertising. This was true even in the five tobacco-producing states.

Morris's point was that a national legal campaign against smoking needed to be focused on stopping kids from starting. That was a winner politically—for members of Congress, and especially for a president up for reelection in 1996. Focus on the kids, Morris said, and you'll be fine.

Clinton's eventual support for concerted action against Big Tobacco was also influenced by Morris's polling. But it was cinched by Vice President Al Gore, whose sister had died of lung cancer. "Mr. President," Morris said, "I am deeply convinced that if you do this, it is not going to hurt you politically. It's not going to cost you Tennessee, and it's not going to cost you Kentucky. This is going to be a very important advance in America's public health."

The industry and the federal government had been living for decades with the grim statistics on teenage smoking. I explained to my brother-in-law that many in Washington considered the tobacco industry "untouchable." I asked him: "What have you guys got that will compete with that?"

"The power of the courts," Scruggs answered with considerable bravado. "Remember, Senator," Moore chimed in, "the industry has never been hit with this much muscle. They have been fighting one patient at a time with a half-decent lawyer. They swatted those aside as if they were gnats."

But the power of the courts was not enough to provide the political force they would need to reach a multibillion dollar settlement. Favorable verdicts from the courts seemed dicey at this early date in the tobacco wars. I reminded Mike, "They've never lost in court."

"I'm not worried," he replied.

But he was worried—especially given popular sentiment in Mississippi against anti-smoking lawsuits filed by adults. That's one reason his case was filed in state Chancery court, where judges, not juries, determined the verdict. Chancery court, a throwback to English common law that survived in only three states, is usually the province of divorce cases and truancy complaints. But Scruggs was interested in this low wattage because of one of its peculiarities: In Chancery court he would be allowed to use gross statistics to make his argument on the health costs of cigarettes. He wouldn't be burdened by the task of providing evidence on every single smoker's ills.

Because I had worked with tobacco sporadically, I knew something about how swiftly the industry's moods could change when it came to reform. I asked Dick Morris about the current attitudes of the cigarette companies. Morris felt they knew that an overwhelming number of Americans—approaching 80 percent—distrusted them, and believed that they had covered up specific findings showing how addictive tobacco was. "They finally understand they can no longer escape retribution for the health havoc they are causing," Morris explained. "They have decided that it is only a matter of time before judges and juries punished them with multibillion-dollar judgments. Trent, some of them fear bankruptcy."

Still, there was great skepticism in Mississippi and Washington that Scruggs and Moore would prevail. In fact, the tobacco attorneys were thrilled when the Mississippi case was referred to Judge William Myers—named to the bench by Moore's nemesis, Republican governor Kirk Fordice. Their joy, however, was fleeting.

Myers was a taciturn justice. He rarely asked questions, and even more rarely addressed or even looked at the tobacco lawyers. In their dark and expensive suits, they sat around on uncomfortable plastic chairs in that homespun Chancery courtroom, waiting to be called to a makeshift lectern fashioned from wooden boxes, with a microphone perched precariously on top.

The judge listened intently, however, and took reams of notes. He gave no hint of his verdict. "Y'all will receive my rulings in the mail," he said before shooing off the roomful of attorneys. When the tobacco lawyers checked their mail, they found several terse paragraphs that contained an unwelcome surprise: Myers had overruled the industry and sustained the state's claim.

Scruggs phoned me to describe the downcast faces of this high-priced talent. And it didn't get any better for them on appeal. On March 13, 1997, the Mississippi Supreme Court upheld the lower court's ruling on every motion. In twenty-four hours, the stock price of Philip Morris (now the Altria Group) fell 8 percent. The ruling meant that there would be only two issues at trial: whether the industry was improperly enriched by selling a dangerous product, and how much Mississippi should be repaid to pay for the damages. The companies feared a wave of similar judgments.

Chester Trent Lott, Sr., one year old

At age three (*right*) on Tucker Street in Pascagoula, Mississippi

At the University of Mississippi, 1961. I was head cheerleader for the Ole Miss varsity squad (*below, second from right*).

With Tricia, dressed for our honeymoon, December 27, 1964

With President Nixon and Congressman Bill Colmer
at Colmer's annual seafood luncheon, 1971

Debating Nixon's impeachment before the House
Judiciary Committee in Washington, July 25, 1974

Arriving with President Gerald Ford at Beach Park in Pascagoula during the presidential campaign, 1976. Backing President Ford over Ronald Reagan that year was one of the most difficult decisions of my political career.

With President Reagan during his visit to Jackson, Mississippi, 1985. For my generation of conservative politicians, Reagan was a bellwether and an inspiration.

Having fun in Dallas at the Southfork Party, 1984 Republican National Convention

Moving from the House to the Senate was a culture shock of the first order—
but with the help of a like-minded "kitchen cabinet" of fellow conservatives,

My family: Tricia, Tyler, Chet, and my daughter-in-law,

I knew George H. W. Bush in every one of his positions in government—from congressman to president; Tom Daschle and I were glad to welcome him back to the Capitol for the Leader's Lecture Series in 1999.

With House Speaker Newt Gingrich, 1996: He taught the House Republicans the art of staying on message.

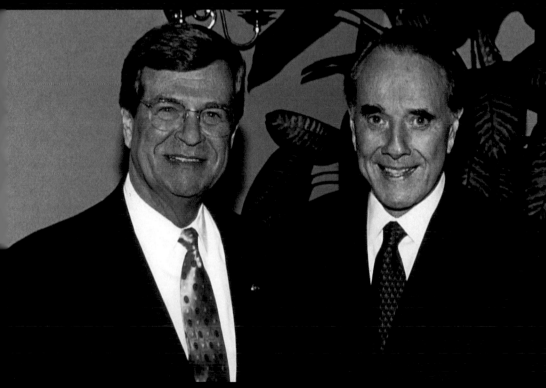

At the White House with President Clinton and Vice President Gore. Dick Morris helped me work with Clinton to pass welfare reform, but Gore's political aspirations may have scuttled the 1997 tobacco settlement.

With Bob Dole, my predecessor as Senate majority leader

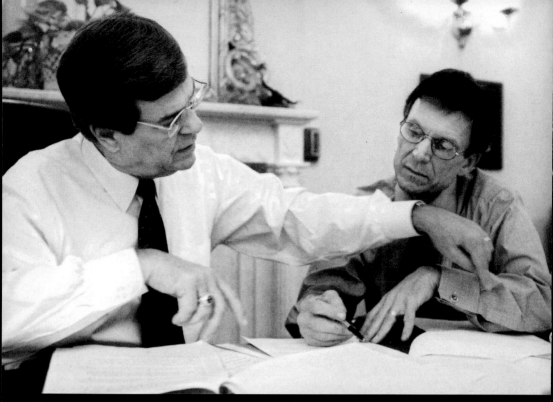

Discussing the details of power sharing with Tom Daschle after the 2000 election. Our working relationship helped both sides deal with challenges from the Clinton impeachment to 9/11.

With President George W. Bush, 2001. Of all the presidents, Bush was the closest to a true friend I've known—though his administration's handling of the Thurmond crisis left me disappointed. *Below*: Meeting in the vice president's Capitol office with my old friend, Dick Cheney.

The Senate Republican leadership team of 1996. Senator Paul Coverdell of Georgia, Republican Conference secretary; Senator Larry Craig of Idaho; Senator Connie Mack of Florida, Republican Conference chairman; Senator Lott, majority leader; Senator Don Nickles of Oklahoma, majority whip; Senator Strom Thurmond of South Carolina, Senate pro tempore; Senator Mitch McConnell, chairman, National Republican Senatorial Committee.

Performing with the Singing Senators: Larry Craig of Idaho, John Ashcroft of Missouri, and Jim Jeffords of Vermont. One of the reasons I'd founded the group was to give Jeffords an informal setting to bond with his fellow Republicans; it didn't stop him from leaving the party.

Arguing for the Bush tax cuts on the Fox News Channel, 2000

Leading a prayer on Capitol Hill with other members
of Congress on the afternoon of September 11, 2001.

On December 6, 2002—the day after our Senate birthday party for Senator Strom Thurmond—
Tricia and I joined Dick Cheney, Strom, his daughter Julie Thurmond Whitmer, and the two
Presidents Bush at a White House celebration. The furor over my remarks had not yet begun.

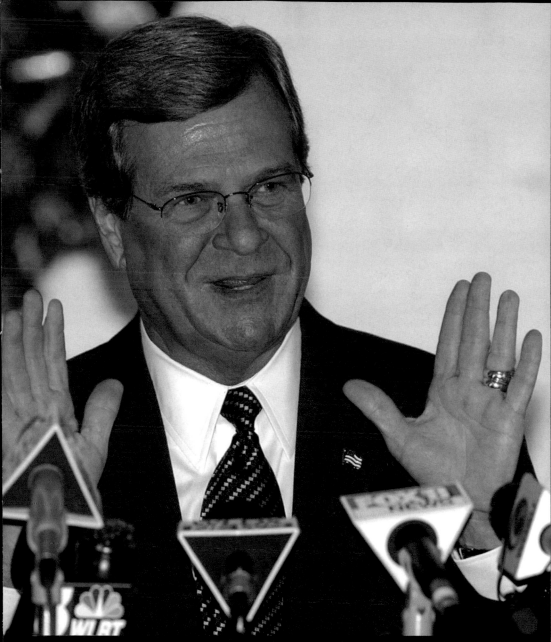

At the news conference in Pascagoula, apologizing
for my remarks at Strom's Senate birthday party.

Christmas 2004 with our children and grandchildren at our farm outside of Jackson, Mississippi. (*From left*) Matt Armstrong holding Addison, Tyler Lott Armstrong with Shields, Chet Lott, Diane Lott with Lucie, Tricia and me with Trent III.

Elation over the victory was contagious. Within a matter of weeks, other states joined what became a national effort, causing Scruggs and Moore to expand their legal army to handle the load. Dick called me. "We are now in a position to deliver peace in the form of settlements," he said. "But Trent, are these companies willing to make public health concessions in return? I want a heck of a lot more than money out of these settlements. These corporations are so global, and so wealthy, that enormous cash awards in court won't make them remove the death sentence they are delivering to American children. They are panicked and desperate."

That's when he asked me to use my influence with Congress and the White House to push for support as they faced federal decisions that could make or break whatever was gained through lawsuits or settlements.

But I had to let my brother-in-law know the low regard I had for such class actions. First of all, I didn't have a vested interest in being for or against the tobacco companies. I have several very close friends who work for the tobacco companies, and I've developed strong sympathy for the plight of tobacco farmers, who must now compete with cheaper tobacco from foreign countries. By choice, I had smoked a pipe since 1963. In doing that, I'd made a conscious choice. I don't believe that anybody should be able to sue some small pipe company in Virginia if I should die of lung cancer.

I like my brother-in-law: He's a close friend, and he's terribly charming and capable. But I still don't like plaintiff's lawsuits. I'm old fashioned, I guess. I'd be more comfortable if you took an X-ray, showed me something growing in my lungs that could kill me, and then proved that the damage was related to smoking.

However, as I studied the documents uncovered for the Mississippi case, the indisputable and gross misconduct of these firms overwhelmed my prejudice against class action lawsuits—*in this particular situation*.

What finally brought me on board was the fact that Scruggs and Moore were targeting tobacco's ceaseless attempts to woo teenagers and children. Although I'm a conservative, I'm also a pragmatist. I believe in getting things done. In this, as in many of my other causes, I looked for a way to defend my ideals while allowing me to live to fight another day. As close as I was to several tobacco leaders, I needed to recognize that some people did have legitimate claims. And Scruggs and Moore were offering the tobacco companies the option of settlement—a tactic preferable to the ruinous lawsuits that were spreading across the country.

One afternoon, Scruggs showed me the television and print commercials the tobacco companies were using to attract kids. I thought they were wrong. If you are a man or woman who cares about children, you cannot help but be offended by that kind of venal marketing. So what do you do about it?

In my case, it made sense to steer the Senate to find a solution that would give benefit to those hurt by the product, without totally destroying the tobacco companies. I was aware that the tobacco conglomerates had become food companies as well. For instance, Philip Morris owned Kraft Foods; RJR Nabisco manufactured a wide range of products beyond cigarettes. Why wipe out all of those other jobs by an action that toppled these corporations?

I could help the process for both the lawyers and the tobacco industrialists—making certain that everyone, particularly the media, understood that I would abstain from voting on any part of the legislation. Within days of the first legal meetings of state attorneys general, Dick and Mike asked if I would help bring all the players to the table—including the White House, the tobacco industry, and the Senate.

The talks I set up resulted, almost overnight, in negotiations that would last nearly three months—from early April through

June 1997. Because the meetings were formally closed to them, the media couldn't get enough of the gossip and speculation that attends any high-stakes private session. As a result, they printed and broadcast rumors that would later haunt us. At various times, the press announced that the lawyers and the cigarette barons were fashioning a series of monumental taxes on retail tobacco products; that the attorneys and the Clinton White House were planning to grant the industry immunity from all future civil suits; and that tobacco would end up *getting* federal and state money to launch anti-smoking campaigns for teenagers. Though this gossip was demonstrably false, it ended up following the settlement to the White House, and from the White House to Congress.

My main ally at the White House was Erskine Bowles. But I also talked occasionally with the president, who was decidedly upbeat about a settlement, and with the vice president, whose hatred of Big Tobacco was well known. At the very start of the multistate summit of attorneys general, Dick Morris and I were still in contact—although he was operating from outside the White House, connected to the West Wing powers by phone. Scruggs, who wasn't privy to my backstairs relationship with the pollster and the president, was surprised at Morris's rapt enthusiasm for the settlement.

Scruggs and Moore convinced Morris to present his evidence to the still-jittery attorneys general and their plaintiff's lawyers who had gathered in Washington. "Dick, there is still the possibility that we'll have to sue if these negotiations fall apart, sending all forty-six attorneys general back into court," Moore warned. Morris's bottom line remained the same: "Stick with the issue of kids, and you cannot go wrong."

Later that day, Morris reported to me that the attorneys general were hyped by the youth issue. From that moment forward, my brother-in-law's settlement talks centered on the general theme of smoking and children. They had picked the one misdeed the industry couldn't defend.

S hortly after Morris's session with the state attorneys general, Scruggs phoned me with a serious dilemma. A huge faction of state AGs had come to him as a group and let him know that they were very nervous about approving any settlement—no matter how good it might be—unless President Clinton himself signed off on it. Many of these attorneys were Democrats who were already being criticized because I would be overseeing the agreement as it wound its way through the Senate and the House. Though they apparently had nothing against me, they felt they just couldn't sign on unless the president gave them cover. He was the leader of their party, after all, and if he blessed the deal, their own constituents would rally around it.

The AGs wanted someone from the White House, ideally someone very close to the president, to attend all the sessions. And they demanded that Clinton release a strongly worded document— a press release would suffice—before they lined up behind any agreement and saluted. I suspected that numerous Democratic senators would feel precisely the same way.

The army of attorneys, tobacco industry executives, and state attorneys general swelled to more than one hundred when formal negotiations began in Washington on April 3, 1997. Moore and Scruggs led a pair of negotiating teams that met daily, including many weekends. Delicate decisions were made wisely, in most cases, balancing some historic concessions by the tobacco companies with far-reaching limitations on the amounts of monetary damages that could be assessed against the companies in future legal actions.

By talking with Scruggs as often as twice a day, I was able to feed my Senate colleagues' likely concerns into the process. After I made another call to the White House urging that someone at a high level participate, the president himself began contributing regularly through his presidential counsel and close political confidante, Bruce Lindsey.

I can still remember the excitement in Scruggs's voice when he called me on June 17 to say that they were only forty-eight hours and several crucial impasses away from what sounded like a landmark settlement deal. But he confided that a touchy political situation was threatening the underpinnings of the deal.

Two days earlier, the *Wall Street Journal* had used the words "judicial immunity" to describe the legal concessions being offered to the tobacco companies. That characterization was picked up by the Associated Press, which sent it to daily newspapers across America. A sizeable contingent of the AGs, especially the Democrats, were now balking at signing the $318 billion settlement. Scruggs and Moore had worked for more than a year on the civil liability limitations. Originally, the industry had demanded total immunity. A hard-fought compromise still allowed suits within state tort systems, but prohibited multibillion-dollar damage awards. In addition, class action suits were outlawed. This is what the *Wall Street Journal* labeled "immunity."

It was clear that the Democratic AGs might bolt without some backing from the president for this sure-to-be-controversial condition. I made several calls to the White House, as did Scruggs and Moore. Bruce Lindsey rushed into the breach and pressured the tobacco industry into kicking in another $50 billion for punitive damages. The president's attorney also promised the balking state officials that the additional money allowed the Clinton administration to provide political cover for the so-called immunity.

In several conference calls, Lindsey promised that the White House would issue a glowing press release the day the settlement was announced, enthusiastically endorsing all of its provisions, praising in particular the big cash trade-off for the limited judicial provisions. Initially, Lindsey was as good as his word. In a conference call to the delegates on the afternoon before the settlement was to be signed, he read a glowing, two-page press release to be made public just minutes after Scruggs and Moore held their press conference. The attorneys general and their plaintiff's attorneys listened and nodded in relief.

The next morning, June 20, 1997, Moore and Scruggs, flanked by legions of lawyers, announced the historic settlement, adding that the president would express his approval later in the day.

The pact they unveiled was a magnificent public health document. The tobacco industry—the Philip Morris companies, RJR Nabisco Holdings Corp., B.A.T. Industries, Brown & Williamson, and Loews Corporation's Lorillard—agreed to pay $368.5 billion over the next quarter century in compensation for smoking damages to the states. They also agreed to drastically curtail their marketing practices—especially when it came to the youth market—and to voluntarily submit to the regulatory demands of the Food and Drug Administration. It was a stunning turnaround: Big Tobacco was agreeing to be tightly supervised by an agency it had been fighting for decades.

The agreement bought the tobacco companies freedom from future class action suits and capped the industry's annual payout at $5 billion for past wrongdoing. Under the terms of the sixty-eight-page proposal, the manufacturers would pay out $10 billion up front to be followed by annual allotments growing from $8.5 billion to $15 billion over the first five years. The annual payment would then stay at that level for the remainder of the twenty-five years. In addition, the cigarette companies would pay $60 billion in punitive damages. Of that, $25 billion would be placed in a trust fund to be used for public health programs, with some of the remainder purchasing coverage for uninsured children.

This was another shocker. It was essentially an admission of wrongdoing, a blockbuster reversal for an industry that for forty years steadfastly refused to accept any responsibility for the health consequences of smoking.

Though some newspaper editorials were already calling it the most historic public-health achievement in history, some warned that a sharply divided Congress must still approve the deal. I knew this wouldn't be an easy fight—particularly with a handful of strong liberal congressmen grousing about concessions to the tobacco industry, and a like number of conservative congressmen complaining about caving to health-care groups and activists.

As Senate majority leader and inside power broker for the deal, I needed strong and consistent support from President Clinton. I was worried that the Democrats might be unwilling to publicly stand up for tobacco liability limits without the White House propping them up. I needed Clinton to do what he had personally pledged to me during our phone conversations concerning the settlement. But my hopes of White House backing disappeared into thin air two hours after the settlement was announced.

Bruce Reed, the president's domestic policy adviser, called me in a panic. The promised press release—read by Bruce Lindsey the previous day to more than a hundred negotiators—had failed to materialize. There was no press conference by Clinton. In fact, the president and Lindsey had disappeared overnight on "a political trip to Western states."

Scruggs and Moore hailed a cab and raced across town to meet with Reed, who had inherited the tobacco portfolio in Clinton's and Lindsey's absence. Serious and close-mouthed, Reed accepted the signed tobacco settlement and handed the lawyers a four-paragraph press release. It referred to a *proposed* settlement and announced that the White House would "study it." Scruggs and Moore were flabbergasted—and furious. Moore angrily asked what happened to the press release that had been read to the settlement commission a day earlier. "This is what I was authorized to give you," Reed said. "That's what I was told to say."

"Surely they're not going to disavow this bill," Scruggs said plaintively. "They helped write the final document." He was referring to the last-minute $50 billion that Lindsey, with Reed's help, had convinced the companies to kick in.

"This is anything but an endorsement," Scruggs told me later. "Trent, this is the way I read it: 'Nice try. We'll look at this and let you know whether or not we'll back it.'"

Erskine Bowles didn't return my calls. I thought there might be some explanation for this about-face, and whatever it was, I wanted to make it right. I had no idea that the White House endorsement had stalled because the president of the United States was using the settlement to play White House politics, pitting one group of staffers against another.

Clinton apparently had pulled Lindsey off the case, making him merely a consultant to the president on tobacco affairs, and appointed a task force headed by Reed, who generally favored the pact, and Donna Shalala, the Secretary of Health and Human Services, who despised it. As the *Washington Post* noted, Reed and Shalala were a political odd couple who often pitched tents on opposite sides of divisive issues facing the president. Clinton found the tension liberating, the *Post* said—a way to hang back while others waged intellectual war until he was ready to make the final decision.

Shalala held the tobacco companies in contempt, as did Gore, and thought the settlement let them off far too lightly. Reed was more of a pragmatist, championing the cause of a settlement because the historic opportunity shouldn't be missed.

My heart fell later that afternoon when I got the full text of Clinton's statement. It was almost hostile to the agreement: "Will approving this proposed settlement protect public health—particularly our children's health—to the greatest extent possible?" The query had a dubious tone.

It continued, "We have not had the opportunity to review the actual terms of the agreement, and we have not concluded whether it is in the interest of public health. This must be subjected to further study."

Thus the critical conclusion in the Clinton press release was a lie. Clinton and his team had been involved in this settlement every step of the way. They had strong representation on the settlement committee. And just days earlier Erskine Bowles had indicated to me that the settlement was familiar to the president, who was fed frequent briefings on what was occurring in the meeting rooms.

But his new statement was a clear signal to congressional Democrats: In approaching this agreement, watch your step.

I sat back in my chair and prepared for what would be a ferocious battle. The settlement required a lot of government involvement—congressional oversight, policing, and alignment with the nation's antitrust laws and regulations. Public reaction was generally favorable: People seemed to feel that, in the interest of public health, we should do this if we could. I had to prepare the Senate to welcome the massive settlement, and assure that it would get a fair shake in the badly polarized body. This was exactly why I had followed each step in the settlement process so carefully: I knew that the whole thing would eventually wind up in the hands of the

Senate. The House was disinclined to introduce the pact; in fact, they made it clear that they were going to wait and see what happened at my end of the Capitol.

Since we had no legislation ready to go, it was critical that I select the right committee, with a staff of political heavyweights who could pull a bill together. The Senate Judiciary and Commerce Committees were the only ones who met the requirements. Because of the judicial guarantees offered to the tobacco industry, many thought Judiciary the natural choice. And Committee Chairman Orrin Hatch made a strong bid for it. He insists till this day that the bill would have passed if his committee had been given the charge.

But I had serious reservations. Senator Ted Kennedy was next in line to become chairman, and the Democrats on Judiciary were among the most liberal in the Senate. I was afraid if I sent it there they would just drive up the amounts Big Tobacco had to pay, and increase government involvement to the breaking point.

Commerce Committee Chairman John McCain also was fired up to pass this bill and implement the settlement. So I sent it to Commerce.

Initially, there were glowing reports about the committee's bustling activity. There seemed to be an immediate rapport among McCain, the public health community, and the world of tobacco, whose executives were invited into a public hearing process that began only weeks after the settlement was signed. But appearances were deceiving. My relationship to Scruggs obliged me to stand back from the actual process, and I probably missed some of the undercurrents that soon began eating away at the settlement's foundation. I did notice that Scruggs and Moore had been invited to take part; setting up shop in the Commerce Committee quarters, they began working directly with the committee staff. Something about that didn't look right, but I brushed aside my feelings, because I believed the tobacco companies and the public health community had equal access. But they didn't. I was wrong about that, and I should have pulled Scruggs and Moore out of there and sent them back to their offices.

One reason for the president's reluctance became clear when Clinton's main advisers on tobacco, former surgeon general Dr. C. Everett Koop and former Food and Drug Administration czar David Kessler, spoke out publicly against the settlement. Their early shots were only the beginning. These two veterans of the tobacco wars would soon lead the public health community's greedy drive to push up the monetary awards and strengthen the judicial penalties against the industry.

I soon learned that Koop, Kessler, and Vice President Al Gore had led an informal White House panel formed to guide Clinton's reaction to, and implementation of, the tobacco settlement. And Gore, apparently, held the reins. Kessler later admitted on the PBS show *Frontline* that "The vice president made all this happen. Clinton had been somewhat reluctant. We told Mr. Gore what we knew, what our conclusions were, and what the research said, and the vice president took it into Clinton."

Dick Morris, who was once again acting as an ex-officio adviser as his sex scandal began to fade, told me that the vice president probably kept Clinton from signing off on the press release for Scruggs and Moore. The pollster confided that Gore's true goal—backed by his friends Koop and Kessler—was nothing less than the complete death of the American tobacco industry. "They wanted tobacco gone," Moore told me.

I believe that the reasons were even more politically crass. My sources in the Clinton White House indicated that Gore wouldn't let the tobacco bill through because he planned an assault against Big Tobacco during his 2000 presidential campaign. This settlement wasn't strong enough to give Gore the boost he wanted.

Do I believe that Al Gore killed the tobacco settlement to bolster his chance at the presidency? Absolutely.

As long as the settlement was in the hands of Clinton and
Bruce Lindsey, the administration maintained its public support.
Once it fell into the hands of Gore and the public-health zealots,
the White House skittered away from the deal. Thereafter, Gore,
Kessler, and Koop won their long, hard fight to drop the deal's immunity provisions. After one key meeting, just as the settlement
was to make its appearance on the Senate docket, Clinton told
aides that he could now be categorized as opposing the legal guarantees. He never mentioned them again.

The McCain Bill that emerged from the Commerce Committee
was much changed, with higher penalties and fewer judicial guarantees to the tobacco industry. It sailed out of the committee on a
vote of 19 to 1. It was a bipartisan bill, with significant Republican votes behind it. It really looked as if we could navigate this
through the shoals of the Senate.

Then Koop and Kessler, by now the dean of the Yale University School of Medicine, set up operations right across the hall
from the Senate chamber in offices provided by Ted Kennedy.
From there they led an all-out assault by the public health community to drastically increase the penalties against cigarette companies and to diminish tobacco's judicial guarantees until they
were worthless.

The bill was amended more than eleven times, until the benefits to the tobacco companies were almost totally eroded. One of
my aides described it as "bloated, gutted and stripped to the
bone." Tobacco executives not only expressed their displeasure;
they threatened to switch sides and attack the settlement they
themselves had helped to create.

I had removed myself as an active, on-the-floor participant
and would abstain from voting, but I could pass along warnings to

McCain, President Clinton, and the senators still backing the bill—and I did. I told my Senate colleagues that they would be steamrolled in their own districts. And I put the White House on notice that the industry would not turn back once it opened up its considerable war chest.

In early April 1998, just before the industry began its bombardment, most players had heard from me that this lull might be the only time they could save the settlement—probably in any form. Then, on April 8, Steven Goldstone, the chief executive officer of RJR Nabisco, washed his hands of Washington in a dramatic appearance at the National Press Club. He accused the White House of being effectively leaderless, and castigated the public health community for running away from a settlement that should have been a public health advocate's dream come true. "The extraordinary settlement reached on June 20 last year that could have set the nation on a dramatically new and constructive direction is dead," Goldstone said.

In the spring of 1998, tobacco interests would spend just under $100 million trying to sink the bill and tarnish its supporters. The onslaught began with $43 million in television advertising—much of it in states or congressional districts of the settlement's supporters. The TV ads depicted the bill as a half-a-trillion dollar tax increase, disguised as an improvement in public health. In the ads, the industry also promoted a toll-free number that viewers could call to register complaints against the bill; those who called were immediately connected to one of their senators' offices in Washington. The campaign began April 25, and, from that day onward the industry connected an average of eight to ten thousand callers a day to Senate offices.

Senator Christopher Bond, a Missouri Republican, received four hundred calls supporting the tobacco bill and fifty thousand opposing it. His experience was not unusual.

At the same time, the industry launched a massive lobbying effort that included such influential and high-priced talent as former Texas governor Ann Richards, a Democrat, and three former Senate majority leaders: Republicans Howard Baker and Bob Dole and Democrat George Mitchell. In all, tobacco sent 192 lobbyists to the Hill—roughly one lobbyist for every three members of Congress. The price tag for the campaign was $43 million, or more than $80,000 for every legislative voter.

The White House, now aboard the anti-immunity bandwagon, unveiled what amounted to an official Democratic version of a settlement that, as former Federal Trade Commission Chairman Michael Perschuk noted in his book, *Smoke in Their Eyes,* "conceded the tobacco industry nothing"—no relief at all from legal liability. In the end, the amendments to the McCain bill that radically increased penalties on tobacco companies also imposed greater regulatory burdens on the federal government and sent the total cost of the legislation to $516 billion, nearly $148 billion more than the original settlement. At that point, the bill was barely breathing.

Still, I kept the bill on the floor for a full month to make certain it got a fair chance. Normally, a measure with that many outlandish amendments would have been jettisoned in a matter of days. At last, I decided to call a meeting of the Republican Conference and ask, "Okay, what do you want to do? Or is this now a hopeless cause?" The consensus was that we would never be able to pass the tobacco bill: It was too big, and too costly to the government itself. Meanwhile, House leaders were telling me they wouldn't even take up the bill in its current form. Even if the Senate should pass it, it was going nowhere. On June 17, 1998, nearly a year after the settlement was signed, the bill came down to a vote on the Senate floor over a filibuster. Fifty-seven senators voted to put the bill to a vote—three votes short of the sixty senators needed. Forty-two voted against. The bill was dead.

More than five months later, on November 23, 1998, the forty-six states that hadn't settled suits signed an agreement with the tobacco companies worth an estimated $250 billion. The plan did not require congressional approval, because it involved no federal regulatory changes. It did not impose restrictions on how the states could spend the money—some used all or a portion of their windfalls to balance their state budgets—and didn't do much in the way of legal immunity. The settlement did require the tobacco giants to make changes in their marketing methods and to underwrite programs aimed at getting kids to stop smoking, or not to start. But all of this was nothing compared with what might have been. The public health would have been better served if Congress had passed the settlement my brother-in-law and Mike Moore had engineered—instead of falling victim to the petty infighting, and ambitious politicking, of those in the Clinton White House.

# 12

# WILLIAM JEFFERSON CLINTON ON TRIAL: PART ONE

I have served as a member and leader in Congress with seven presidents in my lifetime, and in my view each in his own way and time has been a great man. These men reached the highest office in the land, often by tortured or accidental routes. They all loved their country and did the very best they could. They were not kings or dictators, and often came from very common backgrounds. Each one has embarrassed us on occasion, but on the whole they have served us well. The Republic has survived.

Maybe because I wasn't even thirty years old when I first met President Nixon, I was in awe of him. My boss at the time, Congressman Colmer, greatly admired Nixon. Contrary to popular perception, he was warm and personable, certainly in my and Tricia's experience. On the few occasions when I sought his advice, I was impressed with his response and grateful that he always took my calls. In 1988, when I was running for the Senate and Nixon had been out of office for fourteen years, he attended a fund-raiser for me in New York City on the Amway

Corporation yacht, *Enterprise*. Our children went along, but they were mortified at being trapped on a boat and having to listen to all the political speeches. But when the former president spoke—and gave a boffo tour of the current geopolitical scene—they were enthralled. At the time, Chet was twenty and Tyler seventeen; both were old enough to recognize a sage mind at work. Afterward, they agreed that they had never heard a wiser man in their lives.

When I won the Senate race in 1988, Nixon followed up with a thoughtful and kind note that said in part: "Of all those elected this year, you have the greatest chance of leadership."

I've already written much about my relationship with President Ford. I knew him personally, but it was the relationship of a president to a young congressman. Obviously he backed into the job, but he gave it his all. I supported him and voted for all his vetoes but one—a veterans bill. I just never felt that he had a strong enough philosophical rudder to steer the ship of state and inspire the people.

Ronald Reagan, of course, was my philosophical soulmate, and I think he should go down in history as one of our greatest presidents. I met with him dozens, maybe hundreds, of times, and I loved every one of those meetings. But somehow I never felt really close to him as a person. Perhaps it was because, when I was around him, I always felt I was in the presence of someone truly special. That feeling created something of a wall between us that I, frankly, found impenetrable.

President George H. W. Bush and his wife, Barbara, were always gracious to Tricia and me. Tricia loved Barbara because she is what she is—a straight-talking and kind woman. I knew her husband in every one of his positions in government: as a congressman, head of the Republican National Committee, director of the Central Intelligence Agency, vice president, and president.

He was a bit too moderate for my blood, but he was a good president. He should never have issued that infamous challenge: "Read my lips, no new taxes," and then raised them. But nor should the American people have turned their back on him in 1992—not when he had the courage to throw Saddam Hussein out of Kuwait. Instead he never managed to get a grip on the 1992 election, and the charmer from Arkansas won the day.

When I was majority leader in the Senate, the first President Bush's son George was a presidential phonemate, who generally called early in the morning—at seven-thirty or so—with business or a question on his mind. As president, George W. Bush comes right to the point, never dallying once he got the answer he sought or the information he needed. Yet, even given his all-business phone manner, he's the closest to a true friend of the seven presidents I've known. His Texas twang is always a welcome sound to brighten up the morning. It's a comforting high-level bond in a town that's full of phony and mercenary conversations.

Bill Clinton liked the phone, too. But he was probably the oddest president I have known. He professed to reporters that we "weren't friends," then contradicted himself by calling me dozens of times late at night. Often, like President Kennedy before him, he merely wanted to talk; sometimes his calls ended in silence as he suddenly replaced the earpiece. One night he phoned about one-thirty in the morning and began a fast and uninterrupted lecture on problems in El Salvador. Hearing only my replies, Tricia noted that I'd answered "Yes, Mr. President" dozens of times. Finally, to my great relief, the chief executive hung up, and I sank back under the comforter.

"What did he want?" Tricia asked.

"I have no idea," I said before falling back to sleep.

I seemed to offer some sort of rare zen role for Clinton— the careful listener on the other end of the line who politcly acknowledged the high-level ramblings of the commander in chief, and just as promptly forgot them.

My leadership positions in the House and in the Senate brought me close enough to the presidents to form some indelible remembrances of these men who have occupied the highest office in the land. They were all remarkably dissimilar in style, political philosophy, looks, and even their basic outlook on life. So it is with our presidents. But no president in my adult experience was as personally reckless, and as disappointing, as William Jefferson Clinton.

My antebellum home in Pascagoula is usually an almost perfect hideaway. It sits atop a slight knoll with the churning Gulf of Mexico at its front and a 350-year-old live oak at its back. It's far from a mansion, but the architect—a man who was far ahead of his time in 1854—managed to harness the southern exposure's blinding light without sacrificing privacy. Huge windows spread across the front of the house, framing a panorama of water and sky. But the living areas in each room are set far back. Behind the house, that sprawling oak protects a large southern garden and secludes my office.

This coastal home, which I laughingly call "Lott's Landing," is my only refuge from the frantic pace of power politics. In the few measured days I'm able to spend there—several at Christmas, a few more in the spring, a vacation in late summer—I'm able to rest and recharge for the legislative battles that are always only a few weeks ahead.

I limit my calls to Washington while I'm there, and try to avoid television with its forest of political talk shows and repetitive news channels. When Washington squalls blow up and attack my routine, they're usually fleeting, polished off in a few hours of work. Sometimes, I rush out for television tapings. But I'm always back home for supper.

However, within half an hour after I flicked on television the morning of Saturday, December 19, 1998, I knew that my holiday escape was essentially over. And I sensed that the private Pascagoula house—a home off the beaten path—would soon become advance headquarters for the trial of President William Jefferson Clinton.

The television day began with infrared shots of United States bombers wreaking havoc on Baghdad during the final hours of President Clinton's Operation Desert Fox. The air war had begun three days earlier and on cue—just as the president's impeachment battle reached fever pitch on the floor of the House of Representatives.

Despite the incandescent lure of Desert Fox, the twenty-four-hour news stations quickly shifted their cameras to the House of Representatives, where a committee of congressmen known as the House Managers was about to reveal to the assembled members and the rest of America whether they were going to impeach the forty-second president of the United States or acquit him of all charges. But when the networks began broadcasting from the floor of the House, another sort of political meltdown was under way.

Like most senators, I'd heard rumors that Louisiana representative Robert Livingston, a Republican, was preparing to resign. Three days earlier, Larry Flynt, the publisher of *Hustler* magazine, had released evidence that Livingston had been unfaithful to his wife—a minor violation compared with Clinton's indiscretions, but a fast-growing scandal just the same.

Livingston was the speaker-in-waiting of the House, replacing the fallen Newt Gingrich, himself accused of conflict of interest and fiscal irresponsibility.

One hour before the impeachment verdict was due, Livingston rose in the chamber and delivered a historic congressional speech. With four network cameras directed at him, he began to speak haltingly: "I very much regret the enmity and hostility that has been bred in the halls of Congress over the last months. I want so much to pacify and cool our raging tempers and return to an era when differences were confined to the debate and not a personal attack or assassination of character."

The acting speaker adjusted his glasses and called upon President Clinton to surrender his office. "You should resign, sir," Livingston cried out.

A host of Democratic congressmen answered with stentorian boos: "No, you should quit, Mr. Livingston. *You resign!*"

An obviously shaken Livingston bellowed his reply: "I must set an example that I hope President Clinton will follow. I will not stand for speaker of the House as I'd planned to do on January sixth, but rather will remain as a backbencher in this Congress that I so dearly love."

Silence enveloped the chamber as the powerful Republican, then chairman of the Appropriations Committee, continued to speak: "I was prepared to lead our party's narrow majority as speaker and I believed I would do a fine job. But I cannot do that job now."


This was the loss of a great leader, I thought, for both the House and the country. I watched the events from Pascagoula in sadness, as Livingston became another victim of the contentious impeachment process that was tearing Congress apart. It had only been six weeks since my friend Newt Gingrich turned in the speaker's gavel and vacated his House seat as well. He had been burned by a partisan firestorm of fiscal charges and countercharges, most of them unproven. I didn't think either man should have resigned.

CNN called for an interview. Connected via satellite to both Washington and New York, I told the weekend anchors that I was surprised by both the timing and the nature of the resignation. But I wasn't surprised that Bob put the interests of his country above any personal considerations he may have had. "We are losing another Republican stalwart," I said.

Personally, Tricia and I were crushed. Bob and his wife Bonnie had been our close friends for years, going back to my days in the House of Representatives. We'd been in each others' homes; we knew their children and they knew ours. Bob was also my legislative neighbor: His Louisiana congressional district abutted my old congressional district in Mississippi.

Less than an hour later, while I consulted on the phone with stunned fellow senators, the House Managers filed slowly back into the chamber. Henry Hyde, chairman of the House Judiciary Committee, led this group of congressmen, who would serve as prosecutors of President Clinton. Exhaustion was evident on their faces; the full brunt of the Monica Lewinsky scandal had settled onto their shoulders.

Hyde was the right man to lead this prickly and difficult proceeding. He was experienced, respected, and an articulate spokesman. Later, his treatment at the hands of some Democratic senators and by the president's lawyers was a stain on the records of the Senate trial.

The managers had considered twelve articles of impeachment against Clinton. But they carried only four to the floor of the House of Representatives.

I settled down on the sofa with Tricia in our den and waited for the House votes. The first article accused President Clinton of lying to a grand jury—as clear a case of perjury as I've ever seen. Many of the members agreed. The vote was 228 for Article I and 206 against, the margin split along partisan lines. Silence greeted the vote tally—a welcome respite from the craziness and anger that characterized the impeachment debates preceding the vote.

The second article, charging Clinton with perjury in the Paula Jones sexual harassment lawsuit, was defeated by 229 to 205.

Article III, alleging obstruction of justice, carried by 221 to 212; the fourth, a harder-to-prove charge of abuse of power, was easily defeated.

After the public turmoil that had accompanied Special Prosecutor Kenneth Starr's investigation of Monica Lewinsky, the vote itself was clean and quick—almost surgical. Representative Bob Barr, a Georgia Republican, predicted confidently "that the American people will be proud of what they have seen on the floor for the past couple of days."

The *Washington Post* television critic, Tom Shales, printed Barr's statement, but opined that "we're leaving the realm of mere derangement for the wilds of the dangerously disturbed."

Tricia and I sat back in silence as the television drifted into the realm of background noise. Many Americans surely did the same.

In a separate news analysis piece, the *Post's* David Von Drehle accurately captured the moment: "Here, in the last weeks of a dizzying year, was the dizziest day of all. It was a day of memorable speeches and vacuous ones, of gestures grand and petty, of shock, confusion, and sudden shifts in mood and shattered logic, of wrong notes and portentous chords, a day of heroes and opportunists in such a frenzy of maneuvering that they could be one and the same from one hour to the next."

For me, that crazy day was a symbol of what was to come. As we approached Clinton's trial, I believed that the honor of Congress was at stake: the power of the presidency was threatened, and the reputation of the Senate could be won or lost during this last act of the impeachment melodrama. I also quickly accepted the fact that, as Senate majority leader, I was the man who needed to prove that the system still worked.

The Senate, for only the second time in the nation's history, would determine the guilt or innocence of an impeached sitting president. I had hoped against hope that the House would find a way to stop this runaway train. Now, as I watched on television,

I promised myself that the Senate would not follow the House into chaos.

It's not that I didn't empathize with the Republicans in the House. I also believed that Clinton was guilty of both perjury and obstruction of justice, and that there was enough evidence to remove him from office. Like my House colleague Bob Livingston, I thought the president should have resigned. He could have spared the country a trial that would divide and poison the legislative branch. President Nixon had set a fine example during Watergate, but Clinton couldn't find it in his heart to leave gracefully.

In Pascagoula, the looming trial consumed all my thoughts; as Christmas closed in, I wandered around the house lost in concentration, seeking some way to prepare for the inevitable.

On December 23, I telephoned Senate Minority Leader Tom Daschle in Aberdeen, South Dakota. According to news reports, he believed that I was aggressively seeking a full-dress trial before the Senate.

But I already knew that the United States Senate, split as it was between 55 Republicans and 45 Democrats, would never convict Clinton of perjury or obstruction of justice—as charged by the House of Representatives. The Republican senators simply didn't have the two-thirds majority necessary to convict Clinton and remove him from office. And we would never have them.

I concluded that there were three or four Republicans whom we might lose—Olympia Snowe and Susan Collins of Maine, Arlen Specter of Pennsylvania, and Jim Jeffords of Vermont. At best, we might only have 51 votes to convict. If the Democrats sought to dismiss the case before a trial, there might even be enough votes in their column to prevail, depending on which way the so-called moderate Republicans leaned.

I also knew that very few Democrats might consider a vote for removal. I could count them on one hand: John Breaux of Louisiana, Joseph Lieberman of Connecticut, Robert Byrd of

West Virginia, Bob Graham of Florida, and Fritz Hollings of South Carolina.

The pickings were very slim. I figured that the final vote count might be 53 to 47, not enough to convict. Even if we got Lieberman, Byrd, and a few other Democrats with conscience, I reckoned we could go as high as 63—but that was still short of the two-thirds. So unless some new and devastating revelation emerged from the evidence, I couldn't see how we could remove Clinton from office.

That first conversation with Senator Daschle since the indictments was a guarded one. I wasn't about to make a Christmas gift of my professional vote tallies. "Look, Tom," I said, "whether we like it or not, we have to stage a trial. It has to be dignified. And it has to be short. And it has to end in such a way that we can continue to work together when it's over."

Tom seemed relieved. He told me later that I'd lifted a considerable weight off his shoulders. He'd been convinced that I would try and drag Clinton through a long and demeaning trial.

Earlier in the year, Daschle had been furious with Clinton over the Lewinsky affair. But his attitude had softened, and he was now zealous to save Clinton's presidency. The ugly reality of impeachment transformed the relationship between us. I told him that the only way we would get through this was to stay in close communication, so we tried to speak every morning during the holiday recess and even more frequently when we returned to Capitol Hill. I finally had a hot line installed in both our offices. That instant connection would figure heavily in the turmoil ahead.

I wanted the shortest impeachment trial I could get. At the same time, I couldn't afford to alienate my fellow senators who prided themselves on the depth of their convictions. As soon as the trial was over, we would have to rebond quickly and assemble an agenda to sell voters in 2000. So I determined to show the House impeachment managers considerable respect.

The trial could be over in a month, I was certain. But a truncated procedure could infuriate the "red meat conservatives," so I acted with caution as I cobbled together a workable plan.

Coincidentally, Washington senator Slade Gorton called to say he had conceived of a shorter but dignified schedule for the trial. Gorton was a good friend; he had also been the attorney general of his state, where he was known as a first-rate lawyer. I put my chief of staff, David Hoppe—formerly Jack Kemp's chief of staff—on the case, and hired Mississippi attorney Mike Wallace, a graduate of Harvard and the University of Virginia College of Law, to serve as my principal legal adviser. Wallace came equipped with an additional credential: He had clerked for Supreme Court Chief Justice William Rehnquist, who would preside over the Senate trial.

Gorton was one of my closest friends in the Senate—a man I trusted implicitly. He'd been one of the first senators to get serious about impeachment. "This is coming at us like a freight train," he told me early on, "and most of the senators are in serious denial. They don't even want to talk about it." He agreed with me that all major decisions leading to the obvious verdict of acquittal should be as bipartisan as we could make them. Gorton confided that Democratic senator Joe Lieberman had suggested an idea to him. "Joe has a plan to end the trial fast," Gorton continued. "And, as you know, he's got one of the best legal minds in the Senate."

You couldn't find anyone with more integrity than Lieberman. He was one of the great Democratic insiders—a close personal friend of the president. But that political intimacy hadn't prevented Lieberman from speaking his mind about the Lewinsky scandal on the Senate floor. In what was obviously a painful speech, the senator from Connecticut had condemned Clinton "for his immoral and disgraceful behavior in this affair." Now, he joined forces with Gorton and got right to work on what would be known as the "Lieberman-Gorton Plan."

My guidelines for the trial were simple: Any bipartisan compromise had to satisfy the impeachment demands of the Constitution; the trial had to be short; it had to be dignified; and it had to
slake the House Managers' thirst for justice.

"I'll get back to you soon," Gorton promised.

As the holidays approached, Republican senators were keeping
in touch through literally scores of conference calls. I was running
the Republican Conference through my desktop phone, and Gorton and Lieberman were burning up the phone lines to craft their
battle plan. Daschle also was talking to his Democrats—all of
them, I would later learn, by New Year's Day.

Three hours after our first post-impeachment conversation,
Slade Gorton boarded a Delta jet with his family for a holiday in
Hawaii. A day earlier, the Liebermans had packed up and headed
for his native Connecticut. As soon as Gorton's Delta jetliner
reached its cruising altitude, Slade picked up the Airfone in the
back of the seat in front of him and dialed Lieberman's cell phone,
reaching Joe while he was driving on a rural Connecticut road.
That was typical. During the next ten days, these two moderates
from different parties and different coasts talked on the phone
every day, faxed dozens of memos back and forth, and drafted
what would prove to be a revolutionary proposal to bring the impeachment trial to a rapid end.

On Christmas Eve, I called Lieberman myself. "I think you
know that Slade Gorton and I are very close," I told him—a pre-
arranged signal that I was lending my official approval to their private attempts to reach a mutually agreeable plan for the trial.
Later, the senator from Connecticut told me that he "understood
that call and its message to be the majority leader's seal of approval on their negotiations."

By December 27, Gorton, drenched in Hawaiian sunshine,
and Lieberman, shivering in Connecticut, had drafted the basic

components of what they termed "a rapid and reasonable impeachment trial." Their plan was to allow each side a day to present opening arguments, followed by a day of questioning by senators. Then, on the fourth day, the Senate would begin to determine whether the president had committed impeachable offenses. With each senator allowed up to ten minutes to speak, the deliberations could stretch into a fifth or sixth day. At the end of the sixth day, the senators would vote on whether to launch a full trial, including witnesses. The vote on going to a full trial would require a two-thirds majority, the same margin required for conviction after the trial itself. If the vote fell short of that, the senators would adjourn the trial and move to consider a bipartisan resolution censuring the president—a move highly favored by the White House.

Lieberman typed out the plan on his computer. It said, in part: "The above procedure completes the trial within a week, and debate and votes on a censure resolution within no more than another week, allowing the nation and the Senate to return to our normal business without having brought the sordid details of this case onto the Senate floor." Joe told me later that he "never imagined that two-thirds of our colleagues might vote for a full-fledged trial."

I approved of the plan in general terms. Still, I wondered how my colleagues would react to this judicial departure, which abandoned some of the rules laid down in the 1868 impeachment trial of President Andrew Johnson and some of the more modern requirements enacted during the Watergate affair. But I looked forward to presenting it to a special meeting of the Republican Conference on January 5, 1999, when the Senate reconvened.

On December 30, however, details of the plan leaked to the press. Worse, the Associated Press, taking advantage of a slow news day, dubbed it the "Lott-Lieberman Proposal"—a label that stuck for weeks. Suddenly and ferociously, the ultra-conservatives in the Senate tore into me, flooding my telephone with calls and sending me unambiguous messages through the press. Led by Senators Phil Gramm of Texas and Spencer Abraham of Michigan, they attacked me for "short-circuiting the trial" and charged me with "pandering to Clinton," a man I'd worked closely with for more than four years.

A *Time* magazine story hinted that my leadership position was being threatened by the party's conservative wing. It claimed, in part: "The country doesn't want a long trial, but the right wing of Trent Lott's party is hungry for witnesses, evidence—and perhaps the President's removal. The question now is which Senator Lott will prevail: the pragmatic Dustbuster or the partisan who has his roots in the Southern GOP."

*Time* even quoted a key (but unidentified) colleague, who said: "If he doesn't get his compromise plan through, he'll be perceived as a weak leader. If he does, he'll be despised by his closest friends."

It wasn't *that* serious. But my conservative colleagues and even some of my constituents were making it very uncomfortable for me.

During my traditional two-day trip to the Cotton Bowl in Dallas, I was besieged at dinner by a group of influential Mississippians, who told me bluntly that I shouldn't let Clinton off the hook, that he had embarrassed the nation and sullied the presidency. In my box at the game, Texas senator Kay Bailey Hutchison spent almost an hour pleading for a full-scale trial. Her passion on the subject got my attention: It was obvious that she spoke for many other senators who were grumbling off-camera.

Later that same day, a conservative watchdog outfit, Judicial Watch, posted a bulletin on its website that began: "What is Trent Lott afraid of?" It went on to assert that "conservatives and other Americans concerned about law and order won't stand for a Senate cover-up of Clinton corruption." Larry Klayman, chairman and general counsel of the organization, warned that "Lott's efforts show a disrespect for the House's role in the impeachment process by implying the articles of impeachment are unworthy of Senate consideration."

When I returned to Pascagoula, a stack of urgent press messages awaited me, all from journalists who sought my reaction to an angry letter sent to me by chief prosecutor Henry Hyde, the chairman of the House Judiciary Committee. I rifled through the increasing mountain of impeachment mail, but found no letter from Hyde. Nor did I find a phone message from the harried congressman.

Several reporters sketched out the bare details of what was a three-page attack against my sponsorship of the Lieberman-Gorton plan. I answered the charges gingerly. "Nothing has been decided yet," I told them. "And the House manager will have a strong voice in what occurs at the trial." I then grabbed the phone, found Hyde, and laid into him. "You ambushed me," I told him. "This is not a good way for us to begin. If you have any problems with me, call me instead of the press." Hyde's response was frosty: "I needed to get your attention, but I should have withheld the letter from the press until you received it. It was a grandstand play. Let's talk more."

"We're talking now," I replied.

After an hour, Hyde was satisfied that I wasn't simply going to let Clinton walk away scot-free But he already had released the most damaging parts of his "open letter." And that opened the floodgates to a revolution among conservatives in the Senate.

In part, Hyde's letter stated: "I agree that we must move with all deliberate speed to resolve this matter. However, we must not act so hastily that the President and the House of Representatives do not have a fair opportunity to present our case and the Senate does not have a fair opportunity to review a meaningful factual record. We believe that a proper presentation of the evidence will likely require the appearance of a limited number of witnesses. We also believe that the President and his counsel may wish to call witnesses as part of their defense."

Hyde continued: "We are especially concerned by your proposal to cancel a trial entirely if a third of the Senate votes to do so."

The commotion kicked up by Hyde and the other House managers convinced a small core of senators that I was planning to give the impeachment process short shrift. A handful of them were thoroughly convinced that a shorter trial was inappropriate. I understood how they felt, but the Lieberman-Gorton plan was one way to give impeachment some public attention before an actual ballot to see if there were even enough votes to convict. If there weren't, a motion for dismissal would certainly hit the floor of the Senate.

A parade of grumbling House Managers and dissatisfied senators tumbled onto the news talk shows and sounded off to television journalists. *Time* depicted my dilemma: "Word began to leak to the House from the other side of Capitol Hill that the Senate leadership was floating a plan to get rid of the whole mess—fast. They heard that Republican Majority Leader Trent Lott and Democratic Minority Leader Tom Daschle were negotiating for a test vote that would likely lead to censure and nothing else. The maneuvering may seem like the usual Washington dance, interesting to only pundits and political junkies, but there is something serious at stake: whether the first trial of a president in 130 years will be quick and civilized or long and dirty.

"The man in the middle is Trent Lott and he's under heavy pressure from all sides."

By then, angry and confused Republican senators were talking to each other by phone as they headed back to the nation's capital. My chief of staff, Dave Hoppe, tried to gauge their mood, and reported back that "a healthy majority wanted to move ahead with some form of impeachment trial." Members of the party's conservative core in both the Senate and House were making it clear in press interviews that they wanted a full-scale trial, complete with plenty of witnesses—ten, twenty, twenty-five, whatever it took to make the case against Clinton.

As I say, I knew how they felt. I was disgusted by Clinton's conduct, and I thought he had committed impeachable offenses. From a purely political standpoint, I could have pushed for a full and lurid trial. But the outcome would have been the same: There were so many liberal senators in the Democrats' ranks that we couldn't get sixty-seven guilty votes, no matter what the evidence before us. But in the process of that long trial, with its certain outcome, we could embarrass the institution. We could embarrass ourselves. And we could even ruin our ability to do anything for the country. Looking back, I really think that this was one of the things that came back to haunt me during the Strom Thurmond crisis. In the Clinton case, I didn't draw blood—and the ultra-conservatives blamed me for it.

I decided to fight back. First I jettisoned the Lieberman-Gorton plan. Obviously, any completely bipartisan plan for a businesslike trial would have to wait. I had run into the reality of the Republican Caucus: You can usually get your colleagues to do many things, but sometimes they just rare up and say, "We don't want to do that." So you have to be able to say, "Let's go to Plan B." And that's what we did.

In this case, Plan B involved starting the trial with no real plan at all. We would dive into impeachment, with no backup chute. On Wednesday, January 6, with the trial set to open the next morning, I met with a jostling and nervous pack of Republican senators in my office hideaway, just fifty yards from the Senate floor. I shouted reminders at the rebelling senators that we had to be fair. "I am not going to let this become a circus," I told them. Many erupted in anger. Over groaning protests, I made myself heard. "We don't need witnesses in this case. The assembled evidence is sitting before us. Let's study it, debate it, and then vote."

"I won't do it that way," answered Susan Collins of Maine, a moderate member of the caucus. Rick Santorum of Pennsylvania, a far more conservative figure, seemed just as angry: "I am more interested in how the history books will judge me." Then he looked right at me: "Senator Lott, if you are trying to help me, please don't. Think of history."

I was thinking of history, too. But many GOP senators failed to see that I also was trying to guide our part of the impeachment process with an eye on the 2000 elections. We had just received a discouraging report on the 1998 vote from Linda DiVall, the party's longtime pollster. The news was bad; Republicans had lost the moderate vote decisively, she said, and voters focused on issues such as education, health care, the economy, and Social Security were breaking for the Democrats. Make no mistake, she warned: Impeachment politics are driving down the image of the Republican Party.

# 13

# WILLIAM JEFFERSON CLINTON ON TRIAL: PART TWO

On Thursday, January 7, in a stark and somber atmosphere, the trial formerly opened in the Senate chamber. Most senators wore dark, formal suits, and a respectful hush greeted the call to order. The charges were read. Chief Justice William H. Rehnquist, in a dramatic, medieval-style robe, took his oath. We were then sworn in as jurors. It was an effective pageant. But soon it all was rendered meaningless, as the trial skidded off its tracks shortly after the half-hour opening ceremony. With the Senate deadlocked on rules, the impeachment trial of President William Clinton couldn't begin. We regretfully recessed. In only the second impeachment trial in history, we couldn't even agree on how to begin.

I looked across the room at Daschle—who seemed just as stunned with his flock of Democrats as I was with my crowd of Republicans. Tom and I naturally gravitated toward each other, and started up a two-way conversation on how to end this embarrassing impasse. We reviewed the steps that got us into this fix, and began throwing out ideas on how to proceed. Several senators crowded around us, then several more, until finally a bipartisan mob completely circled us. Soon, members of my caucus had surrounded me; Tom was all but buried in his.

Majority Whip Don Nickles of Oklahoma, my second-in-command, held his hand aloft and yelled: "I'd like to make a motion for the two party caucuses to meet together. We can gather in the Old Senate Chamber—no press, no spectators, no cameras, no tape recorders." The crowd murmured its approval. I immediately saw this as an opportunity to avoid in the Senate the bloody confrontation that had just consumed the House. I looked across at Tom Daschle. He nodded his head in approval.

Nickles recognized that we shouldn't gather in the current Senate chamber, which was now an official court of law, and I agreed. So I scheduled the meeting for the next day, in the historic setting that housed the Senate from 1810 through 1859. I spread the word through my caucus, and asked Democratic senator Danny Akaka of Hawaii to open the meeting with a prayer.

As the lawmakers began to leave, several still-dissatisfied conservatives ambled alongside me. I kept walking straight ahead and said, for all to hear, "You know, the Republican senators must stick together, or *they*"—and here I nodded my head at the Democrats—"will pass a motion to dismiss."

There was more grousing, and one of them barked out: "We're not on trial here!"

"Yes we are," I shot back.

Daschle hesitated and asked for more time for the Democratic senators to consider the Lieberman-Gorton plan. If that resolution failed to find favor, the minority leader told me he would bring his troops to the Old Senate Chamber.

I also decided to give the compromise plan one more chance to succeed. Perhaps now there were enough votes to somehow force it through. I set a meeting for 5 P.M., where I offered up a limited version of the Lieberman-Gorton compromise. The House managers and White House lawyers would have five days to present their cases, I told them. The Senate would have two days to pose questions. Motions to dismiss or to call witnesses and enlarge the trial would then be considered. "This does not mean the trial would simply be shut down," I said.

The room stirred angrily. "No. This is a mistake," said Olympia Snowe of Maine. Both Arlen Specter of Pennsylvania and John Chafee of Rhode Island pleaded that the joint caucus would offer a solution acceptable to both parties—and, though they didn't say so specifically, would also provide political cover. "Drop this plan and wait until tomorrow," Chafee concluded.

I'd had enough. "Look," I said, "I've stuck my neck out for bipartisanship. I stuck it out and some of you chopped it off." With that I shut down the meeting abruptly, leaving some senators with unanswered questions. Many believed the rumors that Daschle was somehow blocking the bipartisan action. One of them, Arizona's Jon Kyl, stood before ABC cameras on the steps of the Capitol and impetuously blamed the Democratic minority leader for "killing off the joint caucus." At that moment, the minority leader was perched on a chair in the anteroom of my outer office waiting to huddle with me over the caucus plans for the next day. Unfortunately, the television was turned to ABC. Hearing Kyl, Daschle bolted from his chair and ran from the room, shouting over his shoulder, "Tell Lott I've gone back to the floor."

I returned to my office a moment later, and immediately ran back out again to tackle Tom and smooth things over. I reaffirmed my plans for the joint session and shook his hand.

"Trent," he said, "the only way you and I can resolve this is if we go to the press gallery together." We bounded off shoulder to shoulder. During our hastily arranged press conference, I said,

"Senator Daschle and I are not dictators. We are merely leaders who are getting some latitude through conferences and caucuses, but we have to bring along ninety-eight other senators." High on this bipartisanship, I grabbed Tom's hand and thrust it up in the air—as if we were at the podium of a political convention.

Downstairs in the Republican cloakroom, watching on television, several conservatives recoiled—particularly Rick Santorum. At the sight of my gesture, I was later told, he yelled: "There goes Lott again, caving in to the Democrats."

Rick was a bright and persuasive forty-year-old Pittsburgh conservative, elected to the Senate in 1994 after two terms in the House, where he had been close to the Republican revolutionaries. To mend Republican Conference fences, I asked Santorum to accompany me on one last appearance before the House managers. I hoped he was young enough, and tough and brash enough, to reach them.

We found them across Capitol Hill in the Rayburn Building, angrily wrestling with the possibility of a bipartisan agreement that they believed would undermine them. Deep in their hearts they still hungered for a full-fledged trial, with a score of witnesses and six months to showcase them. Their hatred for Clinton was clouding their reason.

We came uninvited and unannounced and unwanted. I could see that the House managers viewed me as the enemy. No one offered us seats, so we sat down on either side of Henry Hyde. I told them we'd come over to explain the Republican proposal—in effect, my modification to Lieberman-Gorton—and to convince them of its practicality.

I put it in plain terms: Each side would get twenty-four hours, spread over five days, to present its case without witnesses. The senators would have two days for a question-and-answer session, and then motions to dismiss the case or to call witnesses would be considered. If the Senate voted to reject witnesses, final votes would take place by February 5. If we called witnesses, the vote would be on February 12.

"Well, we have a problem with that," Henry Hyde answered. He then turned to Representative Chris Cannon, a manager from Utah. "Chris, haven't you got something to say about that?"

Cannon, a legislative firebrand, erupted: "This deal is designed to screw us. You are cutting the managers off at the knees. This is a whitewash; this is a sellout. The president has tampered with witnesses. He's obstructed justice and he has lied on the stand. Do we just let him go?" Then he turned and shook his fist at me.

I tried to be gracious: "Believe me, I understand what you're going through."

"No you don't, and you don't really care," Cannon continued. "Well, you should know that we're a co-equal house here. The worst thing that could happen here is you could give us rules we won't follow."

Fiery Georgia congressman Bob Barr, as far to the right as any of the managers, turned to me next. "I have a problem even calling this a trial."

"You're just dealing in semantics," I replied.

"Use any words you wish," said Barr. "But this is not a trial."

Looking at these congressmen, I tried to put myself in their position—ensnared by time and coincidence in a scandal not of their making. I empathized: "I was in the House. I was where you guys are. I sat on the Judiciary Committee during Watergate. I'm not against you guys. I brought Rick along because I thought you would really respect his judgment."

Santorum jumped in on cue: "Trent's one of us. He's not here to cut everybody off. But he's got to run the Senate. He's not the speaker. He's the majority leader; he has to lead. I want you to have witnesses. Work with us!"

They weren't swayed; nor were they civil. They told us to leave the room while they discussed their choices—which were fewer than they suspected. The debate that followed, I later learned, was frantic. Some wanted to walk out; others wanted to go public with their outrage.

But they decided they would hold out for live witnesses, and would use only eight hours for opening arguments—no more.

Eight hours? "You need a lot more time than that," I told them when we were back in the room.

"You're putting us in a box," Santorum said.

"You're putting *us* in a box," said Barr.

I was crestfallen, but promised to trek back to the Senate to see if I could sell this to Daschle. But I turned back around and warned them: "Don't use up all of your time arguing for witnesses. You'd better go ahead and make your case."

Several days later, the *Washington Post* commented on my ordeal. "Trent Lott's party leadership was on the line," reporter Peter Baker wrote. "With so many Republicans balking, he did not have the 51 votes to force his plan on the floor. After his unilateral negotiations with Dick Morris and President Clinton and the Democrats, some Republican senators do not trust their leader."

I don't think my leadership was on the line. If it was, I never sensed it. But I was totally focused on achieving my mission. As my chief of staff, Dave Hoppe, told a reporter for *Time,* "Senator Lott was walking a tightrope. He had to constantly check the moods, the shifts, and the mind-set of each senator to guide his course. And, with each step he took, he had to know what the boundaries were. It was more an act of diplomacy than a power play."

Aside from Hoppe's analysis, the press misread my problems. My troubles during the early days of the impeachment trial resulted strictly from some core conservatives who wanted to come down hard on President Clinton.

But soon those dissenters would face the reality of the Democratic wall they faced.

The senators who filed into the 1810 Senate chamber on Friday morning, January 8, 1998, seemed humbled. Again, they had dressed in dark suits as they sank into the Victorian armchairs beneath the gilded ceiling. The Old Senate Chamber thoroughly reflects the late Napoleonic era in which it was built. Draped in crimson French brocade, furnished with elegant chairs and desks, it mirrored an era when legislative ceremonies were governed by stark rules of decorum.

The silence seemed even more impressive when Senator Akaka voiced his prayer, a message of hope that the Senate could surmount the impeachment crisis. "Heavenly Father," he intoned, "We are in trouble and we need your help. We've come to a point where we don't know what to do." A respectful hush followed Danny's simple prayer.

The night before, I'd asked Tom Daschle to help me assemble speakers who would both command respect from their peers and preach in a manner that conveyed reverence for our institution. We decided to limit the number to three senators from each caucus—highly respected men determined to cross party lines in order to solve our problems.

The historic session opened with a show of pyrotechnic oratory, staged to light a bipartisan fire under the now-discouraged senators. West Virginia's Robert Byrd was the elegant dean of congressional orators. His forty years in the Senate, his mane of white hair, and his courtly manner of dress combined to make him the picture of the old school senator—perfectly matched with the gilt edges of the chamber itself.

Byrd stood up slowly as the room fell silent. "The White House has sullied itself," he said in a deep and dolorous voice. "The House of Representatives has fallen into the black pit of partisan self-indulgence. . . . And the United States Senate is teetering on the brink of that same black pit."

Byrd, the Senate's official historian, paused to straighten a tower of books he'd brought with him—books that discussed the impeachment issue and impressed his audience.

"We look very bad," he continued. "We appear to be dithering and posturing and slowly disintegrating in political quicksand. We can start by disdaining any more of the salacious muck which has already soiled the gowns of too many. If we can come together in a dignified way to orderly and expeditiously dispose of this matter, then perhaps we can yet salvage a bit of respect and trust from the American people for all of us, for the Senate and for their institutions of government."

Florida's Republican senator, Connie Mack, gave a stirring pep talk: "We've learned a big lesson here, and that lesson is that we senators should open up to one another and express our true fears of what lies ahead."

Joe Lieberman was up next. The plan he had developed with Slade Gorton had been set aside, but that hadn't dimmed his perspective. "There will not be sixty-seven votes on this set of facts" to convict, he told the room. "We must do what is necessary to achieve a fair trial and a fair vote and then simply move on."

I wondered about the effect of Lieberman's honest assessment on my own troops. The only hope Republicans had of reaching a two-thirds vote depended on Democrats such as Lieberman. And he'd already concluded that the president would be acquitted.

Lieberman brushed past the issue of witnesses. "They should not be brought in if they aren't necessary because they would prolong the trial and bring into the Senate the sordid sexual details we so fervently wish to avoid." He closed by stating: "This is a political trial, and we are politicians. We can handle it."

After similar orations by Senators Chris Dodd and Slade Gorton, Texas's brilliant senator Phil Gramm took the floor.

Gramm stood and motioned for quiet. Since he had made it abundantly clear that he was out for Clinton's blood, curiosity filled the chamber. Yet his message was intriguingly simple: Why don't we just move to start the trial, and then vote on the other issues as they come upon us? "Let's just take the first steps upon that road and worry about the intersection ahead later," he said. In an echo of the Lieberman-Gorton plan, he suggested that the managers and the president's lawyers each be given twenty-four hours for their presentations.

Both Democratic and Republican heads nodded at the brevity and practicality of Gramm's suggestion. Senator Ted Kennedy of Massachusetts seconded Gramm's proposal, then suggested that the witness issue—the real bone of contention—be voted on later down the road.

That was all I had to hear. These few phrases, I saw, were building blocks for a later consensus. "I think we have a bipartisan agreement here," I said. "Let's vote." Because I grabbed onto this so quickly, no second thoughts marred the moment.

Later, Dave Hoppe compared my bipartisan leap to that of a general who grabbed up the colors and shouted, "Charge!" I did realize one thing: There might not be another moment like this one to forge all the senators together in this sad enterprise.

As journalist Peter Baker noted in the *Washington Post,* however, the moment of bipartisanship would be fleeting. "For the second time in two days, Lott had seized the moment to preserve bipartisanship and forced the independent-minded senators to keep paddling in the same direction," Baker wrote. "But he had only kept the situation from falling apart for another few hours." I saw it more as a lucky break, one that gave me the time to bundle Kennedy, Gramm, chief Senate lawyer Tom Griffith, my legal adviser Mike Wallace, and Dave Hoppe off to a conference room to stitch together a binding resolution out of what the senators had said. Leaving Hoppe in charge, I began lobbying senatorial support for the resolution to come. The gang ended up scrapping for almost two hours, as Lieberman, Gorton, Jon Kyl, Mike DeWine, and Ted Stevens joined what was becoming a crowd.

In the end, Daschle and I had to jump in to hammer out a final compromise: The House managers would be allowed to make their full presentation about the need for witnesses before the Senate voted on any motion to dismiss.

At four o'clock that afternoon, we all trooped from the Old Senate Chamber to the Senate floor, where we conducted our regular business and voted. The Gramm-Kennedy Resolution passed one hundred to nothing—a daunting display of unanimity that startled both the House managers and the White House lawyers. The trial was officially scheduled to begin six days later, on Thursday, January 14.

In the days before the trial, I began poring over the evidence given to us by the House managers. It was extensive. It was overwhelming. It was saddening. I started carrying a notebook around with me so that I could assess, for myself, the conduct of President Clinton and his relationship with this young woman.

The evidence wasn't new; it was the same information that had so fascinated the media for the past year. But I was still stunned by the sheer amount of data that proved the president's indiscretions and his duplicity.

My face must have reflected my growing concern after each study session. One afternoon, my old friend and adviser Mike Wallace came up to me and asked if the evidence was getting to me.

"Your opinion of President Clinton is shifting, isn't it?"

I nodded.

He later told me that he'd seen my face register deeper and deeper disappointment in the man that I had engaged so closely over the past four years. I had thought I understood Bill Clinton. We were both sons of the South. We came from the same place—blue collar homes off the beaten path. And we'd both risen from those small towns to national prominence—he, of course, more than I. That's why we were able to form that secret bond, linked only by Dick Morris. But the more I read, the more I realized that I hadn't understood or even known this man at all. The man and president who committed the acts outlined in the mass of evidence couldn't be the man I thought I knew.

That his crimes had involved a young woman was even harder to understand. That was part of the story I began to feel personally, as Dave Hoppe soon figured out. "You're thinking about your daughter," he noticed one day when he saw me reading some of the evidence involving Monica Lewinsky. "She's about the same age."

I looked back at him. "Yep, I guess I am."

I was appalled at the immorality evident in this middle-aged man's attention to a woman less than half his age. It sent an awful signal to the nation.

But there was little time for such personal thought as the trial proceeded and partisan politics reared up again. In the midst of a question-and-answer session involving the House managers and White House lawyers, aides handed us a freshly printed press release. It was headlined: "Statement by U.S. Senator Robert C. Byrd—a Call for Dismissal of Charges and End of Trial." After several scorching paragraphs concerning his abjectly low opinion of Clinton, Senator Byrd was calling for dismissal merely because "the necessary two-thirds for conviction are not there."

Byrd angrily dismissed the need to call witnesses. "That would only foster more of the small hallway press conferences and battle of press releases that are contributing to the division of our parties and our nation."

Chief White House lobbyist Lawrence Stein passed a note over to the president's attorneys, the press later reported: "Don't smile; don't gloat," the note said. "It's over." As the *Washington Post* and others noted at the time, Byrd's move signaled that the Democratic caucus would hold: As I'd known all along, the votes for conviction just weren't there.

But we still had a constitutional duty to perform. To end the trial this way, in a partisan manner and without a vote on the articles of impeachment, didn't bode well for the reputation of the Senate. So, for the time being, my job was to make sure Byrd's motion was defeated. For all my work with Minority Leader Daschle, the Democratic caucus had blindsided us. Using one of their tactics, I sent a message back through the press.

Standing before a bank of cameras just outside the chamber, I told reporters: "The Senate will vote, perhaps as early as Monday, on dismissing the charges. Keep in mind that if you cut it off, you don't have the opportunity to vote on subpoenas; you don't have depositions; you don't have a chance to debate whether or not you'd have a single witness. That's a big leap of faith. And I'm not sure the Senate is ready to take it yet."

The lead prosecutor, Henry Hyde, bellowed at the unfairness from the floor of the Senate. "We tried to be fair because we understand you need a two-thirds vote to remove the president. We needed Democratic support. So far we had none. That's okay. Let the process play itself out. We were fair. Everyone needs to know that."

And then, in comments directed at the Republican Conference and me, he added: "By dismissing the articles of impeachment before you have a complete trial, you are sending a terrible message to the people of this country. You're saying, I guess, perjury is okay if it is about sex. Obstruction is okay, even though it is an effort to deny a citizen her right to a fair trial."

Hyde adopted a mocking tone as he concluded: "I know, oh, do I know what an annoyance we are in the bosom of this great body. But we are a *constitutional* annoyance, and I remind you of that fact."

With Byrd's premature objection to any witnesses at all, the bipartisan ship that Daschle and I had kept afloat for so long foundered. From that moment I had to use our superior numbers, both to kill the motion to dismiss, and to try and provide a partisan conclusion to the trial we had started together.

After counting my own votes and failing in one last attempt at a bipartisan resolution, I readied a proposal for limited witnesses—winnowed down to three, on video rather than in person—and led my caucus into a contentious session of the full Senate late on the evening of January 25. Rather than allow the world to witness our partisan selfishness, I motioned to close the debate. But Daschle and the Democratic Caucus wanted it open. The secret session, which would last almost five hours, was approved by a mostly party-line vote of fifty-seven to forty-three. History and the Constitution were on my side. The secrecy rules were the same drafted for the only other presidential impeachment trial—that of Andrew Johnson in 1868.

Although there were some minor compromises, we returned to open session on Wednesday, January 27, to vote whether to dismiss or continue the trial under our Republican-drafted guidelines. These included a provision for three witnesses on video—Monica Lewinsky, presidential adviser Sidney Blumenthal, and Clinton's friend and adviser, Vernon Jordan.

Again, as with the joint caucus in the Old Senate Chamber, the senators of both parties dressed somberly for the occasion, as did the House managers and President Clinton's attorneys. Everyone had a sense that we were rushing down the final path, toward an acquittal that made few senators entirely comfortable, regardless of party.

Senator Robert Byrd's motion was defeated, with 54 Republicans and one Democrat—Senator Russ Feingold of Wisconsin—voting no and 43 Democrats voting yes. The GOP plan for deposing witnesses and continuing the trial was approved by 54–44 in a straight party-line vote.

Technically, the House managers won: The case wasn't dismissed out of hand, and they were permitted to interrogate the trio of witnesses. Some thought the trial was essentially over, since forty-four senators had said we lacked the evidence to carry on—enough votes to prevent the removal of Bill Clinton from office. I didn't see it that way. From the beginning, Mike Wallace had impressed upon me that my main duty was to provide "a trial" to consider the charges against President Clinton. "It's very important how you define a trial," he told me one afternoon. "We must all decide what the requirements are for this court proceeding and then fulfill them." After several long conferences with Wallace and chief Senate attorney Tom Griffith, I understood that I needed to ensure that the House managers could adequately present their evidence—no matter what form it took.

But that gave me great leeway to measure this evidence in light of what had already been assembled by special prosecutor Kenneth Starr—two moving vans full of documents, depositions, and exhibits. The House was merely proposing to *recall* witnesses who had already been deposed by the $40 million Starr investigation. That's how we convinced the House managers to winnow the list to three—the three that most influenced the charges of perjury and obstruction of justice.

Then the House managers made a couple of grandstand plays and created a ruckus over Monica Lewinsky—the sort of thing I'd been working to avoid. They sent word to the Republican Conference, and through us to the entire Senate, that they were happy with the television depositions being given by Jordan and Blumenthal. But they pleaded to bring Lewinsky to the Senate floor.

The furor increased when Representative Henry Hyde, for reasons best known to him alone, went back to Kenneth Starr and asked him to force Monica Lewinsky to give a pretrial interview. The Independent Counsel's office agreed, and petitioned a judge in Washington to issue the order. Two days later, Judge Norma Holloway Johnson commanded Lewinsky to answer questions submitted through Starr's lawyers.

When Lewinsky arrived in Washington from Los Angeles later that afternoon, the media and the European paparazzi mobbed her at the airport as she tried to grab a taxi. An even larger crowd was milling around the entrance to her hotel, the Renaissance. She'd tried unsuccessfully to disguise herself in an oversized black coat, tucking her signature hair into a baseball cap.

In a Sunday piece for the *Washington Post*, journalist Michael Powell aimed his darts at the House of Representatives: "A more prosaic haplessness attends to the House Republican impeachment project. There is now in the statements of the House players a sense of an endgame, of actors desperate to forestall a final act. They summon Lewinsky in the manner of a desperate opera director dialing a diva: She must breathe life into a flagging production."

Powell pointed out, as I knew well, that we already had the transcripts of twenty-two interviews with the world's most famous intern. And now we had her newly taped video. We quickly screened it and instantly realized that it contained nothing new. In fact, everything she said seemed to strengthen Clinton's hand. The Democrats were ecstatic. After watching it, even some conservative members of my coalition began pleading for a rapid end to the trial.

The House managers' attempt to put Lewinsky on the floor, and the paucity of the evidence in the video depositions, allowed me to paste back together the bipartisan league of senators who had joined to do battle back in late December. Daschle and I engineered a few votes that defied party lines, and helped bring the trial to a dignified conclusion.

First, nearly half of the Republican senators joined Democrats in a 70–30 vote to keep Monica Lewinsky out of the well of the Senate. Then I persuaded a core of key members in my caucus to drop "findings of fact" resolutions that would have detailed instances of wrongdoing by the president without actually convicting him of anything. From the start, most Republican senators had claimed there would be Democratic support for these actions. "I just don't see it," I said at a testy meeting. "Show me the Democrats who will support this, because we aren't going out there alone." No one ever showed up.

Finally, on February 4, with Daschle's support, I was able to pinpoint a final date for the votes—February 12. I was off by twenty-four hours.

On February 13, after two days of Senate questioning, a series of fifteen-minute speeches by almost every senator, and a day of deliberation, the United States Senate acquitted President William Jefferson Clinton of both perjury and obstruction of justice.

Article I, alleging perjury, was defeated, with all 45 Democrats and 10 Republicans voting to acquit and 45 Republicans voting to convict. Article II, charging obstruction, failed on a fifty-fifty tie. Five Republicans joined all 45 Democrats in supporting acquittal of that charge.

Tom Daschle and I were the final speakers before the vote. The Democratic minority leader was very generous. He gestured to me with his right hand and said, "Perhaps more than anyone in this chamber, I can attest to the steadfast commitment to a trial conducted with dignity and in the national interest. He has demonstrated that differences—honest differences—on difficult issues need not be dissent and in that end the Senate can transcend those differences and conclude a constitutional process the country will respect, and I do."

I could have said the same of him.

In my final words, I admitted what my chief of staff, Dave Hoppe, had detected long before—that this whole matter had been very personal for me. "My own daughter is the same age as the young intern Monica Lewinsky, who was used for sexual services just off the Oval Office by the president of the United States."

Then I put down my notes and said: "Let's vote."

# 14

# ELECTION 2000 AND JIM JEFFORDS

In the middle of the summer of 1999, I spent considerable time at my desk in Washington reviewing reams of documents and crunching numbers. The information included poll results, detailed maps of every congressional district, and fat dossiers on incumbent Democrats and likely challengers to our incumbents. The overall impression wasn't good, I thought: We could easily lose our majority.

Most of our young senators were running for their second terms—a capricious and notoriously dangerous time for a first-termer. These were senators who had come to power in no small part because of the revolution inspired by Newt Gingrich in 1994. All had been boosted to power by Gingrich. But Newt was no longer there to help them; they needed our help on the Senate side of the Capitol.

After they got to our side of the Capitol, we in the leadership gave them a crash course in senatorial protocol and began to introduce them to the Senate's movers and shakers—in both parties. Now it was time for a heavy dose of Campaigning 101. We had our National Republican Senatorial Committee to help them, and we made it clear that we would provide assistance in any way we could. We advised them to raise as much money as early as possible. "I'll stump for you guys whenever you need me," I told them. I made campaign appearances for most of them, even getting the quartet of "Singing Senators" I founded to perform in Missouri on behalf of one of our members—John Ashcroft.

I don't consider myself a superstitious man, but so many bad things happened before, during, and after the 2000 election that I began to wonder whether we were somehow hexed.

First, one of my best friends in the Senate, Florida's Connie Mack, decided not to run again. Then, on July 18, 2000, GOP senator Paul Coverdell of Georgia died suddenly of a cerebral hemorrhage, and the current governor of the state filled the slot with former governor Zell Miller, a Democrat. And that was only the beginning. We went into November 2000 with fifty-four seats, enough to keep our majority. But would we be able to retain that margin, or even a majority, through the election? I had my doubts—well justified, as it turned out. It was a bloodbath for us. In Michigan, first-termer Spencer Abraham lost to Debbie Stabenow. In Minnesota, first-termer Rod Grams lost to Mark Dayton. In Washington, my friend and confidant Slade Gorton, who had served three honorable terms in the Senate, was defeated by millionaire Maria Cantwell in a razor-close contest. And perhaps most ignominious, first-term incumbent John Ashcroft of Missouri lost to a dead man—the popular governor Mel Carnahan, who had perished in a plane crash on October 16, 2000.

In four months, we went from 55 to 50—dividing the Senate right down the middle. Our only consolation was that newly elected vice president Dick Cheney would take on the role of president of the Senate and serve as the tie-breaking vote in the event of a party deadlock. As for me, I was presiding over a shaky and fragile Republican Conference. The enormity of it didn't really dawn on me until the furor over the Bush-Gore vote died down. It was bound to be unsettling, with each party fighting over the few crossover votes to pass new legislation.

During the Christmas holiday that year, I began to think seriously about how we would muddle through in a split-decision Senate. Shortly after Christmas dinner in Pascagoula, I left the family gathering and ducked into my office to call Tom Daschle in South Dakota. I wanted to assure him that I was ready to work with him in running an all-but-deadlocked Senate. I wanted to make the first move to draft a bipartisan procedure, so that the newly elected president, George W. Bush, had a chance to move around this potential logjam and advance his legislative agenda. I assured Daschle that we'd work out the details in January. He assured me that the Democrats wouldn't undercut me. Then I returned to our Christmas celebration.

It was a parlous moment in many respects. The Senate, of course, figured to be bitterly divided regardless of my and Daschle's best efforts. And the crisis in Florida provided the finale to a rough, contentious presidential election that left everyone hanging for more than a month. Personally, I never doubted that Bush would be declared the winner. There was never any indication of fraud or of stealing votes, but considerable damage was done before the allegations of tampering were discounted. In the wake of the election, the nation was traumatized and confused.

The presidential election shouldn't have been that close. Al Gore was a poor candidate—stiff as a board—and Bush should have won it going away, because his themes were closer to the American mainstream. But to me it seemed that Karl Rove, Bush's chief campaign strategist, and the candidate himself got a little cocky at the end and coasted a bit more than they should have. It should never have come down to five hundred votes in Florida.

\*   \*   \*

I knew my Republican Conference wasn't psychologically ready for this new fifty-fifty world in the Senate. We had been in the majority for six productive years and had fought a fierce campaign to hold onto that power. My senators hated the idea of any sort of power-sharing agreement with the other side. But we needed to construct a serviceable arrangement with Daschle and the Democrats if we were ever to move legislation through the Senate. For the good of the country, we had to demonstrate some maturity.

Two days after I returned to Washington after the Christmas holiday, I set up a meeting with Daschle and began researching my options. In fact, they were few in number. Technically, we held the power when it came to voting. Since Vice President Cheney held the tie-breaking vote, we could win the roll call on straight, party-line votes. But given his daily obligations at the White House, we couldn't expect the vice president to be in position on a permanent basis. That meant, in theory at least, that in his absence I could be a majority leader without a majority to back it up. I vowed that I wouldn't hesitate to summon Dick Cheney to the Senate if that's what it took to win a crucial vote.

Meantime, Florida was still on the minds of some Democrats, who were making noises about stalling confirmation of Bush's political appointments and sandbagging his initial legislative proposals if they weren't accorded complete equality in the Senate. In effect, they were proposing that we have two majority leaders. *Roll Call*, the Capitol Hill newspaper, duly reported one bizarre proposal: Daschle would be majority leader in the morning, and I'd take over after lunch. When Elizabeth Letchworth, then secretary to the majority, told me about that one, I told her, "Not until there are flowers growing in the Potomac."

On January 2, I consulted the Senate's parliamentarian for an official ruling, Even though there hadn't been a split Senate in fifty-three years, he assured me that the rule was clear. Since the Republican Conference had Vice President Cheney's vote to break any ties that came along, I would be recognized as Senate majority leader.

Armed with this ruling, I began negotiating a power-sharing plan with Tom Daschle. I knew that the words *shared power* would anger a considerable segment of my conference. But I had to take the high road; I had to find a way to make the Senate work under extremely difficult conditions.

For a while, Daschle himself had apparently toyed with the idea of a co-majority leader role. He dropped that, but he gave me a list of "demands"—some of which seemed reasonable, while others, frankly, needed to disappear. Most worrisome was a proposal to share the priority right of recognition. The Senate majority leader always has the right to be recognized first by the presiding officer—the vice president. That places him in a critical position to propose legislation and amendments. What Daschle proposed was that we would alternate in the priority right of recognition. To satisfy my own skepticism over this notion, I asked Letchworth for her analysis. She concurred: It would put an end to my ability "to control the legislative process . . . during floor consideration of any given legislation." Not a chance, I resolved.

It took us three days of bargaining, but Tom and I reached an agreement that was approved by the Senate on January 5. The plan awarded Democrats equal representation on all committees, as well as equal budgets, staffs, and office space. But Republicans held the committee chairmanships, and by law and precedent, the vice president retained his tie-breaking privilege. Moreover, the agreement was designed to avoid stalemates by empowering either party leader to bring a bill or a nomination to the floor from a deadlocked committee. A four-hour debate would follow, after which the measure or nominee would be placed on the legislative calendar for further consideration on the floor if the full

Senate approved. Sharing priority right of recognition was not part of the program.

I had difficulty selling the deal to my fellow Republicans, and it was especially tough to have some of my longtime buddies buck me on the issue. They thought we should have insisted on having a one-seat margin in the committees because of the vice president's vote. But as I told them, the Democrats would never in hell have agreed. Daschle had made that crystal clear. Phil Gramm of Texas was particularly adamant, arguing that the arrangement was "a prescription for mischief by Senate Democrats. I see this as a 51–50 Republican majority." But it wasn't, not according to the Senate parliamentarian. The vice president could break ties; he was not the 101st senator.

What I also told Republicans was that we had to remain sensitive to the needs of the Bush administration. The agreement may have involved a few compromises, but it helped the White House avoid what might have been a long, contentious, perhaps paralyzing battle on the floor over the organization of the Senate—a battle Daschle had vowed repeatedly to undertake—just as the president was settling into his office.

The sharing plan I authored also created bipartisan responsibility. If the committee divided fifty-fifty between Republicans and Democrats failed to function productively, then I could talk about obstructionism. And one way or another, the American people would know who was trying to make it work and who wasn't.

The power-sharing agreement was a classic case of extending the hand of friendship and of good faith, while knowing a thing or two about your negotiating partner. My long-term relationship with Tom Daschle had proven to me that he was a man I could trust. I knew Tom in the House before he came over to the Senate in 1987—two years before I was elected. Once he got there, he adroitly hooked himself to Senate Majority Leader George Mitchell and soaked up the veteran leader's way of doing things.

When Mitchell left in 1994, Daschle was elected by one vote over Chris Dodd of Connecticut to be the Democratic leader.

I found him to be a formidable opponent, and a committed Democratic partisan—a prairie populist. But there's a side of him you can trust. You may fight every day, but you don't just gut each other at the end of the day.

To steer our difficult détente, we established an all-but-constant communications network, meeting frequently in my Senate office or his and talking by phone every morning. We had a secure line installed that linked us instantly with the push of a buzzer. Not even our staffs knew about it. And we managed to guide the angrily divided Senate as smoothly and profitably as was possible under the circumstances.

Two years later, I found myself seated next to Tom at a Pentagon ceremony. I leaned over to him and said, "You know, we've been through a lot together, and while there have been times when I've attacked you and you've attacked me, and our relationship has been strained, we've gotten through all of this together. People will never really know what an accomplishment that was." Daschle nodded in agreement.

In his book, *Like No Other Time,* he wrote, "To Trent's credit, he was sometimes able to resist forces within his own party who wanted to close off all lines of communication between us many times." The point is, Tom and I made it work. And Republican senators were able to cautiously guide Bush's early legislation through Congress.

But just as the power-sharing agreement seemed to be working well, something came along and blindsided us.

On a late Friday afternoon in March 2001, Republican senator Jim Jeffords was lingering in the office of Democratic senator Chris Dodd of Connecticut. They were discussing a child care amendment, but Dodd noticed that Jeffords seemed to have another agenda. Changing the subject suddenly, he began talking about his friction with the Republican leadership. During a pause in the conversation, Jeffords quietly asked Dodd: "Do you think there is any room left for me in the Democratic Party?" Chris later told Daschle he could barely remain in his seat. Suddenly the Democrats had a chance to take over the Senate and establish Tom as majority leader.

In truth, raiding parties from both sides had been scouring the Senate practically since the day after the election, looking for dissatisfied members who might cross the aisle and explode the current balance of power. The Democrats were having serious discussions with the staffs of John McCain and Rhode Island's Lincoln Chafee, who was appointed to the Senate after his father, John Chafee, died in October 1999. "These were all very informal discussions but nonetheless very serious," Daschle later wrote. "And the reports I was getting by late March were that it looked as though something might happen with McCain or Chafee."

We had posses of our own trying to rope in a very dissatisfied Zell Miller of Georgia and Ben Nelson of Nebraska. We were rushing Miller in a very serious campaign, piloted by Senator Phil Gramm of Texas—a friend of the Georgia senator. (Miller later wrote a book, *A National Party No More,* about the deficiencies and erosion of the Democratic Party.)

None of this was new or newsworthy; both sides had been trawling for turncoats for half a century.

Daschle met with Jeffords once, then a second time. In their second meeting, Jeffords volunteered that he could never become a Democrat; the tenets of the party didn't jibe with his basic philosophy. But he *was* willing to become an independent, caucusing and voting with the Democrats. That would give the Democrats the majority and boost Daschle into the leader's office. Daschle didn't want Jeffords to get away, assigning his senators to stay with him from the time he arrived in the morning until the time he put on his coat to go home. If they could have camped out on his lawn, or in his living room, they would have.

We were just as busy. I met with Jeffords several times, as did Phil Gramm, Don Nickles, and Pete Domenici. We were in a particularly nasty bind. Debate was underway on Bush's budget, and the votes were lining up almost dead even. Jeffords knew how important he was, since the president's proposed $1.6 trillion tax cut—one of his key campaign promises—was coming up for a vote as part of the overall fiscal plan.

Several weeks earlier, Jeffords had inserted himself into the process by asking me to earmark $200 million for special education. After the Senate whittled the tax cut down to $1.35 trillion, I phoned Jeffords and offered him $180 million for special education. Seven days later, with Jeffords's vote, we passed the federal budget and the tax cuts without a vote to spare. Though the package included the funds for special education, it wasn't enough to halt his march into the arms of the Democrats.

Actually, I'd been handling Jeffords with kid gloves ever since we were colleagues in the House. He was always one of the most liberal Republicans, and probably voted with the Democrats more than any other member of our party. And he'd always had a habit of bartering his vote on crucial legislation for his own pet projects—from special childhood education to perks for the Vermont dairy industry. The haggling began shortly after I was elected House whip. Simply put, Jeffords was a loose cannon.

In fact, one of the reasons I founded the Singing Senators was to bring Jeffords aboard, which allowed me to get to know him better and put him more at ease. He told me soon after that he finally "felt a part of everything." And the move seemed to help his team-player instincts a bit: Every once in a while he would vote with us, and the quartet gave me opportunities to pressure him on a more personal basis. I remember one nip-and-tuck tax vote we faced late in the Clinton administration. The House had passed the measure, and we were down to about two votes in the Senate. The daughter of one of our senators was getting married, and he couldn't be there. We were likely to lose two or three more. I went to Senator John Chafee of Rhode Island. "John, without your vote we're going to lose."

"If it's that important, Trent, you'll have my vote," he said.

Now we were down to one vote.

I walked over and sat down next to Jeffords. "Jim, we have to have you this time or we're going to lose."

Jeffords was ready for me: "If you will add a billion dollars for a child health care program, I'll vote with you," he said.

"Whew," I told him. "I don't know what I can do, but I'll try."

Since the House had already passed its bill, I went see Speaker Dennis Hastert and leveled with him. "Mr. Speaker, here's the deal," I told him. "To get Jeffords, it's going to cost us a billion dollars."

"I trust you," Hastert answered. "I'll start the process." When the money was guaranteed on the House side, Jeffords voted with us, and we carried the Senate. Unfortunately, Clinton vetoed the bill, making the exercise moot.

In another case, I successfully bartered for his vote by increasing and extending grants to Vermont's dairy industry—a move that hurt the industry as a whole.

In the early months of George W. Bush's first term, the bartering continued. At one point, Jeffords wanted hundreds of millions of dollars for a child health program to be attached to another bill. The White House said no, but we needed Jeffords's vote. Cheney and I sat him down in the vice president's office and got him to vote with us. But by the time I got back to the Senate floor, he had done a 180-degree turn on me. "I can't do it," he said, and again asked for the money. I reminded him that it was impossible, and lit into him. "Jim, we're going to get the vote one way or the other. But we are not giving you any money." It got pretty ugly. And I told him, "Jim, this one is going to hurt, and I'm not going to forget it for a long time."

All of this is just to suggest that there was a history here. So, in retrospect, it probably shouldn't have surprised us that the Democrats were able to get Jeffords to leave the Republican Party. It came down to another Jeffords trade-off: Senator Harry Reid finally reeled him in by offering Jim his own senior position on the Senate Environment and Public Works Committee. With the Democrats in the majority, Jeffords would become chairman.

The consequences were huge. And I was stunned at first. I had raised money for Jeffords; in 2000, I had even campaigned for him in Vermont. Six months later, this was the way he repaid me. After his announcement, I tried repeatedly to talk him back into the fold. Fellow GOP moderates, including Olympia Snowe, Arlen Specter, and John Warner did the same.

I'd gotten to know his wife, Elizabeth Daley, fairly well. She was very liberal, but a very nice lady; I had campaigned with her in Vermont, and we'd become friends. So I appealed to her for help in stopping her husband from making such a dramatic move—a move that would affect Congress, the presidency, and the country. "I agree with you," she told me. "Jim should stay a Republican. But the decision is his."

I even appealed to his son, Leonard. "What's he doing here?" I asked. "Doesn't he realize that he's going to overturn the majority?"

"I'm with you," Leonard responded. In fact, he was disappointed; he didn't understand his dad's motives. But his hands were tied, too.

Jim's motives confused many members of the Republican Conference; most of them hadn't been privy to his incessant demands for money for projects to assuage his own constituents. Amazingly,

Jeffords even tried bargaining for budget concessions in meetings with both President Bush and Vice President Dick Cheney over his defection. He later told Phil Gramm he was angry that the president and the Senate, which had cut taxes by $1.35 trillion over ten years, couldn't produce major funds for education.

Later, when his autobiography was published, Jeffords told the press: "I voted against the budget agreement, but my disappointment was more profound than that one vote indicated. Here I was, the chairman of the Senate's education committee, and I couldn't find any additional money for education despite the fact that a major reform was about to take place." It was the year of Bush's "No Child Left Behind" initiative.

As far as I was concerned, Jim stuck it to his party and his country just to pick up another committee chairmanship. By sensing his dissatisfaction, Daschle and Reid engineered a major coup.

Phil Gramm summed it up in a press conference: "I think this had to do with one member who wanted things that we could not give him. Everyone tried to reach out to Jim Jeffords. I don't think anything could have been done here that would have changed things. I think Senator Lott deserves a gold medal for going the extra mile."

On May 24, the Democrats began preparing to take over. We were moving into what we thought was an uneventful summer, including the long August recess. We'd be back after Labor Day—in early September 2001.

# 15

# THE TERROR AND THE HEALING

At nine o'clock in the morning on Tuesday, September 11, 2001, I was shaving in the sunny bathroom of my Washington townhouse and still thinking about the mess Jim Jeffords had created. I'd returned from Mississippi the night before, excited about the remainder of the president's legislative agenda. He was ready for a second round of political rock 'n' roll. I was listening to radio station WTOP, as usual, when a reporter interrupted the broadcast for breaking news from New York. An airplane had crashed into one of the towers of the World Trade Center in lower Manhattan, he reported. But first reports suggested it was an accident, and that it involved some sort of small plane.

I paid little attention to the story as I dashed out the door and headed for the Capitol, only a few blocks away. A few minutes later I was at my desk in the majority leader's second-floor office at the Capitol, buried under the avalanche of paper that had piled up during the August recess. About fifteen or twenty minutes past the hour, a young staff aide, Corban Gunn from Ocean Springs, Mississippi, knocked insistently on the door and burst into the room uninvited. "Leader, you should turn on your television."

I flicked it on—and found myself looking at a panorama of fire, destruction, and death. Looking at those two towers on fire, and the explosions of the two commercial jets that crashed into them, I thought immediately, *This must be a terrorist act*. I watched transfixed for a few minutes, then turned to face the big bay window spread out behind the leader's table, where the Council of Trent deliberated, and noticed black plumes of smoke billowing up from the vast Pentagon complex on the Virginia side of the Potomac River.

Gunn had come into the room again, and this time I grabbed his arm. "You know, Corban, I think America is under attack. And we're next. Let's get out of here." I slipped behind my desk and hit the direct-dial button for Tom Daschle. "Tom, we're under attack. We've got to do something quick."

"I'll do it," Daschle interrupted. "I'll take care of everything in the next few minutes." Then he abruptly hung up the telephone.

As if on cue, my security men invaded the room. "Leader," one of them barked, "we've been ordered to evacuate immediately." I grabbed my briefcase and a sheaf of important papers, and followed security out the door into the chaos of the hallways. People were actually sprinting to the stairwells and heading down to the first floor, some of them taking the marble stairs two at a time.

The security details were taking the congressional leadership out of the building, up the street to the Capitol Police Command Post tower, where we were left milling around in a group. The walls were covered with outsize television sets and security monitors. One of the stations suddenly announced that a fourth plane full of terrorists was still in the air—United Airlines Flight 93. "It appears to be heading for Washington, D.C.," said the news anchor. The Capitol Police checked with the Federal Aviation Administration, who confirmed that United 93 was still airborne and still headed toward Washington.

"Has anybody ordered that plane shot down?" I asked. The police and some in the leadership looked at me as if I'd gone mad. One of them seemed to wince, as if I had slapped him in the face.

"I'm not kidding!" I yelled. "That plane is headed for the White House or the Capitol. They need to shoot it down!"

Less than five minutes later we learned that United 93 had gone down somewhere in Pennsylvania—thanks to the heroic acts, we later learned, of some of the passengers onboard.

Still, everything was in disarray, and no one seemed to be in charge. I tried to reach Tricia, who was in Jackson with Tyler, and Chet, who was supposed to be at a meeting on Capitol Hill that morning. But the cell phones got nothing but busy signals; the satellites were jammed. Within an hour I finally reached Tricia and was reassured about Chet, who'd barricaded himself in our house, trying to call and reassure his wife Diane in Kentucky. I also was able to contact my mother, then in her late eighties, to tell her I was all right and not to worry.

I was doing what came naturally. One of the things I've learned about myself over the years is that my immediate reactions to crises, tragedies, or other major events aren't always emotional; my initial reaction is usually that my mind starts turning, trying to assemble what I need to do. Sorrow or remorse can come later—in a day or a week or a year. On that September morning, I was thinking: Are we in the right place? What are the chances of further attacks? Should we be in session tomorrow?

Another hour passed and there we were, stuck indefinitely in the police tower. My security agent, former Air Force sergeant Clark Morton, said quietly that he thought I might be "very vulnerable." I looked around and saw he was right: We were sitting ducks, silhouettes behind the transparent glass of the Capitol Police tower, right in the center of Capitol Hill.

By that time, we knew that President Bush, Vice President Cheney, and Speaker of the House Dennis Hastert, who was next in the line of succession, were in secure places. We needed to be in more secure locations, too, certainly until the immediate emergency was declared over. "Get the car," I told Morton. "I'm going to Andrews Air Force Base." It had come to me in a flash: Andrews, which was on the Beltway southeast of Washington in suburban Maryland, was protected. Its communications lines were secure, and it was close enough that we could return from there to Congress in short order.

Don Nickles, my number two in the Senate leadership, jumped in with us, and we circled by my townhouse to pick up Chet. The traffic on the way to Andrews was heavy, but Morton drove aggressively and with great skill, using flashing lights and the occasional curb or sidewalk to get through what amounted to an obstacle course. In a secure office at Andrews I breathed a little easier, probably for the first time since those television images of the Twin Towers first crossed my line of vision. Using the Andrews phone bank, I checked on just about everyone I knew, and then settled down to ride it out.

My security officer ran into my room a short time later. "I just got the word, sir," he said. "You're being choppered out of here." What if I didn't want to go? I surely didn't think it was smart. But this was no time to countermand orders or to buck quick decisions made higher up the ladder—at that point, I suspected, by the vice president. Soon a military helicopter carrying Tom Daschle and his whip, Harry Reid, touched down at Andrews, scooped up Nickles and me, and immediately lifted off. The flight provided a spectacular view of something none of us could have anticipated a few hours earlier—the capital of our nation preparing for war. Ground was broken for the Pentagon's construction sixty years earlier—to this very day—and now that symbol of America's military might was burning beneath us, one corner of it collapsed like a cut wedding cake as one cave-in followed another. Flashes of electrical fires glowed deep within wreckage. Contingents of uniformed personnel dotted Capitol Hill and the streets of Washington seemed filled with military and police vehicles.

We were headed to an underground facility carved out of the cliffs in West Virginia or Virginia—a desolate place that seemed to consist of square, barren rooms shoved up against each other and stretching back beneath bedrock. At the time I was unable to get any real concept of its size or whereabouts; to this day I still do not know its exact location.

In the bunker, Daschle finally set up a senatorial command post and communications center. When he talked with the thirty-seven senators and representatives who were still crammed into a basement room at the Capitol Police Building, a majority of them wanted to go back into session. I took the microphone to express my disapproval: "The very thought of going back into session is outrageous. We don't know where this threat is coming from. We don't know what's going on with the investigation; we're totally in the dark. Let's see what's going on before we make a decision about going into session." That seemed to calm many of them down.

Finally, in the middle of the afternoon, Dick Cheney made a conference call to a number of groups, including us. He told us what he knew: that it was a terrorist attack; that it was carried out by al Qaida and directed by Osama bin Laden; that thousands were dead in New York, and hundreds more at the Pentagon. Though some concerns still existed, the immediate danger had abated. Then the vice president initiated three or four private conversations, including one with me. "Mr. Vice President, I want to go back to the Capitol," I told him. "That's where we belong."

"No, Trent," he said. Along with the rest of the leaders, I was grounded on the orders of the vice president. Imagine: the veep telling the leader of the Republican Conference in the Senate, *No, you can't go.* I urged him to keep us informed, because we felt very out of touch.

Later in the afternoon, I'd finally had enough. I told my ground security to leave for the Capitol, and *now*—"because I'm not spending the night here." I had this decision radioed back to the vice president's people, and the others pulling the strings. They finally relented and arranged to have us ferried back to the Capitol by helicopter.

Before we boarded the chopper to head back, Daschle, Dick Gephardt, the House minority leader, and I planned a press conference for about 5 P.M. on the Capitol steps to put us back in touch with the American people. But the senators and representatives we told about the press conference had other ideas. *We intend to be there, too,* they said. They didn't ask permission; they simply said, when you arrive, we'll be waiting.

And they were. In all, they were more than two hundred strong—Republicans and Democrats alike, waiting for us on the west front of the Capitol. Speaker Dennis Hastert had joined the leadership group on the steps, and the assembled members of Congress lined up behind us as Hastert and Daschle made brief remarks meant to reassure both our colleagues and the nation. Then, just as we started down the steps to leave, one congressman started quietly singing "God Bless America." Several others joined in, then scores, and finally the whole two hundred, singing out as the evening shadows played across our faces. This time, I did react: Our voices rising as one gave me the chills. *We're not going to be daunted by this,* I thought. *We are one America and we're here in defiance of these attacks. We'll be in session tomorrow and I'll be proud to be a part of it.*

\*   \*   \*

We were in session the next day, and in the weeks and months that followed. The representatives and senators who reconvened in September, October, and early November 2001 were as bipartisan and single-minded as any Congress in years, perhaps decades; there may have been nothing like it since the days after Pearl Harbor more than sixty years earlier. The outcome was a legislative treasure trove that helped launch President Bush's war on terrorism and usher in a new political era.

First came massive aid packages to New York and other cities, and to the airlines that suffered because of the September 11 attacks. There were some controversial provisions in the $15 billion aviation legislation and the $20 billion cities package, and we got into some minor partisan politics. But the dickering was minimal compared with the usual give-and-take on Capitol Hill. Daschle and I remained in close contact, so finally I picked up my direct line to his office. "Tom," I said. "Let's do it. And let's do it now. Let's you and I go to the floor, call up these bills, and pass 'em."

Tom thought for a couple of seconds, then responded as I knew he would: "Let's do it. I'll meet you down on the floor." We acted like leaders and we acted together. I remember telling the Senate, "We're not going to nit-pick this bill. We're going to take it up right now and pass it." As I recall, it was the resolution to authorize retaliation against those who had attacked us—the Afghanistan resolution. Within minutes it was done, on a vote of ninety-eight to zero. We passed legislation for aid to the victims' families, to cities and states, to the aviation industry that had taken such a hit that day. In fact, we saved the industry by understanding the problem and paying to keep the planes in the air. The aid included $5 billion in direct payments for losses stemming from September 11, and $10 billion in loan guarantees from a new Air Transportation Stabilization Board.

In short order, the Senate then took up the Patriot Act—based on the rough draft of a bill written by Attorney General John Ashcroft and aggressively lobbied by the White House senior staff and President Bush himself. After rewrites and redrafts by a handful of senators, including myself, the measure gave the CIA and the FBI extra authority to track terrorists—something they had needed for years. It made it easier for the agents to seize electronic and medical data on suspected terrorists, with less red tape, and to obtain quick national search warrants to seize electronic evidence. The president called it "a sure fire weapon against terrorists operating both here and in other countries." As far as I was concerned, he was preaching to the choir.

In the course of researching the bill, I was shocked that under the old laws the FBI was forbidden in many cases from talking to the CIA at all. Federal laws were such that the law enforcement side of the government was kept separate from the intelligence side. We had to sweep these requirements out of the federal codes, and give the two agencies authority to communicate more aggressively.

The most controversial section of the Patriot Act made it easier for agents to obtain authority for wiretaps. A lot of people, including libertarians and some conservatives, were concerned about those provisions. But it was good legislation, and to this day I wouldn't change a word of it. Liberals were especially upset, and some of them tried to make a scene on the floor, but we had the wind at our backs: the momentum was so great that they couldn't stop the bill from being signed into law.

I recall walking onto the floor of the Senate during these weeks of bipartisan comity and being encouraged by the attitudes of the senators. Sure, they disagreed frequently along party lines, but they sat down with each other and worked it out. The buzz on the floor reminded me of the House decades earlier, when it was a pleasure to be whip because the representatives acted like professionals, differing among themselves, but without the party hatred that so dominates the legislative scene today. For once, even though it was brought on by an atrocity, we were not Republicans or Democrats. We were Americans.

The American people saw that, too, and gave Congress an 84 percent approval rating—the highest such rating ever posted. It was something to savor—and something that wouldn't last.

During this period, the Senate was drawn even more personally into the war on terrorism by two episodes that will remain vivid reminders of that fateful autumn for the rest of my days on this Earth. In late September, Tom Daschle and I led a large group of senators on a trek to Ground Zero, until then best known to us as indelible images on a television screen and word pictures from others who had been there.

The sky was slate-colored and rainy on that morning of September 20, when we boarded an Amtrak train for the three-hour trip from Washington to New York City. We settled in and steeled ourselves for what we knew would be one of the most painful experiences in our lives. There wasn't much levity on this Senate journey. For the most part we were silent, wondering how we would react to what we saw and how those working in and around Ground Zero would react to us.

A bus took us to the Hudson River and up to the ramps of a boat, where a weary Mayor Rudy Giuliani waited to greet us. It was a quiet salute, marked by tears on both sides. Then the boat pulled away from the pier and headed down river toward the columns of black smoke that spread across the sky.

It was upon us before we knew it. And we stepped onto a huge pad of melted asphalt to find the wreckage of the once-glimmering World Trade Center, crushed now into a horseshoe-shaped behemoth of twisted metal and crushed shards of grass, I felt a mixture of profound sadness and deep anger welling up inside me. The scene was horrifying, a battlefield on hallowed ground in a war we had to fight and win.

Both the firemen and the police at Ground Zero greeted us not as interlopers, but as men and women who could help our nation deal with the terrorists. We had lunch with them and other workers, who told us, with dry-eyed composure, of their comrades and friends—the brave souls who perished when the towers collapsed. It was humbling.

But perhaps the most memorable part of our brief journey was the smell that spread out from Ground Zero and permeated much of the city. As we headed back up the Hudson, the smell seemed to follow us. I couldn't get free of it—even on the train. And I'll never forget it. The trip would succeed in putting the antiterrorism bills into a real and personal perspective. The burden from some of that pain was now on our shoulders.

Less than a month later, Grant Leslie, an aide to the majority leader, began to open a small letter in the mailroom and in the process released a cloud of fine white powder. The powder drifted through the mailroom and settled on her skirt and shoes. Bret Wincup, the intern standing next to her, found his jacket and trousers dusted with the powder as well.

Leslie sat frozen at her seat, aware of what the danger could be and afraid to move and risk the danger of further contamination. Someone else on Daschle's staff contacted the Capitol Police, and an officer arrived within a few minutes. Instructing everyone to stay where they were, he directed Leslie to softly set the envelope down on top of the small knoll of anthrax at her feet.

The mailroom and parts of the Hart Office Building's interior were immediately quarantined, as policemen, medics, nurses, and eventually scientists from the Federal Bureau of Investigation and the Centers for Disease Control arrived at the scene.

Daschle called me thirty minutes after the discovery. Both of us understood that the spray of poison would soon close down Hart—not just part of the building, but all of it. None of us knew how far and wide the trace amounts could spread. Suddenly, the possibility of a successful biological attack against Congress became quite real. No one was seriously injured this time, but we were plainly vulnerable. A small dusting of powder had spread to the furthest corners of Daschle's office suite and beyond. The next afternoon, evidence showed that the powder also had drifted into the adjacent Senate offices of Wisconsin Democrat Russ Feingold. Two members of his staff tested positive for exposure to the biological poison. Still a third letter was buried in sacks of mail to Vermont senator Patrick Leahy, although it didn't turn up until November 16, in a barrel of mail seized by the FBI and quarantined a month earlier. The letter bore the same postmark and handwriting as the terrorist who originated Daschle's envelope.

On Wednesday, October 17, I met with Daschle and we drew up the plans for evacuation of the Hart Office Building for an indefinite period of time. Decontamination experts from the Environmental Protection Agency had begun their work. But Hart was the largest structure ever faced by EPA's scientific teams. Over the next forty-eight hours, fifty senators and thirteen committees from Hart were relocated. The operation involved setting up temporary offices at a new building, connecting six hundred new telephone lines, seventy-three new routers, and more than seven hundred personal computers and one hundred printers. The displaced senators found homes in offices throughout the Capitol. Some senators, such as California's Dianne Feinstein and Barbara Boxer, converted their hideaways in the Capitol Building into staff offices.

Others bunked with other colleagues. Nebraska senator Chuck Hagel made room in his own relatively small suite for his Republican colleague, Ben Nighthorse Campbell of Colorado.

As the autumn deepened, the EPA prepared to fumigate the Hart Building with thousands of gallons of chlorine gas—the same substance that had been used successfully against Legionnaire's disease. But no building the size of Hart, nine stories high, with more than one million cubic feet of floor space, had ever been decontaminated before. In December, the EPA's hunch about the gas paid off. Daschle's offices and the remainder of the building were anthrax-free. In all, twenty-three people had been directly exposed to the biological agent, and all were cured by antibiotics or the new "anthrax vaccine" the EPA spent $20 million to develop.

After the turn of the new year, three thousand displaced workers moved back home.

# 16

# PLAYING DEFENSE, PLAYING OFFENSE

One of the things that contributed to the bipartisan atmosphere through the fall and winter after 9/11 was the way the congressional leadership—Republican and Democrat—were able to engage top officials in the executive branch, starting at the very top. Beginning in early October, Speaker Dennis Hastert, Majority Leader Tom Daschle, House Minority Leader Dick Gephardt, and I had weekly breakfasts with President Bush in the dining room just off the Oval Office.

It was generally chilly and barely daylight when I left for these 7 A.M. breakfasts. Leaving my townhouse at 6:30, I drove past all the great monuments that make Washington, D.C., so special. The Capitol rose from the early morning mist off the Potomac, the Washington Monument towered over the other end of the Ellipse, and you could see the Jefferson Memorial in the distance. Then there was the White House itself. For this boy from Pascagoula, Mississippi, it was still an awesome experience. These were serious and momentous times in the history of our country, and I felt humbled and honored to be a part of them.

I always arrived early, five or ten minutes before seven. My three congressional colleagues had the same idea, so the four of us would sit in the anteroom, waiting to be summoned to breakfast with the president. At seven sharp, the door to the Oval Office would open and the president would greet us. Sometimes the vice president was there, and occasionally National Security Advisor Condoleezza Rice—now our secretary of state—or CIA Director George Tenet. Usually, Nick Calio, senior advisor to the president for congressional relations, was there as well. He would usher us quickly into the room for breakfast.

We would take our seats, Hastert and I on one side, Daschle and Gephardt on the other. The president sat at one end of the table; when the vice president was present, he would take the other. We would order breakfast quickly, and then the president would get down to business.

In an incredible tour de force, Bush would bring us up to date on the war on terror—what the CIA knew, the latest threat assessments, the hunt for al Qaeda operatives and Osama bin Laden himself. The president conducted this briefing solo, using no notes. As we ate breakfast, we would ask questions in response to his presentation on terror. Then, after the first thirty minutes, we moved on to domestic issues—the anthrax investigations, various pieces of legislation, other matters—and by eight sharp, we were done.

These meetings offered me a glimpse of a George W. Bush I had never seen before, and it was plenty impressive. This was a president who was engaged, informed, passionate, who knew what he wanted to accomplish for America. I had never seen him better.

\*   \*   \*

Though the structure of bipartisanship we built after the World Trade Center attacks was strong and sincere, shortly before Christmas cracks began to appear. The Democrats and Republicans suddenly parted company when President Bush's $20 billion economic stimulus package came out of committee. Here was truly an issue where both parties had serious philosophical differences.

Put simply, Daschle and crew wanted the maximum in unemployment benefits for American workers suffering because of 9/11; they also wanted Medicaid benefits for jobless workers and their families. We wanted more tax cuts, and suggested a one-month vacation from the Social Security payroll tax for every American earning a paycheck. We preferred somewhat less in cash payments to the unemployed.

We were miles apart.

Bush's plan was clearly designed to get the economy going again. There was no question that *something* was needed. The economy had gone into a precipitous dive after 9/11 and was still nosing downward.

But I didn't like some of the precedents the president loaded onto his bill. And I found that, on this at least, I couldn't back him.

The president's plan, submitted in October, called for an extension of thirteen weeks of unemployment benefits in the states hit hardest by the al Qaeda attacks, Medicaid for uninsured workers and their families, and a series of tax cuts to individuals and businesses to spur job growth. There also was a plan to send a direct check to every taxpayer. Bush seemed to be trying to satisfy everyone, Republicans and Democrats alike. But I was concerned about the total cost, and whether the program would have much immediate impact.

As the holiday recess neared, Daschle informed his colleagues that he wasn't going to let the stimulus plan come to the floor; he intended to adjourn Congress before any vote on the plan could be taken. When informed of this, Bush used his weekly radio address of December 1 to urge both parties to end their floor fight and vote on the bill. "The holiday is about on us," Bush concluded.

I kept the Republican Conference lined up against the bill, and made no move to fight Daschle. For the first time since tragedy struck, we stalled out on a bill because of our highly partisan differences. Later, we worked out some of the details that had bothered me—mainly, the nature of the onetime payment to taxpayers—and passed the bill in early 2002. But the 9/11 honeymoon was beginning to end.

When the Senate returned to session in January 2002, we were still getting along better than we had before the attacks. But it was also clear that we had entered the 2002 political season. Though the election was still eight months away, both parties had begun their gargantuan struggles—the Democrats to hold onto the majority that Jim Jeffords had given them, and the Republicans to recapture the majority.

The Democrats rolled out a series of measures with the November election written all over them. We dropped into a defensive crouch to stop what amounted to campaigning in Congress, and I suddenly rediscovered the simple pleasures of being a minority leader. I no longer had to go over each bill that came up, to study and schedule amendments, or to produce results in an institution that too often makes it all but impossible to achieve them.

I'd learned all the rich tricks of the trade when I was a minority leader in the House. I knew what you could do to gum up the works, or to move the agenda like clockwork when it suited you. By the fall of 2002, with the help of President George W. Bush, we were giving the Democrats absolute fits. We were making them dance to our agenda, successfully enough that they helped us pass two big legislative initiatives—and lost control of the Senate while they were at it.

The first issue was establishing a Department of Homeland Security. The idea for the new department, truth to tell, came from a Senate Democrat—Joe Lieberman—but he hadn't been able to find adequate backing in his own party in early 2002. Still, it had seemed a good enough proposal for many of us to hang onto the paperwork for future reference. Then, on July 2, I got hit with the proposal by a higher authority. President Bush was hosting the annual White House barbecue before everyone broke for home and a long Independence Day weekend, and he invited Speaker Hastert and me to a private meeting about an hour before the festivities were to begin. As we settled around a table in the president's private quarters, Bush got right to the point: He told us the nation needed a cabinet-level department for homeland security. "I want all of these security agencies combined into one large unit," he said, "and I'm going to announce it this afternoon."

Hastert and I assured Bush that the congressional Republicans would line up behind him. The Democrats had tried to run with the ball on this one, only to fumble and lose it. Before it was over, the history of the Homeland Security legislation would influence the 2002 congressional elections, and help to put the power back into our hands.

When we came back from the summer recess in 2002, the Homeland Security bill was front and center, and it devoured most of the Senate's time right up to Election Day. One of the critical points of contention between the White House and Republicans on the one hand, and Democrats on the other, had to do with organized labor. The Democrats wanted to open up the department to unions and union rules, but Bush wouldn't have it.

Union rules have no place in national security, the president said. "We can't protect the country on nine-to-five schedules." Our message in the fall was that the president was pushing for what the country desperately needed—strong homeland security—and the Democrats were obstructing it. The bill stalled out, hurting Democrats and helping us. It was the main reason we defeated Georgia's Democratic senator Max Cleland, for one, and retook control of the Senate.

We finally passed a more dressed-up version of the bill on November 19, following the election recess. The resulting measure—which incorporated twenty-two agencies within the one Department of Homeland Security—was the most sweeping reorganization of the federal government since 1947, when President Harry S. Truman merged the War and Navy departments. It was the first new department since the Veterans Affairs Department was created in 1989. Included in the consolidation were the U.S. Coast Guard, the Border Patrol, the Secret Service, and two new agencies: the Immigration and Customs Enforcement Bureau, and the Transportation Security Administration.

The combined budget of this governmental conglomerate was about $27 billion a year, and Congress allocated $1.2 billion in 2002 just to pay for the reorganization itself. President Bush gained more personal control over the security agencies in the reshuffle, and appointed former Pennsylvania governor Tom Ridge, who had served as his homeland security adviser, to head the new department. It's still going through the difficulties any brand new bureaucracy suffers, but I believe our domestic defenses are better for its creation.

The second big issue for us was one familiar to George W. Bush's two predecessors—and in fact, to earlier presidents as well. In the summer of 2002, even as the first moves on a new Homeland Security Department were under way, the president began lobbying for an open-ended resolution empowering him to wage war on Iraq.

Members of Congress had heard rumors that the president might be eager to take on Saddam Hussein. And Bush had made clear his intentions to wage war on Iraq in several of our private meetings. But, as late summer rolled around, I didn't feel the administration was moving toward this goal with the decisiveness that would be needed to sell Congress.

He couldn't attack Iraq in the spring of 2003 unless he finessed a resolution through Congress in the early fall. And he was far from that goal in early September. Neither he nor Dick Cheney had said anything in public on the subject for months.

I'd been privy to some of the early presidential briefings on the possibility of a war with Iraq. I knew that the president wanted to go in like lightning, remove Saddam and his family from power, and replace his brutal dictatorship with democracy. Bush wasn't interested in half measures.

Secretary of State Colin Powell and former secretary of state James A. Baker III had been giving frequent speeches on Iraq, but their words seemed at odds, or at least some variance, with what I thought Bush had in mind. If Powell and Baker were surrogates for the president, they were both seeming to indicate that more control should be placed in the hands of the United Nations. But Bush had suggested to me that he wanted to take a less fettered approach to deposing the Iraqi dictator.

Baker failed to note that Iraq had changed, becoming more militarily aggressive, and that despite a decade of work the UN had yet to fully inspect Hussein's weapons of mass destruction. The president was considerate in answering his dad's secretary of state, skillfully using the kind of diplomatic language that Baker himself had once employed so successfully. "The comments are part of a very constructive debate, and I welcome them," he said in one response to a question about Baker's remarks. Bush may have been less tolerant of similar statements from his own secretary of state. Powell appeared to be urging complete coordination with the United Nations. And both Baker and Powell hinted that it might be best to allow weapons inspectors one last try before throwing our military might against Saddam's desert dictatorship.

Because of the president's relative public silence, it might have seemed on the surface that Baker and Powell were speaking for the administration. I felt I needed to intervene. My personal and political relationships with both Bush and Cheney had been enriched by our many breakfast meetings and other intelligence briefings; they made a point of keeping me in the loop and abreast of Bush's latest thinking. Meanwhile, Tricia and I had developed a personal relationship with the president and Laura. He had been to our house in Pascagoula, and I had visited their ranch in Crawford, Texas. They had entertained us in the private quarters of the White House, making it a far closer bond than I'd had with any other chief executive I had known.

On a Sunday in mid-August, I called Cheney from Chet's house in Lexington, Kentucky.

"Dick, I think you may have a big problem here with public perceptions of a possible Iraq War," I told him. "The case hasn't been made as to why we should do it, and, furthermore, the administration seems to be speaking through surrogates."

"Don't worry," said the vice president. "We're about to fix all of that. Just hold on."

Nine days later, on August 27, 2002, Cheney arrived in Nashville, Tennessee, for the 103rd annual meeting of the Veterans of Foreign Wars. Police and other security brought him to the gate of the convention hall and whisked him inside. Cheney was running late, so he jumped right into his speech—the text of which had been completed by his speechwriters that morning. First, he condemned Saddam Hussein for personally bringing a prospective war down on himself by kicking out the arms inspectors in 1998, by not letting them return, and by continuing to stockpile weapons of mass destruction. Saddam was a clear and present danger, the vice president insisted, and he quoted the words of his boss, the president: "Time is not on our side." In so many words, the vice president said that disarmament and regime change in Iraq were essential to the national security interests of the United States. He employed much the same rhetoric that President Bush had spoken on horseback as he dealt briefly with reporters crowded at his Crawford Ranch a month earlier.

Cheney played the nuclear card. "We know that Saddam has resumed his efforts to acquire nuclear weapons. Among other sources, we've gotten this from the firsthand testimony of defectors—including Saddam's own son-in-law, who was subsequently murdered at Saddam's direction. Many of us are convinced that he will acquire nuclear weapons fairly soon."

He also highlighted the dangers of Iraq's proliferation of weapons, citing Henry Kissinger's recent warning that "The imminence of the increase in weapons of mass destruction, the huge dangers this involves, the rejection of a viable inspection system and the demonstrated hostility of Saddam Hussein combine to produce an imperative for preemptive action." America, Cheney insisted, would not "live at the mercy of terrorists or terror regimes."

Cheney also described Iraq as a haven for terrorists, and for the first time described "a plan of action to bring democracy to that country" after Saddam was forcibly removed. "We need to get him before he becomes any stronger," the vice president concluded. Those words brought down the house at the VFW and led the newscasts that night—attracting more attention than the president's own actions that day. As Tricia often says, "Dick Cheney is the E. F. Hutton of American politics. He doesn't say much. But when he does, everybody listens."

The president followed Cheney with several key campus addresses designed to shine more light on Iraq's misdeeds. I understood why Bush had focused so intently on going to war with this rogue nation on the Persian Gulf. There might not be a direct tie between 9/11 and al Qaeda, but the president's plan was plainly an outgrowth of the national tragedy. This president had embarked upon a clear course—going after terrorists wherever they were and the nations that harbored and supported them. I was included in many of the intelligence briefings leading up to our actions in both Afghanistan and Iraq; they included the briefings about WMD—the new shorthand for weapons of mass destruction—by George Tenet and the president himself. I concluded that we needed to take Saddam out—indeed, that we had made a mistake by leaving the job undone during the 1991 Gulf War.

From what I heard in the briefings, I had every reason to believe that Saddam Hussein still had stockpiles of chemical weapons, and had enlarged his capacity to launch them over long distances. And I was convinced that he was continuing his quest to acquire nuclear weapons.

At the request of Bush and Cheney, I became involved early on in the drive to pass the President's Iraq War resolution—the basic text of which the White House sent over to the Senate and the House in early September. I went to work, facilitating the rewrites in the Senate of the resolution that would be put before both bodies of Congress. But my group wasn't alone: Senator Joseph Biden, Democrat of Delaware, and two Republican senators, Richard Lugar of Indiana and Chuck Hagel of Nebraska, were drafting a version of their own.

The day I returned to Washington after the August recess, Jim Baker offered a bit of very public advice on the Op-Ed page of the *New York Times*. He urged the president to slow down and take his plea to the full United Nations, "in order to gain a broad groundswell of world support," much as his father had done at the start of the Gulf War more than a decade earlier. Baker's plea was troubling. I knew that the president wasn't interested in having any war with Iraq partially directed from the chaotic halls of the United Nations. He was seeking the unilateral power to wage war on Iraq and remove Saddam Hussein. And he wanted convincing bipartisan authorization from Congress.

During the second week in September, we had some tense moments at one of our regular White House breakfast meetings. Senate Majority Leader Tom Daschle made it very clear that he would not support the war resolution. In the Senate, we would have to troll for Democratic votes without the blessing of the Democratic Caucus's leadership. But Dick Gephardt, the Democrats' minority leader, said that he would honor the president's request and support a resolution.

House Speaker Dennis Hastert and I began to work aggressively with Gephardt to make the language strong enough. Meanwhile, Bush and Cheney made a special request: They wanted me to see what I could do to kill the Lugar-Biden-Hagel bill, and make certain it didn't pollute the strong language they required.

"We are disturbed by the expansive language in the proposed congressional action," said Biden when he introduced his alternative measure. Rather than authorize the president to "use all means that he determines to be appropriate, including force, to defend the national security interests of the United States," as the draft language in our resolution stated, Biden, Lugar, and Hagel would have limited the authorization of military force to the destruction of WMD installations in Iraq. They also were proposing a two-step process: First, the United States should try to secure a tough new resolution from the United Nations calling for thorough inspections and authorizing enforcement of the inspections by force if necessary. Failing that new UN resolution, they would have required the president to demonstrate to Congress that the danger posed by Iraq's WMD programs was such that only military action was adequate to the task.

In other words, they wanted to require a new resolution before the president would be allowed to declare war—this after Saddam Hussein had ignored a dozen previous resolutions. President Bush reacted angrily: "My question is: What's changed? Why would Congress want to weaken a resolution? I don't want a resolution such as this—that ties my hands." Bush's order to me grew more emphatic: *Derail the Biden legislation,* he directed me, *and make sure its language never sees the light of day again.*

I was already working with a special Senate committee to draft language for the Bush legislation, a group that included Alaska's Ted Stevens and Virginia's John Warner. I was especially concerned about Lugar, then the ranking member of the Senate Foreign Relations Committee. When I called Lugar to ask about his concerns, he told me he was worried that the authorization preferred by the president had a Vietnam-era ring to it. And he wanted to make sure whatever we passed would have a mantle of broad bipartisan support.

"Dick, you know me well enough to know that I'm not going to be a party to locking you out," I said. "But I want you to know that I'm very concerned about the Biden initiative and where the language is going."

"I'm not out to cause mischief," Lugar replied. "And I want to do the right thing, but I cannot guarantee you that I will pull my support from the Biden language." I told him I wanted him with us on this one, and we agreed to talk again in a couple of hours.

In that subsequent conversation, Dick said he wasn't going to be "the skunk in the garden party." I immediately put him on the language task force that had begun meeting.

Within a week, the task force had completed the key clauses in the resolution: "The President is authorized to use the Armed Forces of the United States as he determines to be necessary and appropriate in order to (1) defend the national security of the United States against the continuing threat posed by Iraq; and (2) enforce all relevant United Nations Security Council resolutions regarding Iraq."

At around the same time, Joe Lieberman of Connecticut indicated that he wanted to get on board, but first he needed to see the proposal's language. I dispatched Senators John Warner and John McCain to carry the resolution to Lieberman and try to get his official endorsement. After a quick study of the proposal, Lieberman said he was with us. In Gephardt and Lieberman, we had the Democratic leadership we needed.

We took the proposal public with a press conference in the White House Rose Garden, announcing the terms of the Iraq War resolution and unveiling the new bipartisan team that was now supporting it. Gephardt told the press, "We disagree on many domestic issues. But this is the most important thing we do. This should not be about politics. We have to do what is right for the security of our nation and the safety of all Americans."

On October 9, Biden dropped plans to present his alternative to the Senate. The next day, we guided the Senate to a 77–23 authorization for Bush to wage war on Iraq and Saddam Hussein. Several hours earlier, the House of Representatives approved the identical measure by a vote of 296–133.

As part of the deal with the House, Bush bent to Democratic wishes and pledged to certify to Congress—before any military strike, if feasible, or within forty-eight hours of a U.S. attack—that diplomatic and other peaceful means alone had been inadequate to protect American from Saddam's weapons of mass destruction.

Some of the intelligence briefings we were getting from Bush and Tenet were getting to be pretty scary. I remember talk that Iraq was developing unmanned aerial vehicles for use as carriers of biological weapons. This, and other intelligence break-throughs, had convinced me that the Iraq War resolution was mandatory. Even today, knowing what I know now, I would have voted to give the president the authority to make war. The danger was simply too great.

# 17

# FORTY WORDS: THE STROM THURMOND AFFAIR

On the evening of December 4, 2002, I sat at my desk, sharpening a speech for Strom Thurmond's one hundredth birthday celebration. Snow from an approaching blizzard was already falling as I thumbed through the decades of jokes that had adhered to the oldest and longest serving senator in U.S. history.

Actually, Washington had been toasting Thurmond for almost a month. There had been private and public luncheons, White House ceremonies, and senatorial tributes. Proclamations had been written and recited; trophies and certificates overflowed his desk.

Finally, the Republican Conference put together a party where his peers—the men and women he'd worked closely with for almost fifty years—would offer their tributes. When I was invited to cohost the event with former senator Bob Dole, I considered it a command performance.

For two decades, the legendary lawmaker from South Carolina had treated me almost like a son, particularly when I was a newly elected senator. As I grappled with rungs on the leadership ladder in the Senate, Strom helped to pull me up. During those early years, he frequently stopped by my desk to inquire about my needs and priorities. With his shock of red hair and booming voice, Senator Thurmond created a stir wherever he went, and his attention helped anoint me as a comer.

On the Senate floor, when the occasion called for it, Thurmond's polite banter could give way to fiery oratory. When the Violent Crime Control and Law Enforcement Act of 1994 was being debated, for instance, I watched Strom rise to deliver an emotional speech about the dangers running rampant on American streets and of the horrifying murder rates blighting our largest cities. As he spoke, you could almost hear the cries of wounded children and the rattle of bullets in the night.

A respectful silence greeted his oration as one senator after another began rethinking their stands on the Omnibus Crime Bill. Senator Thurmond was on hand when President Clinton signed it into law on September 13, 1994.

While Strom Thurmond's centenarian status, astounding forty-eight-year senatorial tenure, and power base in the Deep South had all contributed to his legend, he was also lauded for a personal and philosophical transformation. Over the years, he had transformed himself from one of the nation's leading defenders of segregation to an unalloyed supporter of civil rights legislation.

During his first term in the Senate, Thurmond had filibustered for five hours and seven minutes in an effort to block the Civil Rights Bill of 1958. Two years before, he had been the author of the "Southern Manifesto," through which nineteen Southern senators and sixty-four representatives sought to prevent the Supreme Court from mandating integrated schools in the South. President Harry Truman labeled him the "nation's foremost enemy of equality." But the Kennedy and Johnson years had begun to chip away at these segregationist views.

Naturally, I didn't know this earlier Strom Thurmond. He was already eighty-seven years old when I came to the Senate in 1989, and by then he was fully committed to the minorities in his native South Carolina. In return, he received 46 percent of the state's African American vote.

As the years went by, and Strom grew more feeble, my affection for him increased. During the inevitable monotonous lulls in Senate business, I always sought him out. We would huddle together as he recounted tales of old South Carolina and spun proud anecdotes about his children.

But the years weighed upon him as he neared one hundred, and he slipped easily into bouts of depression. I often rushed over to lighten his mood. One way to brighten his spirits instantly was to spin jokes about his run for president in 1948 on the breakaway Dixiecrat ticket, which opposed integration in any form. I was only seven when Strom was barnstorming the South, and I remembered nothing about the election or the furor that surrounded it. So I'd kid him, "You know, you would have made a great president." His eyes would light up, and you could sense that he savored the compliment.

I never mentioned the segregationist platform he supported half a century earlier, and neither did he. I was aware that he had evolved over the years, broadening into a minority-oriented politician. But we didn't talk about that either. To Strom, inequality was part of his discarded past—an ideology he had abandoned.

When the planning began for this senatorial party for Senator Thurmond, the Republicans had just been reelected to the majority, and I was exuberant about the opportunity to reassume the reins as majority leader. Since Bob Dole, my predecessor, would be sharing the rostrum, the speeches were bound to be competitive. I wanted my speech to bring down the house.

My longtime press aide, Susan Irby, prepared a semi-serious draft peppered with many of the tried-and-true Strom Thurmond jokes that had followed the senator for decades, along with a few new jokes fashioned for this celebration. I was ready.

On Thursday, December 5, Thurmond's one hundredth birthday, Washington was snowed in after the worst storm in a decade. I plowed through snow banks to the banquet rooms of the Dirksen Senate Office Building, where I found a standing-room-only crowd of revelers. The tone of the event was irreverent from the start; it was more of a roast than a tribute. A blowsy Marilyn Monroe imitator opened the show by spoofing the movie star's birthday serenade to President John F. Kennedy. Then she planted a crimson kiss on Thurmond's forehead and sashayed from the room. Bob Dole was up next, with a typically sarcastic speech packed with just about every joke in the Strom Thurmond repertoire—including all the ones my staff had used in mine.

I was left with little to say. Irby's paragraphs about longevity and about Thurmond's place as a role model played well. But I was hard pressed to come up with a batch of fresh compliments and gags to match Dole's performance. In my haste, I repeated a joke that Dole had just delivered. Then, in desperation, I started talking off the cuff. In closing, I revived a bit I'd done back in 1980 at a campaign rally for Ronald Reagan in Mississippi. I turned toward Senator Thurmond and repeated it: "I want to say this about my state. When Strom Thurmond ran for president, Mississippians voted for him. And if the rest of the country had followed our lead, we wouldn't have had all these problems over the years either."

The stag-party mood all but drowned out those forty words. There was no stunned silence as I concluded, and no gasp from a rapt audience—though both would be reported thousands of times during the next three weeks. As we piled into heavy winter coats and boots, none of us noticed the C-Span cameras aimed at the rostrum.

Friday morning was calm, just another business day. The storm to come wasn't even on the horizon. In the middle of the afternoon, I took a ride with CNN's Jonathan Karl on the spiffy underground monorail line that connects the Senate office buildings with the Capitol. In an interview for the network's series, "Subway to the Capitol," Karl didn't mention the gala the previous night. He was more interested in my imminent return as Senate majority leader. Within a week, such innocent questions and equally innocent answers would seem supremely ironic.

Karl asked: "Some of your friends up here have said that they noticed that you seemed happier personally because you no longer had the responsibility of trying to run this narrow majority. Is it a lot of headaches? This is a pretty tough place to run?"

I answered: "I've been smiling an awful lot lately, Jonathan. So I'm pretty happy about it."

The journalist continued: "Have you been gloating at all?"

"I haven't had time to gloat," I said. "This is a very humbling experience."

When the segment aired that afternoon on Judy Woodruff's *Inside Politics*, CNN didn't mention my remarks at the Thurmond testimonial. But the fallout had started.

That night, at the close of PBS's *Washington Week*, moderator Gwen Ifill ended her broadcast by playing just the audio portion of the forty-word statement. Then she asked: "That detail brings us to tonight's little history quiz—something we call, 'What Was He

Thinking?' Drop us an e-mail. Tell us what Trent Lott meant by that statement."

My staff took note of this isolated reference, but disregarded it. "She just doesn't seem to know what to make of it," one staffer counseled me.

But in the lower reaches of journalism, a small fire had been set. In the past few years, the growing number of so-called news sites on the Internet had been the catalyst for a number of political free-for-alls, including the Lewinsky scandal. But they had never shaped and perverted a story so grotesquely as they did mine. Much later, after I resigned as Republican majority leader, the *New York Post* proclaimed in a banner headline: THE INTERNET TAKES ITS FIRST SCALP.

The online conflagration actually had begun at 1:54 A.M. on Friday morning, when Timothy Noah, a columnist for the Microsoft Network's magazine *Slate,* posted a story headlined: BLURTED OUT CONVICTION OF THE WEEK: TRENT LOTT. WHAT'S A LITTLE SEGREGATION AMONG FRIENDS? Along with a string of derogatory words, Noah offered sights and sounds. With a press of a computer mouse, Internet browsers could see the C-Span video of my remarks. One more click, and you could hear the audio of Strom Thurmond's 1948 Dixiecrat acceptance speech.

Noah didn't need to write much more. With some fancy audiovisual aids, he had linked my words at the gala to a set of fifty-year-old virulent remarks I was hearing for the first time. His column was labeled, appropriately, "Chatterbox."

About four hours later, ABC journalists Mark Halperin, Elizabeth Wilner, and Marc Ambinder debated the remarks and their supposed meaning on *The Note,* the influential political journal on ABC.com. In addition to the text of my comments, the journalists added: "There is, as you may recall, an election in the Bayou tomorrow, where African American turnout is crucial to the chances of Democratic incumbent Senator Mary Landrieu. Maybe Lott was being jocular. But a plain reading of what he said might generate some anger." (Landrieu was in a runoff election, which she won.)

The network journalists alerted Wade Henderson of the Leadership Conference on Civil Rights. And he responded: "Thurmond ran for president as a Dixiecrat, a segregationist. He gave the longest filibuster in history to try and stop the passage of the Civil Rights Act. In his statement today, Lott also embraced those dubious achievements. Lott had betrayed his role as the majority leader of all Americans." Within hours of my off-the-cuff praise of an aged and dying colleague, a band of journalists was tarring and feathering me as a racist.

A month later, after all the damage had been done, the *Online Journalism Review*, a publication of the Annenberg Center for Communication at the University of Southern California, proclaimed, "Trent Lott Got Bloggered." They were right: The Web logs, and the bloggers who write their columns, did target me. "The mainstream media had to swallow its pride and follow the Internet on the story," the *Online Journalism Review* continued. *Time* also credited the "hum of Internet bloggers who were posting their outrage and compiling rap sheets of Lott's earlier comments."

At the time, however, all of this was invisible to me. As Saturday dawned, the only clue that the story remained alive—if barely—came in the form of a small story by Thomas B. Edsall on page A6 of the *Washington Post*. Ron Bonjean, one of my press aides, had received a call from Edsall late the previous day, asking whether I had used any "code words" in my Thurmond remarks. Bonjean and Susan Irby, my communications director, felt sandbagged by this classic press ploy. Journalists love to call late for comment on a negative story, giving the public official little time to reply. Still, my folks crafted an immediate response to Edsall's question: "Senator Lott's remarks were intended to pay tribute to a remarkable man who led a remarkable life. To read anything more into these comments is wrong."

Edsall included the statement. But he began his piece this way: "Senate Republican leader Trent Lott of Mississippi has provoked criticism by saying that the United States would have been better off if then-segregationist Strom Thurmond had won the presidency in 1948." Edsall didn't note any particular sources of criticism, other than two people he had contacted himself. One of them, William Kristol, editor of the conservative *Weekly Standard,* answered Edsall's query by saying, "This is ludicrous. He [Lott] should remember that the Republican Party is the party of Abraham Lincoln."

Despite the simmering Internet, which now featured twenty columns on what was starting to be called "Lottgate," Edsall's story didn't generate a single media call to my offices.

That night, Tricia and I decided to attend newscaster Sam Donaldson's Christmas party, a favorite of Washington's movers and shakers. We'd been invited three times before, but had never been in town. Now, buoyed by the new GOP majority, we dressed formally and waded into the crowd of notables. As we moved through the throng, Brit Hume edged over and took us aside. "Look," said the anchor of the Fox News Channel's *Special Report with Brit Hume,* "That statement could become a real problem for you. This is a story that could have legs." Tricia and I looked at each other, shocked and shaken. Coming from one of the most conservative political reporters on the air, these were troubling words.

Chris Matthews, another columnist and star of MSNBC's *Hardball,* ambled over a few minutes later with his own blunt take on the subject. "What did you mean by those remarks?" he asked.

"I was just paying an old friend a compliment," I replied in what was to become a stock remark during the harrowing weeks to come. Chris, another old friend, seemed less concerned. And that set me at ease, because nobody has a better ear for the inside story than Matthews. When he posted the quote on *Hardball's* website that same evening, he let the remarks speak for themselves.

Though we weren't aware of it, an undertow of gossip about my predicament was spreading through the holiday gathering. Friends told us later that former executive editor of the *Washington Post,* Ben Bradlee, regaled partygoers with the phrase, "We got him this time." Others said that Terry McAuliffe, the liberal chairman of the Democratic National Committee, said much the same thing. But in Washington gossip is just that, and most of it rarely translates into credible fodder for the media.

Then the politics started to get ugly. On Sunday my press aide Ron Bonjean received a call from the *Chicago Tribune.* Jesse Jackson had just delivered a press release to the city desk labeling me a racist, and urging that I step down as majority leader of the U.S. Senate. "Trent Lott is nothing more than a Confederate with a master-slave mentality," Jackson said in the release. "He should resign." Before Ron could reach me by phone, I learned that Jackson had also called Tim Russert, urging him to raise the question on *Meet the Press.* Russert responded by quickly scribbling a question for the morning's panel.

Columnist Robert Novak offered a spirited defense of me—the last in the media for a long time—when Russert raised the issue on the show. "I think those statements were a mistake, and I don't think that Senator Lott was all that serious," Novak said. "I don't think we should dwell on it. This is the kind of thing that makes people infuriated with the media; they pick up something from a birthday party and turn it into a case of whether he should be impeached."

On Monday afternoon, December 9, former vice president Al Gore was speaking on unrelated topics with Judy Woodruff on *Inside Politics* when, without being asked, he blurted out, "Trent Lott made a statement that is racist. He should immediately withdraw those statements, and I think the U.S. Senate should undertake a censure of the comments. This is not a small thing. His was the very definition of a racist comment." Gore's remarks caught the attention of the mainstream media, which played it big.

Early that evening, Irby, Bonjean, and I huddled together to draft my initial reply to the critics. "My remarks were a poor choice of words that conveyed the impression that I embraced the discarded policies of the past, and I apologize to anyone who was offended by my statement," I announced in the statement. Bonjean gave the apology to the Associated Press, and it first appeared on Aaron Brown's *Newsnight* program later that evening.

"It looks like this story is over for now," Brown declared.

For a while, it seemed Brown was right. Despite Gore's blustery attack, media calls to my office remained muted. At ten in the morning on Tuesday, the Congressional Black Caucus held a press conference in the Capitol Radio-Television Gallery to criticize my comments. Given my apology, though, the press didn't make much of it. We thought the storm had passed.

By then, I had a decision to make. For months, Tricia and I had been planning to travel to the Florida Keys for what was to be our first real vacation in several years. Convening my senior staff, I mulled over the nature of the controversy. I'd issued an apology, and it seemed to have the desired result. Everyone believed we had weathered the storm. "By all means go," said my chief of staff, Dave Hoppe. "This will blow over."

Ron Bonjean escorted a lone NBC cameraman who filmed as I piled into the car. Bonjean waved as I drove off, sighing in relief.

Later that day, Tricia and I were settling into her sister's beach house in Key West when the story began to take on new life. Someone had dug up a 1980 story in the *Jackson Clarion-Ledger,* mentioning a Mississippi rally where I'd used similar words about Thurmond to pep up a Reagan campaign event. The quotation also was cited by historian Joseph Crespino in a book he was writing about race and civil rights in the modern South. Both references were faxed to the *New York Times* early Tuesday evening, leading to a meeting at the Capitol between *Times* reporter Carl Hulse and Bonjean. Hulse handed Bonjean the *Clarion-Ledger* article, which he said had been faxed by a professor from George Mason University, and asked for comment as soon as possible. While Bonjean and Susan Irby hunted for me, the newspaper posted an announcement of the upcoming story on its website: "He Said It Once Before." That set off an unprecedented and unexpected tidal wave through the rest of the media.

Between late Tuesday evening and late Wednesday evening, 288 media calls bombarded my beleaguered Washington staff. The big TV magazine shows—from *60 Minutes* and *20/20* to *Inside Edition* and *Extra*—had crews in the air Wednesday morning, headed for Mississippi. The *New York Times, Newsweek,* the *Washington Post,* and *Time* all flew research teams to the state to investigate my past.

As I learned of all this, that phrase from the Donaldson Christmas party—"We got him this time"—echoed in my ears. This feeling was reinforced Wednesday when the *Post*'s media critic, Howard Kurtz, blasted the media for under-covering the story. "There were cameras at that celebration," he wrote. "It was on C-Span, for crying out loud. When Lott apologized yesterday, the big papers were finally on the story. But why did they wait so long?"

My reply was buried in the bottom of the story: "To read any more into these comments is wrong. The fault isn't with me, it is with the evil commentators who are reading too much into what I said."

Ron Bonjean, Susan Irby, and the rest of my team were desperate to get my face on television to counteract the media firestorm that had erupted. But I was out of reach. I hadn't brought a laptop computer, and the house wasn't wired for cable. Even so, I knew things were desperate by the frantic phone calls from my staff.

And so I sat there in our vacation hideaway, paralyzed by indecision and frantically seeking a way to explain myself. Maybe, I thought, my own view of Strom Thurmond was to blame. By the 1970s, when I befriended him, he had changed a great deal. I knew him as head of the Armed Services Committee, as president pro-tem of the Senate, and as the acknowledged leader of the Republican Party in the South. As the years went by, he hired minorities; he got the minority vote; he helped. That's how I saw Strom Thurmond.

But many people in Washington still view the South as it was during the civil rights era of forty years ago. There has been deep and permanent change since the 1960s. For instance, Mississippi has more African American elected officials than any other state in the Union, and we've progressed further in race relations than many other states—and that includes Northern states. We have made quantum leaps, but few in the media give us any credit for it.

I have had African American staff members since 1975, and not just in low-level positions. In the 1980s, I had two African American women acting as top aides on the House Rules Committee. Right now, many of my staff members are from minority groups—African Americans and others. So how could they accuse me of being callous to inequality? But the media seemed happy to measure me by a civil rights yardstick four decades old.

The furor was stoked by the Internet, by liberal newspaper ed-itors—and even, I believed, by members of the White House staff. My visceral reaction that Wednesday afternoon was to pile into the car, get to the airport, take the first plane back to Washington, and face this thing down. But instead I stalled.

By dallying, I violated all my cardinal rules—the most impor-tant of which was, "ride to the cannons." People thought I was hiding down there. I also failed to keep my own counsel and fol-low my own instincts. A lot of well-intentioned people, in and out of the Senate, were calling and telling me what to do—the wrong things to do. And because I was upset and concerned by the way people were reacting, I listened.

My gut told me to draft one heck of an apology, and deliver it in person. And deliver it *just once*. I didn't do that, either. Instead, I holed up down there and issued one statement that wasn't good enough; then a second, better but still not good enough; then, fi-nally a third. When those didn't work, I held a press conference, where I offered a fourth confession. By rising to the bait, I bungled the whole affair terribly.

Susan Irby and Ron Bonjean were the staff members forced to deal with my stubbornness in remaining in Key West—and they, to their credit, decided to work with it. They scheduled what they termed "a one-two conservative punch"—a hookup to Sean Han-nity's radio show in New Jersey, followed by an audio shot on *Larry King Live*. My remarks on Hannity would be picked up by the rest of the media and spread across the country, while Larry King would promo my appearance as a media coup. We had used such a strategy when Republican senator Jim Jeffords jumped ship, and achieved spectacular results.

On Wednesday afternoon, when the media circus was at its peak, I spoke with Hannity. I said, in part, "Obviously, Sean, I'm sorry for my words. They were poorly chosen and insensitive. I

was surely not defending or endorsing Strom Thurmond's segregation policies of fifty-two years ago. When I think back on Strom
over the years, I look back at a man who was strong for defense
and economic development and balanced budgets. This is a mistake of the head and not the heart, because I don't accept the segregationist past at all."

Hannity asked: "Is this all being driven by politics?"

"That's for others to decide," I answered.

He noted that Senate Minority Leader Tom Daschle had initially defended me, and then, after great pressure, "issued a
strong statement of disapproval." Hannity asked: "Is there a
double standard in the media? After all, former President Clinton had a very strong relationship with William Fulbright—a
well-known segregationist. And Clinton had strong words of
praise for Fulbright, and didn't get called out over it the way you
have been."

"I'll let other people make that judgment," I said.

*Larry King Live* was a bit tougher, but I held my own. He
opened the show with tape of my comment the previous week, and
then asked: What did I think of the furor?

"Well, I was a little surprised. You know, for years I have been
kidding him, you know, saying, 'You would have made a great
president.' "

King continued, "But you can understand civil rights groups,
especially, being very sensitive to that."

"I absolutely do. That's why I have been on the phone and
talked to people such as Congresswoman Bernice Johnson of
Texas, with the Black Caucus and other minority leaders. You
know, in my own state, Larry, I do have a long record of trying to
involve African Americans and supporting our historically black
colleges and universities." I went on to cite other evidence of my
support of African Americans and other minorities in my state.

Finally, King asked the key question: "Senator—are you considering stepping aside?"

"No, I'm not, Larry. Again, I was honoring the man and not his policies. I've apologized for the remarks."

"And winding it up," King asked, "no one in the Bush administration has spoken to you about resigning?"

"No," I answered confidently.

Irby and Bonjean warned me that members of the White House staff monitored both appearances, looking for clues to guide their reactions in the days to come. In a way, I knew I was performing for that select audience—for Bush himself, and for the president's men and women. The president was the only one who could throw me a lifeline. Bonjean, among others, gave me a B for my conduct of both interviews. Later, he counseled: "America could only hear your voice, senator. And you possess a strong, clear tone, a tone that comes across as upbeat and optimistic rather than apologetic."

Once again, it was obvious to me: The American public needed to see my face. Yet again I equivocated and remained in Florida. One simmering Internet site called me "yellow" for "hiding out and addressing the nation on a conservative radio talk show."

I was less interested in media politics than in the complicated, Byzantine, and incessant political games that I now realized were happening within the White House. The Thurmond matter first came up in the White House press briefing on Tuesday morning, December 10. A television reporter asked: "Can you tell us now, whether the president agrees with [former] Vice President Gore that this was a racist statement?"

Press Secretary Ari Fleischer answered: "I think from the president's point of view, Senator Lott has addressed this issue. He has apologized for the statement, and the president understands that this is the final word from Senator Lott. He has apologized for it."

Ari concluded: "The president has confidence in him as Republican leader, unquestionably."

By the following morning, however, many on my staff had grown certain that some powerful Bush staffers had launched a power play to replace me as Senate majority leader. While Bush was professing deep support, several Capitol Hill journalists had warned us, some of his key advisers were telling another story. In the afternoon that same Wednesday, for instance, CNN White House reporter John King told viewers that even as Fleischer talked of "the president's continued support of Trent Lott," elsewhere in the White House "other highly placed staffers were telling me, 'Lott has to go.'"

Since my remarks had become an issue, I'd been consulting as usual with the White House Congressional liaison officer, Nick Calio, and Bush's chief of staff, Andy Card. Both had expressed continued confidence in me, and told me they recognized that I had been placed in a very difficult position. "But you'll weather it," Card said at one point. Each time, they conveyed Bush's high regard for me.

Still, my staff believed that someone at 1600 Pennsylvania Avenue was about to torpedo my senatorial leadership position. One of my staffers, a crackerjack observer of West Wing politics, assessed it this way: "The White House was watching closely. If the senator had demonstrated strong emotion—as he would later do on Friday, when he used the 'segregation is a stain on our soul' speech, the White House would have pulled back. Instead, the thought among presidential staffers was that this was moving out of control. And the decision was made to get him"—that is, to pull the rug out from under me.

The next morning, Thursday, December 12, President George W. Bush struck out at me. In Philadelphia, before a faith-based consortium, the president blasted me in a blunt and angry speech. "Recent comments by Senator Lott do not reflect the spirit of our country," he said. "Any suggestion that the segregated past was acceptable or positive is offensive, and it is wrong.

"He has apologized and rightly so."

I couldn't argue with the words he chose. But the tone he employed was devastating. When Bush said, "He has apologized *and rightly so,*" his voice hammered away at those last three words in a tone that was booming and nasty. Watching from Florida, Tricia and I were totally flattened emotionally. If we hadn't yet realized the desperate nature of our fix, Bush's obvious anger drove it home.

I learned later from contacts on Air Force One that the president was agitated as he told his staffers he'd decided to speak out against an old friend. "This is going to be painful," he told aides. "But we have to do it. It's like lancing a boil." The press reported that Bush decided to withdraw his support for political reasons: If he refused to condemn me for the remarks, it could be perceived as insensitive to the African American voting base.

Several worried callers, my biggest supporters among them, convinced Tricia and me that we had to return to our home in Pascagoula—the Senate was already in holiday recess—and go face-to-face with the press. Then my friend Rick Santorum called. Pennsylvania's junior senator was traveling back to Washington with Bush on Air Force One. While a group of journalists hammered Ari Fleischer in the front of the plane and Bush huddled with advisers in the back, Santorum found a quiet spot in the midsection and urged me over the phone to hold a press conference. "Make your point as strongly as you can. I think the president would appreciate that."

Senator John McCain of Arizona called soon after Santorum, reinforcing Rick's point. "Stay as long as they want you to, and answer every question until they quit asking." By noon that day the press had finally located me on the tip of Florida. And ABC was already broadcasting tape of me walking into the beach house. Ron Bonjean phoned to say that Miami news crews were headed for Key West in a caravan. At last, it was time for action.

We packed quickly and headed for Pascagoula.

# 18

# THE DIFFERENCE BETWEEN FRIENDS AND COLLEAGUES

Before leaving for home, I telephoned President Bush to tell him I agreed with his comments in Philadelphia. I hid my acute discomfort over his tone. The president seemed typically upbeat, and expressed confidence in my leadership. "Hang in there," he said before signing off.

I set a press conference for three in the afternoon the next day at the La Font Inn in Pascagoula—the site of many victory celebrations I'd enjoyed throughout my career. Irby, Bonjean, and I worked through the night on what had to be the best speech of my career. Eventually, dozens of fingers got into this particular pie. But we had a finished draft.

On Friday, the thirteenth of December, my exhaustion was obvious to all as I approached the seven camera crews and nearly fifty reporters at the La Font. They watched in silence as I greeted the journalists I knew, and positioned myself before the dizzying array of mikes clipped to the lectern. The speech I delivered was as close to a manifesto on racism as I would ever give:

Segregation is a stain on our nation's soul. There is no other way to describe it. It represents one of the lowest moments in this nation's history and we can never forget it.

I grew up with it here in the communities of Pascagoula and Moss Point, where we worked hard to overcome segregation and to bring about eventual reconciliation.

Let me be clear: Segregation and racism are immoral, and I repudiate them. I grew up in the First Baptist Church here, where I still actively participate. And, as I have come to realize more and more, you cannot in any way support discrimination or unfairness for anybody. This is just not consistent with the beliefs I feel so strongly about. President Bush was correct when he said that every day our nation was segregated was unfaithful to our founding principles and our founding fathers. I've personally seen what racism and segregation has wrought on the lives of good people.

With regard to Strom Thurmond: He is a friend. He is a colleague. He's legendary. But he also came to understand the evil of segregation and the wrongness of his own, early views.

About the birthday party: In celebrating Senator Thurmond's life, I didn't mean to suggest that his views of some forty years ago were justified or correct. I apologize for opening old wounds, and for hurting Americans who feel so deeply in this area. I take full responsibility for my remarks. I hope that people will find it in their hearts to forgive me for that grievous mistake. I have worked in this town, in this country and in this state to try and help people bring about reconciliation and to reach out to people of all races, colors, and religions to give them a chance to get a better education and to help them obtain decent paying jobs.

We need a color-blind society, in which every American has an opportunity to succeed. We need an end to the entrenched poverty and joblessness that have plagued minority communities and communities of all kinds in this state and across this nation. We need a good education for every child—an education that gives him a real chance for a good life and that rejects the racism of soft expectations.

To those who believe that I implied that the American Dream is for some but not for all, that's just not true. But I apologize to those who got that impression.

Welcome applause greeted me both from the one hundred supporters or so who were on hand, and even from members of the media, many of whom shook my hand as they departed. Following McCain's suggestion, I had stayed for every question.

Yet I drove home from the news conference spent and disillusioned, with the discouraging impression that nothing I said would be good enough. By this time, I was taking counsel from too many people. I also had the feeling that somebody was stirring the pot, priming the media, and feeding the discord. Just who was a mystery to me.

My staff was still pointing a finger at senior White House advisers. But I remained in contact not only with the White House staff, but with Vice President Dick Cheney, a former colleague and now a friend. All of them told me to buck up, that the worst was over. John Warner of Virginia phoned and told me to "go full speed ahead and damn the torpedoes. You'll make it through."

Most of the national coverage of the press conference, meanwhile, moved quickly past my message to speculation about my future. On the CBS Nightly News, chief Washington correspondent Bob Schieffer reported that "influential Republicans, some of them inside the White House, were now urging the president to work behind the scenes to force Lott to step down from his leadership post."

At the White House, no public endorsements were forthcoming. Ari Fleischer, the president's spokesman, reiterated his boss's words: "He apologized and rightly so." Then Ari added: "I reiterate that the president doesn't think he needs to resign." If he's speaking for Bush, I thought, that's pretty lukewarm.

Half an hour after my press conference, Senator Larry Craig of Idaho moderated a conference call of my Senate supporters—from Olympia Snowe and Ohio's Mike DeWine to John Warner and, most stalwart of all, Rick Santorum. The telephone caucus numbered twenty-four, and included less enthusiastic supporters: Senator Don Nickles of Oklahoma; my ambitious second-in-command, Susan Collins of Maine; and Bill Frist of Tennessee.

My speech drew mostly rave reviews from this select audience, all of whom rated my chances of survival as high. The mood was so joyous that Warner interrupted the dialogue to bellow out, "Let's all of us vote to endorse Trent right now. Let's have a vote for Lott right here, right now, and make it public. We don't want to get off this call without supporting him first. What do you say?"

Don Nickles demurred. "Now, wait a minute. Let's see how this plays out first."

"What do you mean, plays out?" asked Warner. "We know how it's going to play out. We're going to support him, and he's going to remain majority leader. Let's vote."

Nickles's monkey wrench quickly attracted support from several others. "He's right. Let's wait to vote," Collins said. Frist also expressed reservations about a vote then and there—a sign of things to come. An angry Warner slammed down his receiver, and the call ended.

I should have suspected what Nickles would eventually do. Ours had been an uneasy partnership. As my whip, he'd made it clear he was after my job as majority leader. He occasionally would appear to be disagreeing with the direction I was taking our caucus, and leaks to the media—especially to *Roll Call,* one of the

Capitol Hill newspapers—often seemed to come from his operation. But I didn't see this sort of thing coming.

My staff concluded that the speech had made all the difference. We had our soldiers—Santorum and Mitch McConnell—headed for the Sunday morning talk shows, and the news calls were tapering off. Ron Bonjean, who'd manned the Washington front lines of the battle, predicted that—barring any fresh developments in the news cycle—Monday might dawn clear and bright with the scandal beginning to fade away.

Saturday *was* free and clear. I did hear a rumor that Don Nickles was circulating some sort of critical memo, and that George Stephanopoulos was going to use it that Sunday on *This Week*. I refused to believe that Don would do that. After stewing for a couple of hours, I said to myself, *No, I'm not going to call him; I'm not going to insult him. Let's just wait and see what happens.*

But the rumor was true. At seven in the evening, Nickles posted the following notice on the front page of his senatorial website: "Majority Leader Trent Lott has been weakened to the point that may jeopardize his ability to enact our agenda or to speak to all Americans. There are several outstanding senators who are capable of effective leadership, and I hope we can have the opportunity to choose one of them."

At six o'clock Sunday morning, while my troops were being prepped for their talk show appearances, a copy of the Nickles website memo was delivered by messenger to the New York studios of Fox News, where an unwary Mitch McConnell would have to confront it. Almost eighteen hours earlier, a telephone tip had alerted the staff of ABC's *This Week with George Stephanopoulos* that Nickles would be posting Saturday night.

Stephanopoulos made quick use of the memo, transforming it into a bulletin on the *This Week* website to promote Nickles's hurriedly scheduled appearance on the show. McConnell was doing the Stephanopoulos show in addition to Fox News. George announced that he would produce, "the person who is going to stick the knife in Senator Trent Lott's back. This is a journalistic cluster bomb."

I became a part of this preposterous scenario when Nickles telephoned me from the makeup room at ABC, where he was to discuss his memo for the first time. I remember very little of that conversation. I wanted to get off the phone and warn McConnell that he was about to be ambushed. Then, almost as an afterthought, Nickles told me that he had alerted the White House the evening before. But he said nothing about the reaction there.

It was impossible to reach McConnell, who already was being interviewed by Brit Hume, the journalist who had predicted—barely a week earlier—that this story might somehow become a problem for me. As I dressed for church, I wondered about Nickles's contact with the White House. They hadn't encouraged his action, but they hadn't discouraged him either. As he hastily told me, the staffers in the West Wing simply told him that they "didn't interfere with legislative matters."

So Nickles made his move, and opened the floodgates to a full-fledged challenge to my leadership. He parlayed his memo into a set of talking points for a number of Republican senators who'd been sitting on the fence. Under our conference rules, it would take five signatories to schedule a vote on the fate of the majority leader. After his lobbying of our colleagues, Nickles clearly wanted to get them.

If I had to pinpoint the day when the ground slipped from beneath my feet, it would have to be Sunday, December 15.

Tricia and I were under siege. The network camera crews and radio reporters and freelance video jockeys who'd come to

Pascagoula for the press conference shifted their raucous base of operations to the quiet lanes surrounding our house. Most mornings there were sixteen reporters and camera crews, but the number fluctuated with the number of news bulletins devoted to the Thurmond story. By now, these so-called news breaks were averaging around seven a day.

Often, to accompany these bulletins, the twenty-four-hour television networks broadcast panoramas of the house—from the gray-blue of the Gulf of Mexico outside our front door to the sprawling, 350-year-old live oak tree in my backyard.

If you haven't experienced a twenty-first century media blitz, it's hard to explain what it does to your life. If Tricia absolutely had to drive to the store, the light packs were switched on; the gaggle began shuffling toward her, shouting questions she could neither hear nor answer. And the pinpoint glare would follow her until she was out of sight. The whole process would begin again whenever my neighbor, Dr. Paul Moore, and his wife, Jean, stepped across the street for a chat—as they had done often during our decades-long friendship. As the days went on, and Christmas approached, the newspeople began to take on the character of vultures. I knew in my heart that they would never fly off until I stopped struggling and gave up my leadership position—in effect, surrendering to them.

The Sunday morning Don Nickles appeared on *This Week*, the media caravan, most of them dressed very casually, followed me down the street to the First Baptist Church, parked their vehicles near mine, and followed me inside with their white hot lights.

It was on the way home that I finally, angrily, answered one of their questions: "Yes, I'm going to remain Senate majority leader. I was a whip in the House and the Senate, and I know the votes are on my side."

"Then why is Don Nickles challenging you?" one of them asked.

"Ask him," I answered. "You've got him staked out, haven't you?"

Having lived a quiet life for thirty years in my small seaside community, it was hard to adjust, much less to think, under this pressure.

Worse, Tricia found it impossible to watch television without running into Trent Lott bulletins or news previews. It wasn't until she finally turned on HGTV, the home and garden cable channel, that she found a network where Senator Trent Lott's name wasn't mentioned for the entire week.

Being a prisoner wasn't easy. I still had to serve my constituents, show up for meetings, and check in at the field office. But I was loath to bring along the magnetized media brigade. One day, I slipped my jacket over my shoulders, ducked through the kitchen and escaped out the back door. My congressional security team had already been alerted, and met me on a side street. By the time the vultures caught sight of me, it was way too late.

I received reports on the morning round of talk shows after I returned from church. On Fox News, McConnell dismissed Nickles's power play: "What Republicans should be doing in the Senate, instead of becoming embroiled in a leadership fight, is pull together to quickly put forward their agenda when Congress reconvenes next month.

"We have a fine leader, Trent Lott, and he's not going anywhere. We should get behind him. We don't have a huge margin in the Senate—we only have fifty-one Republicans. We need to stay together and pursue the president's agenda."

Rick Santorum was eloquent on *Meet the Press:* "Trent Lott is a man of tremendous integrity, of deep faith, and someone who believes all men are created equal."

Santorum, who was chairman of the Senate Republican Conference, told Tim Russert that he was opposed even to calling a meeting of Senate Republicans to discuss a potential replacement. "Our rules don't allow me to do that."

But there had been some slippage of support since my press conference. John Warner, who had been fierce in his support of me on Friday night, had come to believe, along with his fellow Virginia senator, George Allen, that Republican senators needed to vote on my fate; it was an echo of Maine's Susan Collins and the inevitable Don Nickles. According to our Conference rules, it would take five to force a vote. They were only one vote away. Here we go, I thought. Democrats tend to surround their wounded players and try to prop them up, but we Republicans eat our own. It's not sour grapes; it's just the way it is.

Accompanying the media discord out in my oak grove, the phone rang incessantly—mostly from supporters who wanted me to give another speech, go on another show, draft another statement, or call this or that senator. It seemed to me that I'd already done it all. Then, in a weak moment, I took another piece of advice from Maine's Olympia Snowe, who had stayed tightly by my side since December 5. "You need to directly connect with black leaders and American blacks as a whole," she urged.

I balked at first. I'd already given three press statements and two extended interviews, bared my soul in a speech written from the heart, and apologized to both the president and the vice president. I told her I'd think about it for a bit.

Actually, I'd been offered just such an opportunity. It came from Bob Johnson, an African American entrepreneur from Mississippi who had built his Black Entertainment Television from a $100,000 investment into a billion-dollar enterprise. And BET was just getting into news and news analysis. He offered me an open slot of thirty minutes during prime time on Monday night, December 15, to discuss my dilemma and to explain myself to an enormous coast-to-coast African American audience. But it would be, no matter what I said or how I said it, another in an agonizing line of apologies.

I was advised not to do it. "This man and his staff are not your friends. You can only lose," I was told by Congressman J. C. Watts, an African American Republican from Oklahoma and someone I respected enormously. But I was no longer thinking soundly. So I went onto Black Entertainment Television for thirty minutes and groveled through yet another confession. I promised and apologized in every manner possible, grasping at every emotional nuance to make my case.

I remember feeling a huge sense of relief when the interview ended, and I stepped back out into the Gulf Coast air to clear my head. I shouldn't have done it—I knew that the minute I finished. As I drove home, I felt that I'd achieved absolutely nothing. And I might even have made it worse.

CNN immediately characterized my performance as "abjectly contrite and apologetic." Its talking head continued: "Senator Lott called the segregated society of his Mississippi youth 'wicked,' and conceded that he was part of it." CNN noted that I also apologized for voting against Martin Luther King Day, and for opposing some forms of affirmative action—though I had many good reasons for doing so.

But you do, and say, strange things when you're desperate.

I knew one thing: From this point on, the apologies were over. Now it was all about my position as majority leader. And I intended to fight for that position, because the votes were there. There would be no more pandering.

I drove home, smiled broadly at the video mob, and decided to let this congressional drama play out by Washington rules. I wasn't going to quit; I just counted out my votes, almost every day. And I realized that the numbers were on my side: the majority leader's job was still mine.

Then politics at the highest level began to swamp my boat.

On Wednesday, December 18, Governor Jeb Bush of Florida invited his favorite reporters into his historic Tallahassee office and told them that my remarks were beginning to politically damage the Republican Party as a whole. Jeb didn't say I should quit, but he might as well have. "Something's going to have to change," he said. "Trent Lott's predicament can't be the topic of conversation over the entire next week."

This meant that the governor of Florida expected me to exit the public scene by Friday. Was this a direct message from his brother, and my friend, President Bush? To this day, I have no idea. Some advisers told me that it had to come from the president; I was inclined to agree with them. Others depicted Jeb as a firebrand who talked off the cuff whenever he felt like it. I did learn later that Governor Bush had spoken with the president's chief political adviser, Karl Rove, the morning he informed the world of his views on my situation.

Less than four hours later, Bush's secretary of state, Colin Powell, also ushered reporters into his presence to say that he, personally, "deplored the sentiments behind Strom Thurmond's 1948 bid for the White House." Powell concluded, "There was nothing about the 1948 election or the Dixiecrat agenda that should have been applied in any way to any American at that time or to any American now."

That one hurt. Tricia and I had given a brunch to honor Colin and Alma Powell in our home during the 1980s. And I'd also prevailed on the president to appoint their son, Michael, to the Federal Communications Commission; Bush later made him chairman. The secretary of state hadn't taken a direct shot at me, but he could have helped and he didn't. I couldn't understand it: I'd worked with him enough over the years that he should have known I wasn't a racist.

Then rumors began to surface that Senator Bill Frist of Tennessee, a close colleague, was ready to challenge me for the post of majority leader. CNN's White House reporter, John King, announced on the air that "a highly placed White House official" had told him: "The president is not going to defend Senator Trent Lott from any challengers."

From the outset, I saw these as signs of pure White House politics. Governor Bush and Secretary Powell wouldn't have spoken so openly and candidly had they not had the permission of George W. Bush. And the CNN bulletin meant only one thing: George W. Bush was cutting me loose.

At this point, I was hardly in a position to complain. Through the endless statements, media calls, and apologies, I had done as much as anyone to keep the story alive. Now it was just politics. Still, ever the whip, I made the calls, did the math, and was reassured to find that I still had the votes—thanks to a core of loyal senators.

At eight o'clock on the morning of Thursday, December 19, an elegantly dressed Senator John Warner told a crowd of quickly summoned journalists that Tennessee's William Frist, a medical doctor and surgeon whose specialty was cardiology, would challenge me for the position of Senate majority leader.

Frist himself remained silent until ten that morning, when he told a *Newsday* reporter that he only decided to run "because a clear majority of the Republican caucus believes that a change in leadership would benefit the United States of America. Therefore I will step forward for that role."

In his own press conference, Virginia's George Allen added, "This may be very unfair to Trent. It may be tortuous for him, but we have to move forward in the best interests of Congress and the nation." Later, Allen called and told me bluntly that I should resign and put an end to the problem. "It's going to reflect on the party if you don't," he said.

"I'm not going to do it," I yelled back at him. "I'm not going to do it, and I'm very disappointed by your call."

Warner eventually phoned me, stating cheerily that he was on the Frist team; after asking how I was doing, he cut off the call as fast as politely possible.

I considered Frist's power grab a personal betrayal. When he entered the Senate in 1995, I had taken him under my wing—just as other powerful senators had done for me. He was my protégé, and I helped him get plum assignments and committee positions. I had pushed him to President Bush. We'd been friends off and on the floor, and that's pretty rare in a governmental body loaded with lone wolves and immense egos.

When I learned of his move, I felt, and still feel, that he was one of the main manipulators of the whole scenario. No other senior senator with stature would have run against me. In fact, they all took themselves out of the running because of close relationships to me. If Frist had not announced exactly when he did, as the fire was about to burn out, I would still be majority leader of the Senate today.

But Bill Frist didn't even have the courtesy to call and tell me personally that he was going to run. Frist and I had almost ten years of history together, and I had to hear the news from a dejected Ron Bonjean—who apologized about having to tell me.

Once again, I did my whip count and found that I could still beat him in a Republican Conference election. But the vote would have been closer than it should have been. It would have stretched the affair through the rest of the Christmas holidays. And it was already becoming a problem for some of my colleagues who were trying to support me—good people like Senator Pete Fitzgerald of

Illinois, George Voinovich and Mike DeWine of Ohio, and Arlen Specter of Pennsylvania.

Late Thursday night I talked with Senator Judd Gregg, and he reluctantly told me that my leadership had been undermined. "Trent, it's going to be awfully tough for you to do your job." He didn't tell me to step aside, but he made it clear that it was going to be a "big problem."

I prayed over it on Thursday night, and meditated about it at dawn as I looked out over the comforting spread of my live oak tree out back. Sometime early that Friday morning, I decided to give up the leadership.

One question remained: Do I even stay in the Senate? If I'm going to have to do this, why go back and deal with what could become a long parade of indignities? But Mississippi and national politics influenced that decision.

The governor of Mississippi was a Democrat, and if I should leave the Senate he would appoint a Democrat in my place. That would throw the Senate back to fifty-fifty; Cheney would still be there to break tie votes in our favor, but that wasn't preferable to a clear majority. After all my work, I couldn't ruin this shining chance in which the White House, the House, and the Senate would all be controlled by Republicans.

I was a member of the United States Senate, and there I would stay.

After my decision, the clouds moved on, the air cleared, and I was finally able to sit down to analyze the players and the process that had toppled me. And, to give credit where credit is due, several post mortems by the press helped me understand the dynamics of my overthrow, quite apart from the remarks I'd made at the Thurmond celebration.

On Saturday, December 21, an hour-long broadcast on National Public Radio was the first to charge that the Bush White House was mixed up in my removal from office. Mara Liasson, an NPR Washington correspondent, got right to the point: "Of course the White House was involved in Lott's removal. Karl Rove was keeping very close tabs on the sentiment for and against Trent Lott. And he was leaking that information like crazy. White House officials were telling the *New York Times* and the *Washington Post* that Lott has lost the president's confidence, and he can't possibly stay on. There is no doubt in my mind that the White House engineered this."

That same morning, in the *New York Times,* reporter Elisabeth Bumiller targeted the "White House for getting Trent Lott." She wrote: "As President Bush was cheerily shaking the hands of thousands of guests at the White House Christmas parties, his advisers were working overtime to jettison Trent Lott as Senate Republican leader. Washington's political professionals were left awed. They said that Bush and his powerful adviser, Karl Rove, had stumbled at times but had still managed to depose, in eight short days, the unanimously elected Senate leader of their party."

Bumiller also quoted Robert S. Strauss, an elder statesman of the Democratic Party and longtime friend of the Bushes: "They've got a skilled surgeon coming in to run the Senate, and they used a surgeon's skill to remove Lott without leaving any fingerprints. . . . You have to give the White House tremendous credit for coming to town and in two years having this kind of political performance."

Democratic strategist James Carville added, "Yep, it was a clean extraction."

I'm still not sure who stirred the pot during this coup. I did find one of the scalpers: longtime Bush adviser Joseph Albaugh.

He admitted to me that he was one of the "Bush aides" who were leaking statements to the press that I had to go.

When I asked him why, he answered, "For the heck of it. I didn't mean any harm. I thought it was off the record." Really—he actually said that.

The press was still surrounding my home on Saturday, even though I'd resigned as majority leader on Friday. So, wearily, I agreed to their demand for one more photo opportunity, walked out, stood before their cameras and read my resignation speech.

"Now, will you leave?" I asked.

"Yup," they nodded their heads.

And finally they were gone.

I was able to celebrate Christmas at last. And the people of Mississippi were great to me. They came by my house to express their confidence and their sympathy—not just one or two, but scores of them.

Jerome Barkum, a former All-American at Jackson State and a professional football player for the New York Jets, drove up from New Orleans and stopped in the driveway. He leaned down and said, "I know you didn't mean what they've put on you. I know that when my dad needed help years ago, nobody helped him but you. And I'll never forget it." Barkum's father had supported me when I first ran for the House in 1972, a time when it was especially tough for a Republican to get African American votes. Later, when I was in office, he had a problem getting his Social Security check, and I helped him work through the bureaucratic red tape. He never forgot, and neither had his son.

A couple of days later, a big Humvee pulled right into the yard, an anonymous behemoth with darkly tinted windows. The driver bounded out and came around to the front of the car. "I'm

Revered Erskine Johnson from Ocean Springs," he said, "and we just want you to know that we've been praying for you. We know the kind of man you are, and we want you know how we feel."

I was in tears, and in shock, after he left. After all of the nastiness, prayers by somebody else can say it all—and so simply.

President Bush finally called me on Saturday, four days before Christmas. He expressed deep concern about how Tricia and I were doing. He said he felt bad about rumors that the administration was undermining me, and was proud of how I had handled my decision to surrender my office.

I will always remember my response clearly: "Thank you, Mr. President, but the rumors did hurt me, and you didn't help when you could have. But I understand that what we are trying to do for our country is bigger than any one man—me, or even you. I knew what I had to do, so I took one for the cause."

# EPILOGUE

# THE MORNING AFTER

S everal days after Christmas 2002, I ventured into my study in the Pascagoula house and began sorting through the Senate mail. At one point, halfway through a large pile of letters, I leaned back in my chair, thought about those frantic days I'd seen in the past month, and suddenly realized that I was completely at peace with the situation. As the dust settled behind me, I'd gone on to have a delightful time with my children and grandchildren, and managed to ignore the problem entirely.

When the political pundits began airing the possibility that I might resign my Senate seat and just fade away, it was the prospect of turning my seat over to a Democrat that made me decide to stay. But now, the more I thought about it, there were many other good reasons to return to the Senate. I could do my best to have a positive influence on the institution and on the legislative work that it does. What's more, I'm not a quitter. The people of Mississippi and I had a contract with each other.

I'd signed on as their senator until 2006. And, at least until then, I intended to continue doing my job.

In fact, I'd just heard from the people. In a survey of Mississippians who were asked to assess their government officials, I'd chalked up an approval rating of 79 percent—the highest of any politician in recent history. That was a strong enough mandate for me.

So Tricia and I packed up and flew back to the nation's capital, uncertain of the reception that would await us. We weren't alone in our concern. When I walked onto the Senate floor for the first time since I'd resigned as leader, it was painfully obvious that my colleagues didn't know how to react. My friends, particularly those who had supported me, had no idea what to say—if anything. Those who had undermined me were embarrassed by their conduct, for the most part, or seemed to behave that way.

I had to reestablish some sort of rapport with each one of them, especially my erstwhile enemies. I began chatting with them—first one on one, then in small groups—to put this sociological puzzle back together and come to some closure. True, I'd been knifed in the back. But in order to become effective again, I had to shake some of the hands that held the daggers. I'm a firm believer in forgiving, if not forgetting. I also believe that if you dwell in bitterness over people who did you wrong, it'll just eat you up.

Rapprochement was slow and uncomfortable. And it played out before the wide eyes of the Democrats, to whom this was an entertaining matinee. But soon I went underground, to finish old business and map out a new committee career for myself. I went from being the most vocal, Johnny-on-the-spot senator to a shadow—avoiding the media as I tried to establish a new congressional persona.

My own offices—both the majority leader's headquarters and my Mississippi senatorial suite—were in mild chaos. In the former, members of a large and brilliant staff, carefully recruited over the years, lost their positions as soon as I resigned mine. But I was determined to place every one of them in an equal or better slot than the ones they had with me. It took five weeks and lots of phone calls. I placed them all, and many of them ended up with promotions. For instance, my chief of staff, Dave Hoppe, ended up at the blue ribbon Quinn Gillespie lobbying and political consulting firm. And Ron Bonjean, my media representative, became the spokesman for U.S. Commerce Secretary Donald L. Evans.

The Mississippi offices in Washington's Russell Office Building had been under siege since I resigned as majority leader. When word got out that I was back in Washington, men and women from all over the United States began writing to tell me how unfairly they thought I had been treated. Towering piles of cards and letters, more than a thousand in all, were everywhere. I began answering them by hand—as many as possible—and would still be doing so six weeks later. It was a lot of work, but as I tried to relaunch my Senate career, reading all those good wishes was a reassuring experience.

When I began meeting with Bill Frist, my successor as majority leader, I told him I wanted committee assignments where I could get something done. I wasn't interested in sitting around in hearings all day. These were delicate negotiations: After all, if it weren't for Frist, I'd probably still be majority leader today. But he had his own problems to face. Frist had leapfrogged over veterans such as the Senate Republican Whip Don Nickles and Republican Conference Chairman Rick Santorum to land the top spot. Now, thanks to my friend Santorum, I became chairman of the Rules and Administration Committee; I also joined the Intelligence Committee, and remained on the Commerce, Science and Transportation Committee. I also took over as chairman of the aviation subcommittee, putting me in the cockpit of the gargantuan efforts to save the airline industry.

In return, I told Frist, I would help him in any way I could; in effect, I would serve as his adviser without portfolio. Our styles as leaders were different. Frist tended to be cautious and risk averse; I was much more aggressive, ready, and willing to roll people if that's what it took to get the job done. At first, my pairing with the new majority leader raised some media eyebrows. But we were just two veteran senators doing our jobs. There's no use dwelling on how he got where he is or how I got where I am. That's how it is. You just deal with it and move on.

The Intelligence Committee attracted my immediate and sustained attention. I'd been receiving key intelligence briefings for more than six years as majority leader, and had become more familiar with the subject during my six years on the Armed Services Committee. In addition, I'd met almost every foreign dignitary who had journeyed to Washington over the past decade, since a call on the majority leader is usually part of the drill. I wanted to stay in the loop on intelligence and foreign affairs.

I was deeply disappointed by the way the committee had been treated by the intelligence agencies. It was obvious after only a few meetings that they gave us as little information as possible. They treated us not as allies, but as a nuisance—something that got in their way. I quickly developed a deep skepticism about the work of the CIA in particular, and the intelligence community in general.

Most people didn't know that a huge percentage of the intelligence budget went to the Defense Department for agencies only nominally controlled by the director of Central Intelligence. In fact, there were fifteen different intelligence agencies scattered throughout the federal bureaucracy, including one at the State Department. Everything was about turf and control, and it infuriated me. When you're talking about intelligence that may affect the lives of Americans in the United States and abroad, there should be no room for mistakes—or territorial squabbling.

When it came to intelligence committee reforms, I classified myself as a radical. It was a complete mess—designed not to work, and in desperate need for a major overhaul. If there was any doubt about it, the deeply flawed intelligence information on Iraq's weapons of mass destruction should have put it to rest.

I supported the recommendation of the National Commission on Terrorist Attacks Upon the United States—better known as the 9/11 Commission—to name an intelligence czar to break down the barriers and better coordinate the nation's intelligence "product." We passed legislation last year that, among other things, created a new director of national intelligence to fill this role, and President Bush signed it into law on December 17, 2004. Four months later, we confirmed almost unanimously John Negroponte, the president's choice, to be our country's first DNI. He is a seasoned diplomat with considerable knowledge of intelligence work, and he should be up to the challenge. His job won't be easy, given the entrenched bureaucracies and their resistance to change, and no one should expect miracles overnight. But Negroponte should shake things up as quickly as he can. Delay, in this case, could have deadly consequences.

Despite the faulty intelligence, however, I still believe the Iraq war resolution was correct, based on Saddam Hussein's conduct—his resistance to weapons inspectors, and his continuing threat to the region. Furthermore, the reasons for overthrowing Iraq went far beyond Iraq and what was done in that country. The war was also meant to send a message to countries such as Syria and Libya that America stood for democracy, and that we were not going to stand by and have people murdered by dictators unanswerable to anyone. That message has begun to get through. Iraq has an elected government of its own, and other antidemocratic countries in the larger Middle East—Libya, Lebanon, Egypt, and even Saudi Arabia—have started to change their ways, however tentatively. I'm not a dewy-eyed optimist, but it is demeaning to the Arab and Muslim people in those lands to say that their cultures and traditions are unsuited to democracy. Freedom, in my view, is a universal longing.

To outsiders, the Senate Rules Committee may sound like a small assignment for a senator anxious to do big things. But believe me, it is one of the most powerful committees in the chamber. Taking charge of it as chairman means accepting responsibility for the bedrock upon which the Senate rests. Every move a bill makes on its way through the process is governed by rules—some of which date back two centuries. I had made it a point to study the rules in great detail when I first arrived in the Senate; when it comes to the rules, knowledge is power, and I believed that my special familiarity with the rules often gave me an edge over other senators who weren't so diligent about the details. But now, I thought, it was time that we gave all the rules a full and thorough review. How many of them were simply archaic? And were there new rules we could adopt in the interest of efficiency and consensus?

The Senate, in my judgment, had become increasingly dysfunctional. Some people argued that it had always been that way, but the gridlock has plainly worsened over the years. One infamous example was the "hold," a formal tactic that any senator can use to stall a bill or a nomination process. The hold was originally created to signal a senator's special interest in being completely involved in discussions about the individual or piece of legislation. Now, the hold sends a different message. It says: *Look, I'm blocking this nominee or this bill, and if you try to call my bluff, I'm going to filibuster.* In six months or less, any freshman senator has the system figured out. As a body, we've become so muscle-bound with such rules and rights that the Senate has become almost impossible to manage.

The combination of Rules and Intelligence alone, I felt, put me back in the game. I wasn't majority leader, but being the junior senator from Mississippi, free of the responsibilities of official leadership in the chamber, was liberating. One afternoon in March 2003, I noticed that I'd resumed my habit of strolling the Senate halls idly whistling and watching the ebb and flow of Congress. I hadn't felt that carefree in months—certainly since the Strom Thurmond reception.

At that same time, the newspapers that cover Capitol Hill and the ins and outs of Congress began trailing me. They thought they detected a comeback.

In the *National Journal,* Kirk Victor told his readers: "Whether using his perch as chairman of the Senate Rules and Administration Committee to make the case for limiting filibusters, or occasionally drawing upon his experience as a leader to question his party's legislative strategy, or playing a behind-the-scenes role to advise Majority Leader Bill Frist, Senator Trent Lott is showing that F. Scott Fitzgerald got it wrong. There are second acts in American lives."

In *The Hill,* the Capitol Hill newspaper, Geoff Earle wrote: "Months after he was forced to relinquish his Senate leadership post, Lott is recasting himself as a key inside player in the GOP Conference. Despite his diminished role, he continues to consult with key White House staff on floor strategy and provides frequent counsel to GOP leaders."

Under the headline "Liberated Lott Emerges as Broker," *Roll Call* was slightly edgier: "Far from turning into a recluse after his December downfall, Senator Lott has instead delved into a new role as the elder statesman in the GOP Conference, taking on a full portfolio of committee work while also retaining his old position as one of the Senate's key dealmakers. He's been dispatched to key meetings with moderates on the budget. He's speaking out in weekly strategy luncheons. And he's even worked the fundraising circuit, pulling in roughly $200,000 so far this year for his leadership PAC and dishing out checks to the same Senators who voted him out of leadership barely three months ago."

These were nice notices. The Capitol Hill trades were reviewing me as if I were a new Broadway play. As for being one of the grand old men of the Senate, at sixty-one I probably was the youngest to be saddled with that august title. Actually, I was just getting my bearings, dodging the roadblocks, and letting my leadership experience take me wherever it could.

One of my first targets, naturally, was the filibuster of President Bush's judicial nominees by the Democrats. This bitter fight is still underway, and probably will crest as the Senate considers Bush's nominees to the U.S. Supreme Court. But it began, in a sense, when Bush nominated a personal friend of mine, Charles W. Pickering, to the U.S. Court of Appeals for the Fifth Circuit.

Pickering's first nomination and confirmation hearing in mid-2001 led to his rejection by the Senate Judiciary Committee on a vote of 10–9 along party lines. Opposition to Pickering, a Federal District Court judge for more than a decade, had revolved mainly around low ratings and vocal opposition from civil rights groups. The president again nominated the veteran Mississippi public servant; his judicial future was sealed on October 30, 2003.

Zealous Democrats decided Pickering's fate, and established a legislative precedent by refusing to allow a vote for the embattled justice to reach the Senate floor. A vote of sixty is required to end a filibuster and move to a vote. We managed to get fifty-four votes—a good showing, but six short of the requirement.

I was stunned. This was the first time in history that the filibuster rules had been used to block the presidential appointment process for federal judges. Backed by an unrelenting character assassination by Democrats and left-leaning public interest groups, Pickering, who possesses one of the finest legal minds I've ever encountered, could not get a straight up-or-down vote in the full Senate. We had enough votes to get him confirmed by a simple majority, but not the sixty needed to push his candidacy to the floor of the Senate.

To make this shocking vote more palatable, the Democrats and the media were portraying Pickering as a judge who had somehow gone easy in sentencing members of a cross-burning gang in rural Mississippi. The story, of course, had been taken out of context. Some years earlier, three young white gang members had been caught, tried, and convicted in Pickering's U.S. District Court for the Southern District of Mississippi. The younger boys, two teenagers, received probation and the right to have the incident removed from their records in five years. In an attempt to be fair, Pickering sentenced the young adult member of the trio to two years in prison—the lightest sentence available.

The national press was flooded with tabloid-style versions of the story. The media's conclusion: Pickering was soft on cross burners. Despite my warning that they were unfairly staining the name of a fine judge, these stories found some credence with members of the Judiciary Committee and with the Democratic Caucus.

An indignant Alliance for Justice, a left-wing watchdog agency, even attempted to link the judge's fortunes to my own: "Pickering's re-nomination should have been doomed," they declared, "because of Lott's racially-charged comments made at Thurmond's 100th birthday party."

Between then and mid-2005, the Democrats blocked ten of the president's appellate court appointees using the same filibuster rule they'd used to clobber my friend Charles Pickering. There had been occasional filibusters in the air over the decades, but the judges involved eventually had their names withdrawn. With such a fresh precedent in the air, though, it looked now as if the Democrats were prepared to reject any nomination that couldn't generate a full sixty votes—a major shift from the policy of the past.

Nowhere in the Constitution is a supermajority—the sixty votes needed to break the filibuster—recommended or even suggested for judicial nominees. The Constitution isn't the only document clear about the intent of the founding fathers on judicial nominees. A reading of the Federalist Papers, where the drafters debated this very question, again makes it clear that a supermajority for judicial nominees was neither sought nor expected.

As the 108th Congress drew to a close last year, we decided to do something about the Democrats' long-winded tactics. A group of Republicans—led by me, with strategic interest expressed by Frist, also a member of the Rules Committee—settled on a tactic to ensure that judicial nominees in the future wouldn't get the Pickering treatment. It was simplicity itself: We would ask the presiding officer, as a point of order, what vote was required to approve a judicial nominee. The answer, of course, would be a simple majority. The Democrats would appeal that ruling by the presiding officer of the Senate. After that, however, the motion could be tabled by a majority vote. Bam! We'd have a new precedent that would defeat filibusters and give nominees what they deserve—a clean vote, with victory or defeat determined by a simple majority.

This was famously known as the "nuclear option," a phrase that first came from my lips—at least according to some reporters and pundits. What happened, as I recall, is that a reporter told me the Democrats would go nuclear if we tried this ploy. Well, fine, I responded, let 'em go nuclear. In any event, political journalist embraced the term, predicting that the Democrats would pull down the Senate walls and bring the body to a standstill rather than submit to what we were doing. I prefer to call it the "constitutional plan," since it's inspired by prose about appointing judges found in both the Constitution and the Federalist Papers.

In the spring of 2005, Republicans and Democrats went toe to toe over this issue. And, when neither side blinked, a group of fourteen senators—seven from each party—managed to come together and fashion something of a compromise. Five appeals court nominees previously stalled by the Democrats were given votes and confirmed, including two women, one of them African American. Two others were left in limbo. Both sides agreed that the filibuster was dead, except under "extraordinary circumstances." I could be wrong, but it's hard to imagine this arrangement holding if President Bush appoints a principled conservative—or conservatives, if he has more than one opportunity—to the high court when he is given the opportunity. Democrats will declare it an "extraordinary circumstance," and we'll have to reconsider the "nuclear option."

Democrats, by the way, are right when they complain about the way President Clinton's judicial nominees were handled by Republicans. We bottled them up in the Judiciary Committee, which was the functional equivalent of a filibuster. It was crazy, but the cycle of retribution needs to end. The Senate Judiciary Committee, regardless of which political party is in charge, should report out nominees in a reasonable amount of time. If the committee wants to report out a nominee unfavorably, so be it. But barring a huge ethical conflict, a lie about the nominee's education, or some other sin that would be grounds for the president to withdraw the nomination, these judicial candidates should come to the Senate floor for a straight up-or-down vote.

In my years in the Senate, I have been a party to some great accomplishments, much routine legislation, and, on occasion, votes that pained me well past the moment. When I rescued President Bush's omnibus Medicare Bill from death by a Democratic point of order, the *National Journal* dubbed me the GOP's ultimate power broker. Other media outlets painted me as a white knight who saved Bill Frist's bacon. The real story was something else entirely.

The 2003 Medicare overhaul, Bush's signature proposal that year, carried an initial price tag estimated at $300 billion; it was billed as the most sweeping change since the system was created in 1965. It would give private insurance companies a vast new role in health care for the program's beneficiaries. It also included $25 billion for rural hospitals, and a requirement for higher-income seniors to pay more for Medicare Part B—coverage of doctor visits, tests, and related costs. Billion of dollars more would go to discourage corporations from eliminating existing coverage for their retirees once the new government program begins in 2006.

The bill would create a limited program of direct competition between traditional Medicare and private plans beginning in 2010. Its centerpiece, though, was a prescription drug program. Beginning in 2006, seniors would be allowed to purchase coverage for their prescription drugs. Bush officials estimated at the time that the premium cost would be $35 a month, with a $250 deductible. The coverage would pay 75 percent of costs after that until a senior's medication costs reached $2,250. After that, there is a gap in coverage until out-of-pocket expenses reach $3,600, or roughly $4,100 in overall drug expenses. Above that level, insurance would pick up roughly 95 percent of the costs.

By the time the prescription elements of the plan were considered by both houses of Congress, the plan had drifted way off course. For instance, the prescription-drug coverage was made universal. A millionaire would have as much access to the service as a low-income individual. I thought we were going to direct the plan at the low-income elderly who really needed coverage but couldn't afford it. The plan as written didn't make sense.

This bill was fiscally dangerous. The costs were going to swamp our children and our grandchildren. We were moving more deck chairs on the proverbial *Titanic,* destining the Medicare ship to sink under its bloated weight.

But I kept my opposition in check, never intending to go public with a full critique of the proposal. Why? Because I believed we really needed to do something about prescription drug costs. I also was prepared to give Frist, a new leader still struggling with the difficulties of the job, the benefit of the doubt. Eight years earlier, it was Dr. Bill Frist who had come to the Senate from his surgical practice in Tennessee, vowing to reform Medicare. It was his chief campaign promise.

I was well aware of the bill's progress. My longtime friend and neighbor, Louisiana senator John Breaux, had been involved in drafting the legislation six years before it passed. Breaux lobbied me mightily over the years, and made a personal plea when the bill got gummed up in a point-of-order trap sprung by Tom Daschle. "I will never let this measure reach the floor of the Senate," said the minority leader, who objected to the market-oriented elements in the plan. "This is where it will die." Daschle and the Democrats had reason to crow: The Republicans were stuck. They had fifty-nine votes to bring Medicare Reform to the floor, one short of the sixty needed.

Whip research had convinced Frist and the GOP leadership that I was the one senator who might be willing to switch. After all, I'd been a reliable party loyalist who had always rushed into the breach. Several days before the November 24 vote on the health care overhaul, President Bush's chief of staff, Andy Card, telephoned to relay the president's continued strong support for the bill—and its prescription-drug elements.

I told Card to tell Bush that I was still against it, and that I would not come to its rescue from the clutches of a Democratic filibuster. I sent similar messages to the vice president through several White House aides.

About that time, I heard a rumor that the president and his top people may have withheld their support of me during the Thurmond crisis because they felt Frist would have been more likely than I to steer the drug bill through the Senate. They would have been right about that. I would not have let this particular prescription drug plan pass through the Senate on my watch.

The bill was hopelessly trapped the afternoon of the 24th when I interrupted my office work to take my place on the Senate floor. By the time I sat down, the measure had been stuck at 59–39 for about forty minutes.

This was a big test of President Bush's clout on domestic issues, and the Senate gallery was packed. Efficient young White House deputies were stationed in the crowd, ready to relay any news back to the Oval Office. As several groups did face-to-face lobbying, I just kept shaking my head emphatically, "No!"

It was one of the most difficult days in my political life. Many of my colleagues thought this bill was a health-care wonder. I happened to glance over at the Democrats, where Hillary Clinton and Ted Kennedy were standing side by side. Then I visualized the press conference they would hold if Daschle's maneuver held. They couldn't help but gloat at the failure of Bush's first major health care proposal.

I couldn't do it. Not to a president I supported so strongly. I stood up slowly, aware that Washington's eyes were on me. As I passed Frist, I heard him say, "Help us out, Trent." With my head still shaking *no,* I strode up to the clerk's desk and quietly said, "aye." The bill was free of the prison of rules Daschle had tried to erect around it.

Though a few journalists raced after me, I quickly slipped into the Senatorial elevator and returned to my offices. I was miserable that night, desperately unhappy at this catastrophic economic "due bill" we had just voted to leave our children, grandchildren, and great-grandchildren. The final cost is still uncertain, but it almost certainly will exceed $500 billion; by some estimates, it could even approach $1 trillion over time.

The full Medicare legislation passed twenty-four hours later. The vote was 53–44. I was one of nine conservative Republicans voting against the measure. President Bush called within minutes to express his thanks.

"That was the worst vote of my career," I told him.

"That's quite a statement, because you've had a long and distinguished career," he responded.

Tricia told me I seemed more devastated by the Medicare episode than at any time during the Strom Thurmond disaster. It will become a permanent blot on the history of the 108th Congress. And the Republicans will have to undo it soon, or suffer the political consequences.

The 108th Congress, focusing so intently on one piece of legislation, dropped the ball on several important initiatives. We didn't pass a highway construction bill, which would have provided tens of thousands of jobs nationwide and improved America's critical infrastructure. We didn't pass an energy bill, a double whammy of an oversight that will hurt our economy and erodes our national security. We get nearly 60 percent of our oil from foreign countries, some of them relatively unstable. Imagine what would happen, for example, if the kingdom of Saudi Arabia, the world's largest producer, were destabilized by al Qaeda or other Muslim radicals, or invaded by a hostile neighbor in the region. Our dependence on these countries is growing worse, and our failure to act in our own best interests is a blunder of potentially catastrophic proportions.

Our *only* choice is to drill for our own oil and gas on a massive level. Environmentalists snarl over the mere suggestion of a true offshore empire of drilling rigs. The opponents of such measures will scream about pollution. But the rigs are usually drilling for natural gas—not oil. There is little danger to the environment. One of these rigs sits in the Gulf of Mexico, off the same shore I look out on from my Pascagoula home. A reporter once asked me, "How would you like to have an oil rig off the coast of your house?" I said, "Fine. You can't leak natural gas. It's a gas." Then I pointed offshore toward the rig—distantly visible on a clear day in southern Mississippi.

We need a full-court press to find solutions to this problem. Our biggest fossil-fuel reserve, hands down, is coal. We should put more money into clean coal technology, to capitalize on this underutilized resource. Nuclear power is clean and it's safe, but we haven't been able to build a nuclear power plant in more than a quarter century. That, too, must change.

I'm not saying we should ignore conservation. We should press for greater fuel efficiency, and we should explore alternative energy sources such as solar and wind and hydrogen fuel cells. But

I'm not optimistic about these alternatives, certainly in the near term. And I don't think we can "conserve" ourselves into a credible energy policy.

The 108th Congress failed in other areas, too—no budget resolution in two years, failure on nine appropriation bills, and more. Some of our problems, but certainly not all, were the result of brick walls erected by the Democrats. Led by Daschle, the minority party was as obstructionist as I've ever seen. The Democrats proved themselves willing to fight to the death on any piece of legislation that might help the GOP in any way, grasping at any point of order or filibuster they could. It was as if they couldn't get over the fact that they weren't in the majority. They just kept attacking, again and again and again.

The Republicans, however, didn't always act if they were the majority party. They wallowed in ideology, and let chances to pass bills slide by—often until it was too late.

We seem to be doing better in the 109th Congress, passing a bankruptcy bill, tort reform, and a few other measures that had lingered since the early days of the Bush administration. But it's early. The energy bill is still out there as I write this, with the Senate and the House having passed radically different versions, and it's unclear whether a compromise that makes sense is possible. We need to keep moving forward.

On the second anniversary of the Strom Thurmond furor last December, the *Jackson Clarion-Ledger* depicted me as the ultimate political survivor in a splash of stories that started on Page One. Under the headline SKILL, KNOWLEDGE LIFT LOTT FROM POLITICAL SCRAP HEAP, the story began: "Since losing his job as Senate Republican leader two years ago, Trent Lott has used his encyclopedic knowledge of Congress and his deal making prowess to remain one of the most effective members of the Senate." It's true that I am usually prepared to sacrifice some aspect of a piece of legislation in order to reach agreement on a larger objective. In June 2005, I had a conversation with President Bush on two issues then on his plate, and advised him to give up a little to get what he wanted. He sat back, smiled, and said, "Trent, you're a deal maker."

"No, Mr. President," I responded, "I'm a results maker."

Larry Sabato, a University of Virginia political science professor, told the *Clarion-Ledger* that I'd adapted surprisingly well to my new role in the Senate. "The marvelous thing is that the mavericks have more fun in the Senate," he said. "Lott has discovered this."

I put it a little differently in my response to the paper: "You can be a leader without having the title. As a leader, you're too busy trying to move the train, quite often a train you really don't like."

One final quote from that story, from former GOP state senator Con Maloney. "I think quietly some people had major concerns that we, as a state, lost a great deal when he had to vacate the majority leader's post," Maloney said. "But his personal stature remained basically intact . . . he's negated those concerns to a great extent."

I sense that Maloney's assessment is accurate, but sometimes it's difficult to appraise your condition with clear eyes and an untroubled mind. As I look back over nearly thirty-four years in the House and Senate, and as I survey the future, I'm inspired by the image of the phoenix, who rose from the ashes. With God's help, and a lot of support from your family and friends, I've found it's not even tough to do. As former navy secretary James Webb said in his book, *Born Fighting,* you can knock a Scots-Irishman down, but he will not stay down!

I still view my years in Washington as a magnificent experience, with many more mountaintops than valleys for this son of the South. I love my country, and still feel as strongly as ever about the principles that brought me into public service in the first place. The best government is the government closest to the people. Individual responsibility. Fiscal discipline. A strong national defense.

The foundation that supports everything we do is our Constitution. That magnificent document, and the freedoms embodied in it, remain a beacon for people everywhere, and have contributed mightily to the expansion of democracy around the world.

Still, from our beginnings in America, we have made necessary accommodations in the public square to accomplish our larger objectives. And we have argued—sometimes in raised and angry voices—about the balance between unfettered rights at one polarity and the oppressive hand of government at the other. So be it. But men and women of goodwill should echo Thomas Jefferson: "I would rather be exposed to the inconveniences attending too much liberty than to those attending too small a degree of it."

America is the greatest nation ever to have graced the Earth, because its people give fresh meaning to Jefferson's words every day of their lives. The leaders of this exceptional land can do no less.

# ACKNOWLEDGMENTS

In writing a book of any length, there are always those pillars of support, strength, and encouragement to whom you cannot forget to express heartfelt gratitude. The company we keep in energy-demanding times can be the very life-giving source we need to persevere. In every arena of my life, I have always had people who would never hesitate to pour themselves out in friendship and stewardship, lending depth, humor, dimension, and perspective to my life.

I cannot mention pillars in my life without mentioning my mother, Iona Lott, who gave me strong values and a sense of responsibility. My wife, Tricia, has given me love and support on every path we took for forty-one years. Our children, Chet and Tyler, have grown into wonderful young adults and have made us very proud of the strength and values they possess and the support they continue to give their parents. And the newest pillars on the Lott platform—the grandchildren, Trent III, Lucie, Shields, and Addison. They are what my thirty-seven years of public service is all about.

Going back to the formative years in the cultivation of my passions, convictions, and leadership skills, I had the privilege of being exposed to people at the University of Mississippi who would become not only my lifelong friends, but also highly influential in their character. As iron sharpens iron, so we were whenever we got together. I have spent time with so many people through the years, and many have fallen to the wayside—except for the five remarkable and unforgettable men whom I call not only friends, but brothers. These Sigma Nu fraternity brothers, Allen Pepper, Guy Hovis, John Corlew, Gaylen Roberts, and Tommy Anderson, have always been there for me, whether it was running for office on campus, or running for Congress and Senate.

Allen, having the detectable skills of a politician in the making, not only sang with me in our infamous college quartet, but went deeper with me, taking the time to pray in one of the most difficult times in my life. The real talent in the college quartet, The Chancellors, was my friend Guy Hovis. He has a voice that makes young girls swoon and old ladies shake in their shoes. Our families grew up across the creek from each other. Our friendship began in 1959 at the university and continues until this day. Guy has given his voice and his energy to almost every campaign since 1972. And for all the fun I had with Allen and Guy, Gaylen could always answer that with his own version of excitement. My friendship with Gaylen goes back to junior high school, in 1953. Gaylen was always the contrarian on any issue. We have had in-depth discussions on subjects from politics to religion. The quartet still gets together to rehash old times and sing together—and we still sound really good, according to our spouses. John Corlew was the character of the bunch. He was absolutely brilliant, and became one of Mississippi's most competent attorneys. I twice offered him a federal judgeship, only to have him decline the nomination.

Tommy Anderson has lived up to his calling as one of my best and most loyal friends. Not only did he give of himself tirelessly as a worker on my campaign during my first race for the House of Representatives, but he also became my chief of staff after I won that election, staying for twelve years while I served the Fifth District of Mississippi. It was Tommy who managed my very first Senate race, which ended with me taking the seat I have now held for almost sixteen years. If not for the people, it is for friends like Tommy that you persevere in a leadership position—for the energy they put forth, the dedication they show, and because they believe in you. I was proud to become majority leader for the people like him who love me, and have sacrificed parts of themselves for me to serve here.

Stepping out in faith takes an element of strength that, in my opinion, derives more from family, friends, and faith in God's sovereign plan than from any amount of self-fabricated gumption. My decision to run for the U.S. House of Representatives was one of the most exciting I have ever made, but undeniably anxiety-inducing and thought-provoking. To lead in such a high position could only invite challenges that one's family has never before experienced. After winning the seat, I knew I had imminent trials and blessings ahead. Some of the experiences in that role were with Dick Morris and Dave Hoppe. Dick had been around for a long time and he knew the South. He had been involved in the campaigns of Senator Jesse Helms, Governor Bill Allain of Mississippi, and, of course, Governor and President Bill Clinton of Arkansas. He had lots of ideas, and one or two were home runs. I had to have the ability to pick out that one or two. There are few men as fine as Dave Hoppe. He has my utmost respect as a man as he epitomizes faith, family, and values. He was on my staff in both the House and the Senate, and he was one of the best staffers on the Hill. He is a true friend.

As secretary of the majority for the U.S. Senate, Elizabeth Letchworth was instrumental in helping me guide the Senate through the impeachment trial of President Clinton, as well as the everyday running of the Institution. She had basically grown up in the Senate herself, and knew the Rules.

I can never really thank Ron Bonjean, my press secretary in the Leader's office, enough. He was there during the "Strom event," catching all the darts, daggers, and blogs thrown at me. He always kept his cool and as always kept me informed. He has gone on to be communications director to House Speaker Denny Hastert.

My relationship with Dick Scruggs is both family and professional. He is married to Tricia's middle sister Diane. An internationally recognized plaintiff's attorney, he was portrayed in the movie *The Insider* for his role in the tobacco settlement wars. We have wonderful give-and-take discussions, where a consensus is never achieved. He is not only my brother-in-law but a true friend.

Aside from my mother, my wife and my children, I must say that the encouragement and support I have received from Tricia's five brothers and sisters, and their spouses and my staff and former staff over these years in politics, has been tremendous. They laugh with us and cry with us. I love them all.

Special thanks to Judith Regan and Cal Morgan, who believed that I had a story to tell, and to Flip Brophy, Peter Brown, and Michael Ruby, for helping it be told.

# INDEX